The Scope of Morality

The
Scope
of Morality

Peter A. French

Professor of Philosophy
University of Minnesota

University of Minnesota Press □ Minneapolis

Published by the University of Minnesota Press,
2037 University Avenue Southeast,
Minneapolis, Minnesota 55455
Printed in the United States of America

Library of Congress Cataloging in Publication Data

French, Peter A
    The scope of morality.

    Bibliography: p.
    Includes index.
    1. Ethics. I. Title.
BJ37.F63   170   79-19026
ISBN 0-8166-0837-7
ISBN 0-8166-0900-4 pbk.

The University of Minnesota Press
is an equal-opportunity
educator and employer.

To my father, Ernest C. French

Acknowledgments

Some of these chapters have appeared previously in other forms in various journals. Chapter 6 in a shorter form appeared in *The Journal of Philosophy*. Part of Chapter 1, in an earlier version, was published in *The Personalist*. Chapter 7 appears in a Festschrift honoring Professor William Werkmeister and the lengthy footnote to Chapter 1 appeared in a longer version in the *American Philosophical Quarterly*.

I have been most influenced in the development of my views by the writings of Donald Davidson and Julius Kovesi on related topics. The influence of John Locke's account of moral concepts on my own thesis cannot be overestimated. I have greatly benefited from discussions with Donald Davidson, D.F. Pears, Gilbert Harman, D.E. Cooper, Hector-Neri Castañeda, Nicholas Fotion, Haskell Fain, Kurt Baier, Alan Gewirth and J.L. Mackie. My colleagues, Howard Wettstein and Theodore Uehling, who were constantly prodding me to completion, have read and criticized portions of the manuscript. Wettstein, in particular, forced me to see that I just could not say some of the things I thought I could say in the way I wanted to say them. I am particularly grateful to Castañeda for his careful reading of the entire manuscript and for his many valuable suggestions. I have also benefited from being able to read an unfinished manuscript on deontic logic by Bernard Baumrin. I would like to be able to say that errors that remain are the fault of Wettstein, but they are really the fault of my wife, Sandra. She has been a constant bother throughout the development of this book and even now would want me to further explain or expand or delete or change this sentence or that phrase if only she could get her hands on it. That the book is in English at all must be credited to her.

I must thank Cynthia Ostrem, a secretary who is both highly competent and kindhearted, and also Norine Eckstrom and Virginia Clemen, who have worked from my first handwritten scraps of paper, for typing drafts.

I acknowledge support in research funds provided on more than one occasion by the Graduate School of the University of Minnesota.

I should like to thank those of my students who forced me to explain again and again my views on these and related matters. In particular I acknowledge the assistance of Roland Nord, Peter Tritz, Martha Jo Onstad, and James Shekleton. I trust they will recognize the views that have developed in answer to their questions.

Finally I owe a great deal to Charles Dickens. A reading of his masterpiece, *Bleak House*, helped me to see the relevance of the distinctions between moral and euergetical notions, between rightness and goodness, that play a major role in this book.

Preface

> In a discussion of such subjects (ethics) . . . we must
> be satisfied to indicate the truth with a rough and gen-
> eral sketch.
>
> Aristotle: *Nichomachean Ethics.* 1094 b

This book is offered as a general sketch of morality. The primary
focus, however, is on the origin, purpose, and function of the various concepts to be found in a more or less mature morality. This
book is, then, an essay in what has come to be known as philosophical ethics or, sometimes, as metaethics. However, contrary to
the practice in books on such topics, no development or defense
of a normative moral theory is offered. No attempt is made to apply such a theory to related problems, as is often done in books
on, for example, business ethics or bioethics. Furthermore, this
book does not undertake to present and systematically criticize
the major classical and contemporary theories. Its aim is to provide an adequate (and, I think, correct) account of the basic elements of a morality that will contribute somewhat to the general
goal of philosophy: understanding the central aspects of our lives.
Incidentally, it may also provide some ammunition for the combatants in the battle of philosophical theories about morality.

I

In 1837 the Danish Royal Society of Sciences offered a prize for
the best essay written in answer to the following question:

> Is *the source and foundation of morality to be looked for* in
> an idea of morality which lies immediately in consciousness
> (or conscience), and in the analysis of the other principal no-
> tions of morality springing from this, or is it to be sought in
> another ground of knowledge?

The only philosopher to enter the contest was Arthur Schopenhauer. He took the question, correctly, to be "directed to nothing
less than the objectively true foundation of morals."[1] That is, the
Royal Society was asking whether or not morality has an objective
base, whether, on the model of the sciences, more than mere convention is behind sound moral judgment and accepted moral principles. The Society was well aware that the problem that they
posed has been at the center of metaethical controversy since the
days of the Greeks. Plato should be read as defending the thesis
that an objective foundation of morality exists, that it lies in nature or in the nature of things as, for Plato, do all truths. Plato
tells us that Socrates' aim was to discover what is good in itself,
rather than to settle for what is good because men say that it is.
Socrates and Plato were certainly not isolated figures as regards
the quest for a nonconventional foundation of morality. Immanuel
Kant both typifies and dominates the objective foundation tradition in the last two centuries. For Kant the objective foundation
of ethics is found in pure reason, that is, in the practice of reason
unadulterated by the knowledge gained in the empirical studies of
the human race. (The rather lengthy second part of Schopenhauer's
essay is devoted to a searing attack on Kant's views on the foundations of ethics. In their criticism of Schopenhauer's efforts, The
Royal Society, obviously with reference especially to the passages
on Kant, remarked, "several distinguished philosophers of recent
times are mentioned in a manner so unseemly as to cause just and
grave offense."[2])

What Plato, Kant, and, we should add, Hutcheson, Price, Balguy,[3] and the more recent intuitionists share is the belief that
knowledge of what is good and bad, of what is morally right and

wrong, of what one morally ought to do is supported by or founded on some objectively knowable source. The general idea all of
these moral theorists espouse is that moral judgments and principles are founded on values that can in some way or another be
discovered. Opposed to this tide of objectivism is a relatively small
group of philosophers who maintain that there simply is no objective foundation to be located. As Schopenhauer wrote:

> Might it not follow from a retrospective glance at the main at-
> tempts to find a sure basis of morals for more than two thou-
> sand years that there is no natural morality at all that is inde-
> pendent of human institution?[4]

Recently a few philosophers have joined Schopenhauer by
mounting direct assaults on the objectivist's positions.[5] I shall not
follow their lead though I am sympathetic to the motivation for
the venture. Instead I shall try to develop a "nonobjectivist" theory of the origin and function of moral concepts. My position
might be labelled subjectivist, but certain dangers are inherent in
that term, owing to its ambiguity. To some people, subjectivists
are those who try to defend the highly implausible view that every
person ought to do whatever he thinks he ought to do in every circumstance. Others take subjectivists to be saying that moral judgments express the subjective attitudes of their speakers or that
such judgments are equivalent to statements that say that the
speaker has a certain attitude.

Actually the nonobjectivism I espouse is an ontological position,
and my mentor, John Locke. The emotivists must have assumed
an ontological thesis consistent with my own, that there is no objective foundation of morality, but they came to this position by
way of providing an account of the meaning of moral judgments as
mere expressions of feelings that implies nonobjectivism, but is itself not implied by nonobjectivism and is, furthermore, a flawed
analysis of the meaning of those judgments. J. L. Mackie has captured this point well. He writes:

> The denial that there are objective values does not commit
> one to any particular view about what moral statements
> mean, and certainly not to the view that they are equivalent
> to subjective reports.[6]

A morality, on my account, is an invention or a series of inventions, a creation of human minds in community. It is best seen as a collection of conventions designed to guide the choices of persons; those conventions have the not necessarily intended collective effect of being a system of defense against the tendency of any person to act in a way threatening to the future well-being of members of the community. That many of our moral principles inhibit or constrain shows this first purpose for their formation. But prevention by restraint and avoidance is only a part of a morality. Encouragement to do certain things and to develop certain habits plays a none too minor and perhaps longer term role. A morality is a product of human creativity in meeting internal threats to well-being, given a recognition that people are creatures of a certain kind operating in a certain sort of environment.

My thesis is that a morality is a system of guidelines for the act-choices of persons, and of ideals of interpersonal behavior, constructed to foster the shared vision of the flourishing, not just the survival, of persons in our environment. The guidelines and ideals I shall argue emerge in a culture in the form of concepts (of what Locke called the mixed-mode variety) that allow the description (or redescription) of acts, events, and persons in ways that inculcate the generally believed status of the act, event, or person with respect to the maintenance or betterment of the human environment. Using the names of those concepts to describe acts is *eo ipso*, to categorize those acts morally, that is, to locate them in the moral world or to see them from the "moral point of view." That "point of view," that world, then is also the product of a morality and is not reducible without reminder to some morally neutral (objective) descriptions of what persons are, do, or did. The moral point of view (of which in moral philosophy a good deal is said but not much told) is not the antecedent, it is the product of the enterprises of moral concept formation and the consequent use of those concepts. One takes the moral point of view when he regards what someone said to be a lie, and also when he considers whether or not he would be lying if he reports less income on his tax forms than he actually earned, etc.

Obviously, the formation of moral concepts was provoked not only by a desire to ward off certain calamitous events, in part through cautioning against acts believed to cause them, but by a recognized need to capture all like acts under the proscription. It would do little good with respect to the general aim of morality if every moral concept had to be "tailor-made" to each act, event, or person. Also it would surely be judged amiss if we did not identify and similarly treat similar acts. We cannot say that X is like Y in every respect except that a person ought to do X but not Y. If we could, the result would be "Queen's croquet game morality." Moral concepts, however, focus attention on features of acts, events, and persons that may be found in other acts, events, and persons and for the presence of which the act is either to be encouraged or discouraged. In short, our moral concepts help insure the similarity of treatment of similar acts by identifying a respect in which those acts are similar, and it is because of that particular similarity that such acts are to be encouraged or discouraged, that persons are to be praised, credited, or blamed when they perform them, *ceteris paribus*.

In his famous work, *The Spirit of the Laws*, Montesquieu wrote: "Mankind are influenced by various causes: by the climate, by the religion, by the laws, by the maxims of government, by precedents, morals and customs."[7] A number of commentators have, perhaps rightly, rebuked Montesquieu for his emphasis on physical causes such as climate in his account of the "general spirit of the nations," but it is clear that he regarded morality as a primary regulative factor on human life, at least as significant as positive law. He appears also to have held the view that exemplars of good character taken from the literature and history of a people, what he calls "precedents," also play a role in creating the communal spirit that tends to govern human behavior from community, or nation, to community. That Montesquieu was convinced that morality was often the strongest influence on the behavior of a people is evident from his remarks about the reason European countries of his time had maintained "moderate" rather than despotic governments. He writes: "Most of the European nations are still governed by the principles of morality." He adds, "But if from a long abuse of power or the fury of conquest, despotic sway should prevail to a certain degree, neither morals nor climate would be able to withstand its baleful influence."[8] Surely it is not surprising that a factor so significant in explaining the behavior of people should become objectified in their thinking. Nothing would seem to be more natural than the reification of morality or the objectification of the values that form its base. However, the statement of the fact that X plays a major causal role in human activity does not imply or entail a statement to the effect that X is objective or discernible in what the Greeks called nature (as opposed to convention) or that X has an objective foundation.

A number of problems must be faced by the proponent of a nonobjectivist theory of the foundation of morality. Most people, philosophers and nonphilosophers alike, think or at least talk as if an objective basis of morality exists, that, for example, there is a way to establish the truth of moral judgments independent of our conventions or that there is a way to discover what a person morally ought to do that is not dependent on the products of human conceptual invention. These beliefs have surely become ingrained in our ordinary discourse, and they color our intuitions on many controversial matters. What might be called "intimations of objectivity" (though sometimes they are anything but subtle) characterize the tone of the moral assertions and arguments we make. Robert Baum and James Randell's collection, *Ethical Arguments for Analysis*,[9] contains page after page of examples gleaned from the nation's newspapers and magazines that attest to this fact. No account of morality can afford to ignore or deny that moral judgments and intimations of objectivity are ordinarily associated even if no ontological basis can be discovered that warrants that association. Of course, as Baum and Randell's collection makes evident, the currently popular method of "ordinary language analysis" cannot show that there is no objective foundation for morality. However, the intimations of objectivity are, as I shall show, accounted for when we come to understand the formation of our moral concepts, when we uncover the reasons for their invention and the elements interwoven in their construction. We will then see how the belief in the objective foundation of morality came to be established and nurtured in the common consciousness and why it is false.

R. M. Hare recounts a personal experience he had with a Swiss exchange student from Lausanne.[10] The student was religious and "full of the best ideals." Hare had only a few books written in French for the lad to read, but one of the books he presented the student was Camus' *L'Etranger*. After reading that book, the student's habits drastically changed. When Hare questioned him as to why he had begun to act in apparently erratic ways, the student confessed that he had become convinced from his reading of *L'Etranger* that there are no objective values, no foundation in nature for the moral ideals he had been taught to incorporate in his behavior. He had concluded with Camus' hero that in so far as that was true, nothing he did mattered, that *"rien, rien n'avait d'importance."* The exchange student reacted in a way that might well be expected of many intelligent people when they are confronted with a convincing argument that their belief in the objectivity of the morality by which they abide is false. But, of course, it simply does not follow that nothing matters if morality is a product of human invention. Things matter or not because of a broad spectrum of interrelated factors that they do or do not influence. Morality matters and it matters because a number of things matter to each of us. The authority of morality, of which so much is written, lies not in the sham of objectivism but, as I hope to show, in the social necessity of its invention.

II

Moral philosophers tend to emphasize as the primary function of a morality one or the other of two focuses of ordinary moral discourse: the evaluation of acts and events or the evaluation of character or persons. Indeed, typically philosophical moral systems are categorized either as being about the rightness or wrongness of acts or as being about the constituents of a good or bad character. Also, if the moral philosopher believes that morality is act-oriented, then he will treat beliefs about those acts that are proper or required as focal, and character evaluation as derivative. On the other hand, if he believes morality's main focus is the evaluation and improvement of character, then he will treat beliefs about the desirability or undesirability of certain traits and habits as of first importance, and the evaluation of deeds will be regarded as derivative. Observations of the various ways moral discourse is used could even lead one already tempted to simplify matters to conclude that judgments about the rightness or wrongness of acts are really assimilated too, or even only another way of making judgments about the goodness or the badness of persons *or* (unhappily) vice versa. The court of common usage is only a guideline, for it is too susceptible to the bribes of the zealous reductionist. Morality is simply far richer than either an act-oriented or agent-oriented version of its contents will support. I hope to show throughout this book, especially in Chapters 2 and 7, that we have to be satisfied with diversity. A mature morality is a complex collection of concepts and their attendant principles and judgments associated because of a common, though rather general, *raison d'être* that permits the identification of a morality within a conceptual scheme that may include other behavioral guidance principles. As a matter of fact those concepts do quite naturally divide into rather distinct and irreducible groups: those concerning character (virtue) and those about the rightness or wrongness of certain kinds of acts.

Some philosophers who have acknowledged the distinctiveness of these two concerns of morality have correctly ascertained that occasions may arise in which a person is trapped between the Scylla of doing what is right and thereby corrupting his virtuous character and the Charybdis of doing what preserves his virtue and thereby not doing what is right. To insure an inner tranquillity to morality, to preserve its aura of authority, or to fortify intimations of objectivity, a number of clever solutions to handle such apparently paradoxical situations have been proposed. Usually one or the other aspect of morality is put forth as really supreme, but it has also been suggested that there are beliefs in a morality about the relationship between act and character, and that those beliefs provide persons with bridge principles from which guidance, when one is in such situations, is to be gleaned. There may well be a third aspect of a morality that houses certain principles to be involved in morally paradoxical situations, but I have been unable to locate any such aspect or find any collection of concepts that would be associated with it. The idea of a harmonious morality, that is, of a coordination between all of the principles of act and character evaluation, is more of a fantasy than Kepler's *Harmonice Mundi*. The invention of the concepts of morality has not been an orderly process. It has been more like the development of a body of positive law in a state than like the composition of a Mozart symphony. Internal consistency is not guaranteed when the invention is the product of so many hands over so long a period of time. Although the idea of a "trade-off" in moral matters is abhorrent to most of the great moral philosophers of our tradition, the totally confident righteous soul who has not a qualm about his choice of actions is a fiction created by certain philosophers rather than a goal embedded in the motivations of the inventors of morality. Such a character, in fact, is more often than not the villain of popular literature and film. Resolutions of the dilemmas that morality forces on us do not come easy or without price. Morality, as we meet it in our daily lives, is multifaceted; anyone attempting to provide an adequate account of morality should not cavalierly ignore the difficulties.

III

Recently I had occasion to read that masterpiece of the old style of historical prose, William H. Prescott's *History of the Conquest of Peru*.[11] In a chapter devoted to a detailing of the husbandry, mechanical skills, and architecture of the Incas, Prescott concludes by pointing out that many of the Spaniards who first visited Peru, enchanted by outward signs of prosperity and tranquillity, had pronounced the Peruvian social system a mighty moral success. Prescott quotes from Carli: "sans doute l'homme moral du Perou etoit infiniment plus perfectionne que l'Europeen." But such praise is, in Prescott's eyes, sorely misplaced. He writes:

> Where there is no free agency, there can be no morality. Where there is no temptation, there can be no claim to virtue. Where the routine is rigorously prescribed by law, the law, and not the man, must have the credit of the conduct. . . . the Peruvian has the least real claim to our admiration.[12]

Of course I am not in a position to judge whether Prescott's analysis of the early Peruvians is warranted (though his account is convincing). But Prescott's three claims about morality certainly reflect basic beliefs about or associated with morality. Though they clearly are not exhaustive, no adequate account of morality can ignore these claims. In this book the first claim, that free agency is a prerequisite of morality, will be discussed in the first chapter, where the requirements for citizenship in the moral community will be examined. Prescott's second claim: that virtue (moral goodness) is earned by positive acts, that one cannot be accidentally virtuous, will be of primary concern in Chapter 7. The idea that institutions such as the law set nonoptional requirements on action, and hence those who follow the rules are not necessarily to be given much moral credit for the resulting acts, is discussed in Chapter 6 in which the focus is on the differences between moral judgments and principles on the one hand and institutional rules on the other.

IV

A word perhaps is in order regarding my title. Morality is a conceptual system functioning as a behavior encouragement and discouragement device within a community. But what is the scope of that conceptual system? Not surprisingly, a number of important issues and disputes regarding our understanding of morality turn on just such a question.

The discussion of scope in philosophical logic in this century is generally acknowledged to be due to the work of Bertrand Russell.[13] Logicians have found it necessary to draw quantificational scope distinctions in order to properly render ordinary sentences. Modal logicians have, in particular, faced issues of scope (often in terms of *de re/de dicto* readings) in explicating the sense of necessity and possibility, knowledge claims, statements of belief, and so on. The overriding concern of philosophical logicians with respect to quantificational scope is that the quantifier, as Quine writes, "reach out far enough to take in any occurrence of a variable that is supposed to refer back to that quantifier."[14] The determination of quantificational scope may be profitably regarded as paradigmatic of scope distinctions generally. In other words, questions regarding the scope of a term, a theory, a modal operator, a conceptual system or concepts within such a system are, at heart, questions about the limits of application over some subject area that is supposed to be captured by it. If morality were a theory, then we should be interested in the limits of its application in much the

same way that physicists were interested in the scope of the Special Theory of Relativity. But morality is not a theory of the Ein-
steinian variety.

Quine has shown, in a most useful short paper, "Logic as a
Source of Syntactical Insights,"[15] that the mathematician's and
logician's use of parentheses (and other devices) illuminates our
ordinary idiomatic expressions and in particular helps to isolate
significant scope distinctions where they exist in ordinary English
discourse. In ordinary usage, issues of scope arise, for example, in
regard to indefinite singular terms, e.g., "every" and "any," and
the appropriate resolution of these issues is signalled by the way
the logician reduces them to universal quantifiers that range over
the variables in different ways.[16]

Scope questions naturally arise in regard to the use of syncategorematic adjectives. Quine, on a number of occasions, uses the example "big European butterfly"[17] which could be interpreted to mean
that something is a big butterfly and of the European variety; or it
could mean that something is big for the European variety of butterfly. Insofar as we know about butterflies, we do know that "big
European butterfly" cannot mean that something is big and is also
a European butterfly. In fact, using Geach's well-known distinction, "big" is not a predicative adjective at all, it is an attributive
one. So we cannot split the predication into "X is big" and "X is,
e.g., a butterfly." But that information alone does not lead to a
resolution of the scope question here. We need to know what the
speaker intended in order to resolve the issue. Knowing only that
European butterflies tend to be bigger or smaller than other varieties is also helpful but, again, insufficient data. The speaker may or
may not have intended to say that the particular butterfly in question was large for its type. In other words, one needs to know a
number of things to properly capture the scope of many attributive
syncategorematic adjectives (of which "big" is a paradigm) when
they are used in ordinary discourse. In the case of the butterfly,
certain knowledge of butterflies does immediately exclude (or
nearly so, since there is always the possibility that the utterance
coud have occurred in a science fiction horror movie!) certain interpretations of scope, but other questions still are to be resolved.

"Moral" is a syncategorematic attributive adjective when used, for example, in such phrases as "moral judgment," "moral belief," "moral act," "moral principle," and so forth. It is therefore not susceptible to predicative resolutions, i.e., "X is a judgment and X is moral." And disputes over its scope when it is attributively ambiguous must be settled by application of information about morality itself. But "moral" is quite different from "big," for speaker intentions are much less important to the scope question. I shall argue that when we understand the function and structure of a morality, we will have uncovered sufficient reasons to resolve the ambiguity of scope of "moral" when it arises in, for example, such phrases as "moral institutional obligation," so that the phrase is interpreted always as "an institutional obligation that is moral or morally endorsed" and never as "an obligation from the moral institution." In this respect, scope of morality resolutions will be rather different from those of attributions of size. Ambiguous attributions of bigness imply that the speaker has applied some standard of measurement to something and that entails that he has made some comparison of that thing with some other thing or class of things, etc. Things are "big as _____," or "big for _____," or big when compared with _____," etc. In order to capture the intended scope of the adjective one must know what sort of comparison is being made. Understanding the notion of size is only a factor in settling those scope issues. Understanding ambiguous attributive uses of "moral," however, though they also suggest comparisons and even measurements, is primarily dependent upon understanding what morality is—understanding that will allow the exclusion of certain interpretations or at least will support the judgment, "If the speaker meant *that*, he is talking nonsense." For these reasons it is advisable to concentrate attention on the concept-types that make up a morality rather than on the analysis of examples in ordinary discourse of the attribution of "moral."

A second reason may be advanced for thinking of the study of morality in terms of scope: Two errors are typically committed by moral philosophers in interpreting the general scope of morality. What seems to be a majority of moral philosophers have uncritically adopted a terribly broad view of the scope of morality. They write as if nearly every action-choice situation is a moral one, governed by moral principle, on the resolution of which some age-old moral question perilously rests. Hare, for example, brings the division of a bar of chocolate into the moral sphere. He writes: "The just way to divide the chocolate is equally. And the principle of universalizability gives us the logic of this conclusion."[18] But why should morality always have an interest in the dividing of chocolate bars? Might not morality be neutral in many cases? Beneath the surface of this view of the scope of morality lies a fallacy of contrary-contradictory confusion. The contradictory of "X ought to do a" is "It is not the case that X ought to do a." It is not "X ought not to do a." There is a world of difference between these two locutions, and it is simply an unhappy linguistic fact that in ordinary discourse the negative of "ought" is its contrary rather than its contradictory. This fallacy is symptomatic of the scope error that, after Richard Robinson, we may refer to as "moral imperialism."[19] The appeal of this view is obvious and pernicious. It suggests that every aspect of life is governed by moral directives and thereby removes the weight of personal act-choice. Who would want to offend the moral directive? "We are never to be faced with the question "What shall I do?" in a wide open field. The answer to 'What shall I do?' will always be 'Do your duty, of course'; and according to moral imperialism you have a duty to perform at every moment."[20] The Kantians, Hare, and the act-utilitarians all tend to commit some version of this scope error. Its root cause may well be a general disdain for an examination of the purpose of a morality, of the reason we have the moral concepts we do, and of their function in ordinary moral discourse.

The second scope error that must be avoided is, according to Hector-Neri Castañeda, the most egregious in the history of moral philosophy.[21] Many moral philosophers write as if one should expect to find moral reasoning under the aegis of, that is, as a subclass of, practical reasoning or as the crowning glory of practical reasoning. In effect they conflate moral advice and guidance with practical advice, with best-play strategy. Kant's identification of moral directives with the categorical imperative, Prichard's defense of the view that when "ought" is used in an unqualified way it is moral,[22] Hare's universalizability principle,[23] the identification of moral guidelines with "all things having been considered you ought to do —," and, recently, J. L. Mackie's view of morality as a "general, all-inclusive theory of conduct,"[24] are but examples of the expansive literature that testifies to the popularity of one or another version of this view of morality. This view, however, fails to take sufficient cognizance of practical reasoning and of morality. I shall argue in the final chapter that if, as is clearly plausible and indeed recommended by many recent authors, practical rationality is defined in terms of economic or prudential reasoning, then being moral and being rational will sometimes come into unresolvable conflict. What this will further lead us to conclude is that discussions of the theories of prudential reasoning and conduct cannot advance our knowledge of morality. This second scope error, which is often to be found in moral philosophy associated with the moral imperialist error, we shall dub the "conflationist fallacy."

The aim of this general sketch is to offer an account of the scope of morality that commits neither the imperialist nor the conflationist error, while still reflecting our basic beliefs about morality, for example, that it is an autonomous and legitimate counsel whose advice bears a special sort of authority within its community.

Contents

I am grieved . . . that we should all be ruining one
another without knowing how or why and be in constant
doubt and discord all our lives. It seems very strange,
as there must be right somewhere, that an honest judge
in real earnest has not been able to find out through
all these years where it is.

Charles Dickens
Bleak House Chapter V

The Scope of Morality

1
Persons as Agents: Membership in the Moral Community

I

The proper subject of moral discourse is a person. The census of the moral world is the census of persons. But what is it, for the purposes of a morality, to be a person? This is an important and difficult question, perhaps one more properly at home in a treatise on general metaphysics or on the philosophy of mind. Recognizing that much will necessarily be left unsaid in the present context, I shall in this chapter sketch out what I believe to be a defensible account of the idea of personhood interwoven in the fabric of a morality. Much of what I shall say about persons may prove to be controversial, but I shall not attempt a full-scale discussion of the controversies or a refutation of the opposing views, for that would only draw attention away from the primary task of this book. I intend to say only enough about persons to allow the drawing of what I take to be crucial implications for the understanding of morality.

Entangled in our western tradition are three quite different notions of what constitutes personhood: the metaphysical, moral, and legal concepts. The entanglement is evident in John Locke's account of personal identity. Locke writes that the term "person" is "a *forensic* term, appropriating actions and their merit; and so belongs only to *intelligent agents*, capable of law, and happiness, and misery."[1] He goes on to say that by consciousness and memory persons are capable of extending themselves into the past and thereby become "concerned and *accountable*." Locke is probably historically correct in citing the law as a primary origin of the term "person." But he is incorrect in maintaining that its legal usage somehow entails its metaphysical sense, agency.[2]

Whether the legal or the metaphysical sense, but especially the metaphysical, and the moral sense (what Locke characterizes as accountability) are interdependent is surely controversial. Regarding the relationship between metaphysical and moral persons, two distinct schools of thought exist. According to one, to be an agent *is* to be a moral entity. The two notions roughly coincide, so that to understand what it is to be accountable one must understand what it is to be an agent, and vice versa. Locke holds the interdependence view, with which I agree. (Though Locke is wrong in rooting both the moral and metaphysical persons in the juristic person.) According to the other view, being an agent is a necessary but not sufficient condition of being a moral person. Moral persons, it is claimed, evidence certain characteristics over and above those by which agents are identified. The preponderance of current thinking tends to some version of this "necessary precondition" view, and we further find that view reflected in many of our legal decisions about, for example, insanity.

(On the other side of the interdependence view we might locate John Rawls, who develops his two principles of justice through a thought/experiment that incorporates the essential characteristics of a pre-moral, though metaphysical, population and then "derives" the moral guidelines for social institutions that the population would accept.[3] Rawls describes the persons (or parties) in the "original position" as being mutually self-interested; rational; having similar wants, needs, interests, and capacities; and as being, for all intents and purposes, equal in power, so that no one of them can dominate the others. Their choice of the principles of justice can be seen as a dramatic version of the compelling thesis that metaphysical persons are moral persons. I do not, for reasons that will become clear presently, believe that we need to adopt all of Rawls' characteristics in our account of metaphysical persons.)

Let us treat Locke as essentially correct in identifying account-ability as the primary characteristic of moral persons. We may then say that a moral person will be the referent of any proper name or description that can be a non-eliminatable subject of "a responsi-bility ascription of the second type." At least two different types of responsibility ascriptions can be distinguished in ordinary usage (not counting the lauditory recommendational use as in, "He is a responsible lad"). The first type pins responsibility on someone or something, the "who-dun-it or what-dun-it" sense. In the corre-sponding senses of "blame" (discussed in the Appendix) this is the sense that identifies the cause or causes of events thought by a speaker to be untoward. (Although we seem more interested in the failures rather than the successes that punctuate our lives, praise and credit are types of responsibility ascriptions and should not be ignored in a fuller account.) Responsibility ascriptions of this first type are blind to the capacities, dispositions, abilities, or even the metaphysical status of their subjects. Hence, no "ought implies can" arguments can be legitimately worked against their application in any specific cases. What counts is whether or not the subject was indeed the cause or one of the causes of the event in question.

Responsibility ascriptions of the second type are, first of all, parasitic on those of the first type in that they also make a causal claim, but they go further: They assert that their subjects have a "liability to answer," are "accountable" for the event. To have such a liability or to be so accountable suggests the existence of an authority relationship between the speaker and the subject of the ascription. Apparently, for someone legitimately to hold someone else responsible for an event there must exist or have existed a re-lationship of responsibility between them, so that in regard to the event in question the latter is or was answerable to the former. We can imagine that such relationships are created in a multitude of ways, for instance, through promises, contracts, compacts, hirings, assignments, appointments, by agreeing to enter a Rawlsian original position, and so on. We know also that the "right" to hold respon-sible in some of those relationships is delegatable to third parties. However, we do not delegate the right to hold responsible where moral concerns are involved in responsibility claims. This is because moral responsibility relationships are a special subset of responsibility relationships. The doing of or refraining from certain acts is perceived to be of such communal import that, as a defining feature of moral responsibility, no person is excluded from the relationship, that is, moral responsibility relationships are taken to hold reciprocally among all members of the moral community. In ordinary responsibility relationships we should say, for example, that only Z has the right to hold X accountable with respect to Y. It is not the business of anyone else. Imagine Z to be a business executive, X to be his employee and Y to be some ordinary task in the factory. It would appear rather silly if a passerby were to insert himself between the executive and the employee and claim that he was holding the employee responsible for the task. If, however, the matter at hand involves a moral principle, then the matter is no longer purely between X and Z; all persons have a stake in it. The passerby or anyone else can hold X responsible. But even though the relationship is taken to hold for all the population of the moral world, it is still only an extension of ordinary, garden-variety responsibility relationships. If we can supply an account of the requirements for entry into any responsibility relationship, we will have provided the requirements for entry into the moral community.

A responsibility ascription of the second type amounts to the assertion of a conjunctive proposition, the first conjunct of which identifies the subject's actions as the cause of an event (often, as previously mentioned, an untoward one) and the second conjunct asserts that the action was intended by the subject or that the event was the direct result of an intentional act of the subject.

In addition, the ascription implies that the subject is accountable to the speaker (in the case at hand) because of the subject's relationship to the speaker (who or what the speaker is, a member of the "moral community," a surrogate for the aggregate). (Again, a fuller account of the associated sense of "blame," blameworthiness, is provided in the Appendix.) Responsibility ascriptions of the second type clearly focus upon the intentions of their subjects rather than occasions, though not to the exclusion of occasions. J. L. Austin wrote: "In considering responsibility, few things are considered more important than to establish whether a man *intended* to do A, or whether he did A intentionally."[4] I want to argue that having the power to act, and acting intentionally, constitutes a necessary and sufficient condition of moral citizenship. In my view, to be the genuine subject of a responsibility ascription of the second type, a party in responsibility relationships, hence, a moral person, the subject must be an agent, a metaphysical person.

II

To be a moral person is to be an agent. To be an agent is to be able to act intentionally.

Given the bent of philosophy in the past thirty years, one is tempted to try to locate some sure-fire "grammatical litmus of agency"[5] that will not fail to identify persons. But this will not do. We may say that members of the class of agents can be identified as the only proper subjects of responsibility ascriptions of the second type, that is, those ascriptions that hold their subjects accountable rather than merely identify them as the causes of untoward events; we have not, however, explained why such entities should be the *proper* subjects of such ascriptions. But suppose that we say that persons are those and only those entities designated by the nouns, pronouns, etc., that appear as subjects of act-descriptions. Act-descriptions can be characterized as predicates in which the primary verb conveys that what happened was under the control of the subject and was not merely something that happened to the subject or something the subject happened to do. This is, again, a more complicated matter than may first appear. A number of things are done by a subject that we would not want to class as the acts of that subject. A human being may fall off a cliff or sleep or win the Irish Sweepstakes; although these are things he may do, they are not properly classed among his acts. For example, Bjorn Borg on July 8, 1978 did something—he won the Wimbleton Tennis Championship—but that was not one of his acts on that day. If we think of doings, actions, and acts in terms of their scope ranging over behavior, then "doings" will have the widest scope (including reflex behavior), "actions" a narrower scope, limited to movement or a series of movements: to take action is to embark on a series of doings. "Act" seems to be narrower still: to act is to do some *thing* to some purpose, to take or undertake action. Alan White has nicely put this contrast between action and act. He writes: "To act is to bring about something, to cause it to happen; an action is the bringing about of something."[6] "Mere behavior" may be defined as any activity of someone or of an animate object that he or it just happens to do, for example, reflexively.[7]

Though ordinary usage might tempt us, we cannot treat the distinctions between doings, actions, and acts on a Chinese box model. We should not assume that because actions are a species of doings, and the scope of "acts" over behavior ("doings") is smaller than that of "actions," that acts are a species of actions. There are *acts* of inhumanity, cruelty, kindness, murder, or thievery; but not *actions* of inhumanity, cruelty, kindness, murder, or thievery. Here it will not be necessary to say more than that the kinds of behavior ascribable to human beings fall into different though related categories and that we have rather standard ways of talking about behavior of each category. Unfortunately, we cannot use linguistic practice alone as a way of distinguishing the categories. For example, one may be praised or blamed for what one did, such as win or lose a game, even though one's successes and failures are not one's actions or acts. Of course one can be praised or blamed or held responsible for one's acts and usually for one's actions.

Of more interest to the present concern is that many cases can be constructed in which a moment in someone's biography can be appropriately described by an act-description or an action-description or even just a description of what someone did. The upshot is that, although agents are act-description subjects, we are left with having to specify the characteristics of agency in other than linguistic terms or we shall likely be limiting membership in the class of agents. For example, the entity designated by the subject of a sentence with an active transitive verb, or as the object of a passive verb, may or may not be acting in the instance described. Consider, "Dr. Kolletschka contracted childbed fever"[8] or, "Three home runs were hit by Reggie Jackson." Locke urged a direct assault on the concept of action (consequently, we should add, agency) when he recognized the "bewitchments" of grammar where talk of human action is concerned. Locke wrote:

> This reflection may be of some use to preserve us from mistakes about *Powers* and *Actions*, which Grammar, and the common frame of Languages, may be apt to lead us into:

Since what is signified by *Verbs* that Grammarians call *Active*, does not always signify *Action*; e.g., this Proposition, I see the Moon, or a Star, or I feel the heat of the Sun, though expressed by a *Verb Active*, does not signify any *Action* in me whereby I operate on those Substances. . . . Only because of my own choice, by a power within my self, [do] I put my self into . . . motion.[9]

Let us then take this tack. We shall say that X is acting if at least one true description of X's behavior is an act-description. We shall say that for some behavior *y* of X to be an act of X it must be true that *y* was under the control of X (Locke's "because of a choice"); by that we shall mean that *y* was intentionally "caused by" X (Locke's "power within"). To say that "*y* was an act of X" is to make the claim that some description of *y* makes it true that X did that intentionally. Donald Davidson's way of putting this is similar to my formulation. He writes, "A person is . . . (an) agent if and only if there is a description of what he did that makes true a sentence that says he did it intentionally."[10] Act-descriptions then always make implicit reference to the intentions of their subjects. They can always be redescribed to make that reference to intentionality explicit. "Dr. Kolletschka contracted childbed fever" is not an act-description because the event cannot be redescribed in true sentences that say that Dr. Kolletschka got the disease intentionally. That species of doings we have called "mere-behavior" can be characterized as movements of animate objects for which there is no description of what occurred that makes true a sentence that the subject intentionally did it.

We shall say that something *is* an agent if and only if a name or description used to designate it is the subject of at least one true present-tense act-description, or that it *was* an agent if a name or description that we use to designate it is the subject of at least one true past-tense act-description. In other words, X is (was) an agent if and only if a description of something X is doing (did) makes true the sentence "X is doing (did) that intentionally." Failing that, in all cases when X does something, X is not (was not) an agent, and because being a person and being an agent are, according to my account, identical, X is not (was not) a person.

As we shall see later, this agency criterion of metaphysical *qua* moral personhood specifies nothing about rational capacities. Instead, the criterion of agency hinges on the relationship between agency and the possible true description of an event as having been intentionally caused.[11] Intentionally, though a causal notion, is an intensional one and so it does not mark out a class of events. In fact, attributions of intentionality in regard to any event are referentially opaque with respect to other descriptions of that event. In other words, the fact that, according to one true description of the event, what someone did was intentional, does not entail that on every other true description of what he did, he did that intentionally. What was intentional depends on what aspect of the event is being described. We can correctly say, for example, that "Hamlet intentionally kills the person hiding in Gertrude's room,[12] but Hamlet does not intentionally kill Polonius," although "Polonius" and "the person hiding in Gertrude's room" are co-referential. The event may be properly described as "Hamlet killed Polonius" and also as "Hamlet intentionally killed the person hiding in Gertrude's room (behind the arras)," but not as "Hamlet intentionally killed Polonius," for that was not Hamlet's intention: He thought he was killing the King. Thus, a piece of behavior can be an act, intentional, even though under another true description of it, the behavior was not intentional. To find out if someone is acting, is an agent, we must find out if there is a true description of what he is doing that says that he did that thing intentionally. Hamlet's killing of Polonius is an act of Hamlet because he intentionally killed whoever was behind the arras, even though Hamlet's intention was not to kill Polonius.

(It would seem to be a virtue of this definition that a number of the things human beings do, that have often been mistakenly classed as acts and also given epistemic accounts, are properly excluded from the category of acts. Following Locke, I have specifically in mind, seeing. X's seeing Y is not an act of X; what occurred cannot be redescribed as being done or having been done by X intentionally. A number of animate entities just happen to see things.[13])

What persons do intentionally is to perform acts. It sounds odd to say that we perform events; acts are, however, a class of events and we can in fact say that P was the agent of some events, because we can expand some of P's acts by causal redescription to include wider-reaching events. Suppose we are interested in a killing; we may say that P pulled the trigger of the gun, thereby firing a bullet into Q, and thereby killing Q, or we may say that P killed Q by firing a bullet into him. In the first case, what P did, his act, is treated as the cause of a subsequent event. In the second case, the consequence of what he did is incorporated into the act-description. Joel Feinberg[14] has called this linguistic feature of act-descriptions the "accordion effect." If we are asked what P did, we can respond that he pulled the trigger, or we can open the accordion and say that he fired a bullet into Q, or we can open it further and say that he killed Q. P of course did only one thing in the sense that he moved his body in a certain way: he moved his finger on the trigger.

The "accordion effect" seems also to have the virtue of revealing that when we ascribe responsibility for an event we are at the same time saying that he is the agent of an act that was a movement of his body that brought about or resulted in that event. Saying that P killed Q is also saying that P did something such as pulling the trigger of a gun, and that is to say that P's finger moved in a certain way.

Davidson, furthermore, has pointed out that the "accordion effect" can be applied only to the doings of persons. "If Jones intentionally swings a bat that strikes a ball that hits and breaks a window, then Jones not only struck the ball but also broke the window. But we do not say that the bat, or even its movement, broke the window."[15]

The use of the "accordion effect" as a means of demonstrating the unity of what might otherwise appear to be disparate acts is not without its detractors. In fact, a basic disagreement in ontology and metaphysics has focused on just this issue. Some philosophers[16] have argued that if we ask (in our murder case) what acts P performed, we must say that he did a number of things, not that he did one thing that takes various descriptions as the accordion is opened. He moved his finger. He pulled the trigger of a gun. He fired a bullet into Q. He shot Q. He killed Q. (The law sometimes takes a similar view when, for example, one can be convicted of a number of crimes—possession of a deadly weapon, possession of a weapon with the intent to cause bodily injury, and manslaughter—for performing a single act: shooting someone.) The force of the argument against treating what P did, as I have, as redescriptions of the same act, rather than as descriptions of different acts, probably is that we feel constraints against treating two things as the same if they take different nonequivalent true descriptions and appear not to have the same properties in common. But we should all be able to agree that there is only one "initial act" (to use Castañeda's term) in the series in question: Suppose we say that the act is P's moving of his finger. All of the other "acts" in the series depend on that having occurred. With respect to the facts, there seems then to be no real disagreement between the opposing positions. The disagreement exists in considering how we are to regard the post-initial histories of an act of, e.g., moving one's finger, whether as the playing out of the same "accordion" or as a sequence of discrete events. The non-unifiers gain support from the principle of the indiscernability of identicals.

I would suggest, with Castañeda[17] and others that we can resolve on the side of the unifiers what may be identified as the Frege-type problem underlying the contention by invoking a redescriptive technique that treats those initial acts as being viewable under different descriptions in different contexts over time. We can then say that P's moving his finger (the initial act) under the description "P's killing Q" is identical to P's moving his finger under the description "P's shooting Q," and so on, without violating Leibniz's Law. To do this, however, is to treat events (acts) as individual entities analogous to those individuals who we designate by proper names (e.g., Sir Walter Scott) but who we also refer to by descriptive phrases, e.g., "The author of *Waverley*" and "The person of whom there is a statue on Princess Street." We do not usually, of course, use proper names to pick out acts, initial or otherwise. But that does not prove a difficulty. If we regard names, as Mill did, as having no connotations, then we have made a clear distinction between the individual (the entity) picked out by the name, and the descriptive phrases that are either true or false of that entity. Even if we treat names as Frege did, we still can ask for the individual that is the referent of the various descriptions and distinguish that referent from the descriptions we use to refer to it. That we generally use only descriptions to refer to acts is then no detriment to our treatment of them as parallel to that of other individuals. (We might imagine a nameless person to whom we always and only refer by using descriptions.) Unfortunately, a series of other problems calling for metaphysical theory remain, not the least of which is to provide an account of what the act in itself is, that is, the act not under some description or another.[18] The initial act, I think, might be regarded as that entity or individual, analogous to the referent of a proper name, that is the referential nexus of its descriptions (or, following Castañeda, its "Ontological Guises"[19]). But it is more to the point here to say simply that redescription of initial acts by virtue of the "accordion effect" is a prime way in which intention, action, and our moral vocabulary are interwoven in discourse. What P did was murder Q, if P's killing Q was intentional (and certain other conditions hold), if P moved his finger, etc. This is not the proper place to pursue the metaphysical matters. I must acknowledge that the view I am adopting is a controversial one and not without its theoretical difficulties and that there is more to be said in its defense than can be undertaken here.

The "accordion effect," however, does not reveal in what respect an act is intentional and, as we have seen, that is an important matter. For example, it might be important to Laertes to know if it was the killing of Polonius or if it was the killing of the person hiding behind the arras that Hamlet intended. Laertes might have felt that, in the former case, Hamlet was the murderer of Polonius, but in the latter, he was the killer of Polonius though not necessarily his murderer. Without the presence of or the assumption of intention, the "accordion effect" also produces counter-intuitive results. For example, suppose that I think that by digging a hole in my back yard and covering it with branches that I will trap an animal that has been raiding my garden at night. When I check my trap in the morning I discover that the neighborhood burglar is lying unconscious in the hole. I think it would be agreed that I caught the burglar. On the other hand, suppose there just happens to be a hole in my back yard and I have inadvertently thrown some branches over it in the process of pruning trees. Night falls, the burglar is again knocked unconscious by his fall into the hole, and I discover him there in the morning. Although in one sense it is true that I caught him—he is now in my power—it is not true that *I* did something with the intent to try to bring about any entrapment, that _I caught_ the burglar. We need therefore to examine more carefully the concept of intentionality.

Consider an example created by J. L. Austin (his reasons for using the example were somewhat different from my own; the example played a role in his attempt to draw attention to differences in usage of the terms "intentionally," "deliberately," and "on purpose"). "The notice says, 'Do not feed the penguins.' I, however, feed them peanuts. Now peanuts happen to be, and these prove, fatal to these birds. Did I feed them peanuts intentionally? Beyond a doubt: I am no casual peanut shedder."[20] When I say, "I intentionally fed the penguins peanuts," am I saying anything more than "I threw peanuts at the penguins?" What actually did I do? My hand holds some peanuts, my arm moves rapidly, and the peanuts fly from my hand into the penguin cage. But these actions coupled with the ingestion of the peanuts by the birds cause the penguins to die. My feeding those birds those peanuts is initially and identical to the moving of my arms and hands in certain ways; that is what it is for me to feed penguins peanuts, my arm and hand move from peanut bag to an outstretched position over the penguin pit, etc. An event occurs, the correct explanation of which must include reference to my act of penguin feeding. My act is "accordioned" out from the "primitive" actions of my body to events on an event-causal path. But the issue is: did I _poison_ the penguins? What was my intention and, if it was not to kill those birds, does that matter to whether or not I am responsible for their deaths? Austin remarks that "I am no casual peanut shedder." Witty that statement may be, but it surely does not clear up matters; although it does give indication that at least the accordion of my movements expanded to "throwing the peanuts to the penguins" falls under my intention. If we know that action was intentional, does that mean the deaths of the birds fall under my intention as well? Surely if I had accidentally dropped my peanut bag, so that the peanuts spilled into the penguin cage and the birds ate them and died, we would not be able to say truthfully that I was the agent of their deaths.

Some philosophers have argued that only if it is possible to describe my bodily movements as having been caused by me in some direct way, agent to action, will such references to intention as "no casual peanut shedder" make sense.[21] But as Davidson comments:

"There seems no good reason . . . for using such expressions as 'cause,' 'bring about,' 'make the case,' to illuminate the relation between an agent and his act."[22] Agents do not cause their acts. One is an agent by virtue of acting. Let us then not even pursue the idea that a special kind of causality exists between the agent and his acts.

Sometimes the descriptions of the bodily movements of human beings are redescribable as bringing about something, for example, feeding the penguins by throwing them peanuts. But just as often bodily movements can be redescribed as the effects of a prior cause; then they are described as done for reasons, done in order to bring about something, for example, feeding the penguins peanuts in order to kill them. Usually that prior cause is some desire or need combined with the belief that the object of the desire will be achieved by the action. This is what Aristotle meant when he maintained that acting requires desire.

Saying that someone performed an action intentionally is describing him as having had a reason (which is the cause of his doing it) for performing that action. Describing a movement as intentional, then, is redescribing it as an effect of a desire conjoined with a belief. If I fed the penguins peanuts with the intention of providing food to relieve their hunger, then one of the causes of my feeding them was my desire to provide food for those birds (penguins) coupled with my belief that peanuts would suffice as food.

Frederick Dretske has shown[23] that the stress placed on various components of causally sensitive sentences throws entirely different lights on what is expressed. Using Dretske's term, "allomorph," we may list as allomorphs of the sentence about penguin feeding:

A. I intentionally fed the *penguins* peanuts.

B. I intentionally fed the penguins *peanuts*.

A proper causal account of allomorph A is given in the preceding paragraph. Another might be that it was penguins not elephants I knew I was feeding, believing them to be hungry; that my intention was to feed penguins and I used peanuts to do so. Allomorph B suggests (at least) a rather different causal antecedant than A. B suggests that it is peanuts that I intentionally fed the penguins, not that I fed the penguins because I had a desire to provide food for them and happened to have peanuts at hand, believing whatever items I was giving them to be nutritious. Or even that I knew the creatures I was feeding to be penguins. I could have the intention of feeding them *peanuts* only if I knew that it was peanuts that I was feeding them and not, for example, popcorn. Hence if B is true, then it must be true that I had a desire to feed the penguins peanuts and that desire was the cause of my feeding the penguins peanuts. If I am caught by the zoo keeper, it may matter to my defense whether A or B is true.

An obvious objection to the foregoing is that reasons, beliefs, and desires cannot be causes because they are not events, and, as earlier endorsed when we discussed agent-to-act causation, no other type of causation than event causation exists. This objection can be over-come if it is acknowledged that although desires and beliefs or pro-attitudes are not events *per se*, their "onslaughts" (Davidson's term) are. If I am asked why I fed the *penguins* peanuts, I can usually an-swer by citing an event, albeit a "mental event," for instance, "They looked frightfully hungry to me." Sometimes, admittedly, I may not be able to explain right away if at all why I did it. There may have been a good number of contributory reasons. Davidson sug-gests that "In such cases, explanation in terms of primary reasons parallels the explanation of the collapse of the bridge from a struc-tural defect: we are ignorant of the event or sequence of events that led up to (caused) the collapse, but we are sure there was such an event or sequence of events."[24]

Accepting the proposition that reasons are causes, however, opens the door to the determinist's query: "From where do(es) my reason(s) (for feeding the penguins) come?" If my reasons for acting are caused by forces or events beyond my control, then I am surely not free, and the linguistic fact that my actions can be redescribed as intentional will be only a mask of the true situation. Although it is not fruitful here to engage in the free will/determinism debate, it is important to point out that the determinist appears to make a number of unwarranted assumptions, two of which are of particular concern.

Obviously, showing that an act was intentional, that is, done for a reason, is not enough to show that it was determined: One would have to show that the reason for acting was both a sufficient con-dition for the act to be performed in the way it was and when it was and that there are sufficient conditions for having that reason that were present when or just before the act was performed. That I thought the penguins to be hungry is a sufficient condition for my feeding them. Furthermore, we may well imagine that it is possible under certain descriptions for my reasons for feeding the penguins to be determined by features of the situation that are outside of my control. But the sufficient condition for my feeding the birds cannot be both that I thought they were hungry and a set of features outside my control. Presumably, if my reasons for feeding the penguins are caused by features of the situation, I should be able to find out what those features are and how they affect my actions. If I do come to know what they are, however, I would not properly be able to say that I thought the penguins to be hungry so I fed them. I would have to say something like, "I was inclined by those features to think (or believe) that they were hungry." But there is surely no small difference between "thinking that" and "being inclined to think that." The determinist must fail if in order to prove his case he must show both that a sufficient condition of my acting was my reason (I thought P) and that a sufficient condition of my having that reason (conditions C caused me to think that P) was present; for, although in any particular case one or the other condition may be met, both cannot be met in the same case. The only way they could be met simultaneously would be if we would allow the determinist to stipulate that an agent is always systematically forbidden knowledge of the existence of the sufficient external conditions for his reason for doing what he does in any particular set of circumstances. There seems to be no good reason in favor of granting that stipulation.[25]

The second apparently unwarranted assumption of the determinist is that holding the position that reasons are causes of acts commits one to holding the position that reasons have evident sufficient causal explanations. Maybe they do not. But that is not important. Instead, that we have reasons that cause our doing certain things provides no grounds for the view that those reasons must be caused, and especially no ground for the view that they must be caused by something external to the person. Davidson writes:

> Why on earth should a cause turn an action into a mere happening, and a person into a helpless victim? Is it because we tend to assume, at least in the arena of action, that a cause

demands a causer, agency an agent? So we press the question; if my action was caused, what caused it? If I did, then there is the absurdity of infinite regress; if I did not, then I am a victim. But of course the alternatives are not exhaustive. *Some causes have no agents. Primary among these are those states and changes of state in persons, which, because they are reasons as well as causes, make persons voluntary agents.*[26]

Thus, four types of situations exist in which someone can be said to do something:

1. when he does the thing intentionally
2. when he does something else intentionally that can be redescribed as the doing of that thing
3. when he just happens to do that thing
4. when he does something else that contributes to or constitutes his doing that thing.

In situations of the third type we would say that the person is not the agent of the event described. In situations of the fourth type we would say that he did the thing, though it will make no sense to say that he was the agent of it, for instance, winning a tennis match. In the other two cases what he does can be counted among his acts. We then may say that *y* was an act of X if and only if some description of *y* makes it true that X did that intentionally. Redescription of an intentional act by inclusion of its effects expands agency.

Thus two necessary conditions must be met to define an action as a person's act. It is an act if and only if, under at least one true description, it is one of that person's bodily movements and, under at least one other true description, it is intentional.

III

At the end of the first section, I maintained that being an agent is a necessary and sufficient condition of being, for moral purposes, a person, a citizen of the moral world. As we have now seen, that claim is to be regarded as equivalent to the claim that one is accountable for what one did if and only if one did it intentionally. To act intentionally is to do something for a reason, that is, because of a desire and a belief. This definition of action would seem to imply that one chose or decided to do what one did. Further, the implication that one could have chosen not to do that deed seems also to be unpackable from the idea of intentionality. Hence, moral philosophers from the time of Aristotle tend to contrast intentionality with compulsion. F. H. Bradley tells us that the contrast is embedded in the "vulgar notion of responsibility."[27] The notion of choice may invite analysis of intentionality in terms of rationality, and a focus on decision theory, but I think that notion is smuggled in rather than really unpackable. Choices do not have to be rational, in the standard sense of the term, to be choices. One's reasons for acting, that is, one's beliefs and/or desires might not stand the test of rationality or be regarded as "intelligent" but that does not mean one is not acting, is not an agent when one behaves in a certain way because of those beliefs and desires.

A more fruitful notion from the point of view of understanding agency and its relationship to moral citizenship, as Locke maintained, is that of consciousness.[28] Obviously, to do y intentionally one must be conscious that what one is doing is y, and that it is *oneself* that is doing y. By "consciousness" is meant, roughly, "present awareness." But Locke has more to say about the relationship between consciousness and accountability. His view is that consciousness is what Mackie has called "a two-directional unity."[29] He claims that by consciousness, in the sense of first person memory traces of past deeds, a person "owns and imputes to it *self* past Actions."[30] The presence of such a dual-aspect consciousness provides the ground for accountability and, thereby, crediting, blaming, praising, and, especially for Locke, punishing someone for their past acts. In fact, for Locke, a necessary condition for justifiable punishment is that the person must remember the punishable act as *his* act. (This is, of course, related to Locke's theory of personal identity, which we need not discuss here.) In the same vein, Bradley maintains that what he calls "self-sameness" is the first condition of accountability.

> If, when we say, 'I did it', the I is not to be the one I, distinct from all other I's; or if the I now here, is not the same I with the I whose act the deed was, then there can be no question whatever but that the ordinary notion of responsibility disappears.[31]

As is well known, Aristotle in Book Three of the *Nicomachean Ethics* provides an argument that only voluntary actions (what I have called acts) are properly blamed or praised. When behavior is involuntary, "we are pardoned and sometimes even pitied." For Aristotle, behavior under constraint (or compulsion) or due to ignorance is involuntary. Although Aristotle does elaborate on the idea of constraint, more useful to the present concern is an examination of his analysis of that other general plea: ignorance. He distinguishes two primary senses of ignorance. The first is ignorance of moral principle, which, he claims, is not pardonable. "Ignorance in moral choice does not make an act involuntary—it makes it wicked."[32] Aristotle's second major sense of ignorance is "ignorance of particulars," that is, the particulars "which constitute the circumstances and the issues involved in the action."[33] Aristotle maintains that exculpability and pardon depend on what aspects of the circumstances are those of which the person is ignorant. Although Hamlet may know that to intentionally kill a human being who is innocent under the law is murder, he may be ignorant of the fact that the person behind the arras (who he intentionally stabs, believing that the hidden person is the murderous Claudius) is the rather harmless Polonius. Aristotle's point is that a person may be ignorant that his action may take quite a different description than the one he intended. Ignorance in this second sense depends on and helps to illuminate intentionality. As Mackie has noted: "The key to the understanding of the role of ignorance is that an action may be intended under one description but not under another."[34] Recall our earlier discusssion of Hamlet's killing of Polonius.

Consider the following:

I 1. Hamlet moved his arm.
   2. Hamlet thrust his sword into the arras (by moving his arm).
   3. Hamlet stabbed Polonius (by thrusting his sword into the arras).
   4. Hamlet killed Polonius (by stabbing him).

II 1. Hamlet moved his arm.
   2. Hamlet thrust his sword into the arras (by moving his arm).

3. Hamlet stabbed Polonius (by thrusting his sword into the arras).

4. Hamlet murdered Polonius (by stabbing him).

Expansion II terminates in a true description of what Hamlet did only if it is true that he intentionally killed *Polonius* (by stabbing him), that what he intended to do was *to kill Polonius*. In other words, we only allow the substitution of II (4) for I (4), when Hamlet's intention was to kill Polonius by stabbing him while Polonius was hiding behind the arras in Queen Gertrude's room, knowing his victim to be Polonius. Expansion I, on the other hand, is a true account of Hamlet's act if he did either (1) or (2) or (3) or (4), whether intentionally or not. It is characteristic of moral words like "murder," when they are used in descriptions of actions, that they draw the agent's intentions to themselves, the magnet force of moral terms with respect to intentions. Although Hamlet could quite unintentionally kill Polonius, for which he ought not (morally) be held accountable *ceteris paribus*, he cannot unintentionally murder Polonius. If he murdered Polonius, he can be held accountable for the deed; if it was murder, it was intentional.

The foregoing considerations may be related by introducing what we may call the *Primary Principle of Accountability* (PPA): a person can be held accountable for only and for all of that person's intentional acts (that is, one is responsible only for that aspect of one's behavior for which there is a true description of what one did that says that one did that intentionally.)[35]

PPA, however, does not satisfy our intuitions about accountability in any responsibility relationship. We must make a few minor modifications.

Suppose that a person knows himself to have inadequate skill for the performing of some task that when performed by the unskilled usually results in injury or some other harm to someone else. The first time the unskilled person performs the task, he is unaware that harm will result, and the harm does result. His act might be written off as an accident or a mistake or simply as unfortunate. But if the person performs the task again, even if he does not directly include the harmful consequence in his intention, we would say that he indirectly or collaterally intended the outcome and can be held accountable for its occurrence. Mackie prefers to call this "oblique intention." He captures this notion rather well when he writes: "The action will be directly intended under any description that represents a feature he has sought, either as an end or as a means, but obliquely intended under any that represents one that he has not sought even as a means but has thus accepted."[36] We should modify PPA to read (PPA') "a person can be held accountable for only and for all of that person's intentional acts and for outcomes that were collaterally (indirectly or obliquely) intended by him."

A further modification of PPA' to suit common practice and our intuitions about accountability is in order. Suppose we imagine two people, X and Y. If X does a and Y does b in response to X's doing a, and an outcome of Y's doing b, of which X was aware when he did a, is an untoward event, then X can be held accountable for b by reason of collateral intention of a nonoriginal (or second) effect. Of course, in certain cases we will hold Y accountable as well. But if Y's doing b is a natural or a required response (for example, because of the respective stations of X and Y in some organization) to X's doing a, then we should probably only hold X accountable, unless Y's doing b is in itself a violation of some moral principle. We could further modify and complicate the matter of collateral intentions for nonoriginal effects, but our purpose is served by altering PPA' to read: (PPA") "a person can be held accountable for only and for all of his (intentional) acts, and for those events that occur that he indirectly or collaterally intended, including those collaterally intended nonoriginal or double effects that involve the actions of other persons." Knowingly tempting another, for example, would qualify under "collaterally intended nonoriginal effects" for which the tempter may be held accountable, *ceteris paribus*. Other modifications of PPA" would be necessary to satisfy all of our practices and intuitions, particularly those when a person acts out of passion or rage, but these need not concern us here. What we have located is a basic principle that relates intentionality to accountability.

Two strong criticisms of PPA" should be expected. The first challenges PPA" by pointing out that we often hold people accountable for their unintentional acts. For example, a person driving an automobile under the influence of alcohol (that is drunk) is usually held accountable for the havoc he causes. What reason is generally given in defense of such a practice? Most often it is the Aristotelian one that the drunkard could have chosen not to get drunk. But getting drunk is exactly what he should be held accountable for, if not by reason of direct intention, then by reason of collateral intention. If after getting drunk he does someone harm, and it is inappropriate to say that he even indirectly intended to do that harm, it seems unreasonable, indeed offends our other intuitions about responsibility to hold him accountable for the harm. Some practical benefit in the way of deterrence might result if we punish drunks for the things they do when drunk, but then, with Bradley, we should have to urge that the difference between punishment and correction[37] is being overlooked.

The second challenge to PPA″ would come from the other direction. As a matter of course, we do not hold certain persons accountable for their intentional behavior. The usual example is young children. I think such an objection, however, is simply wrong. What we do not usually do with young children is punish them, as we would adults for similar misdeeds. We often treat their misdeeds as the basis for inculcating moral concerns, this Bradley calls "pedagogic punishment." This does not imply that children, if they are capable of intentional acts, are not persons for the purposes of morality. Indeed, it seems to me, that just the opposite should be concluded from the practice. Pedagogic punishment would be absurd if the subject is not a moral citizen. Discipline and moral training are designed to guide the child's future choices, to make it more likely that the child will make the morally endorsed decisions regarding his or her future acts. In other words, pedagogical punishment is holding accountable, but for pragmatic reasons, this accountability is usually backed by less severe punishment. Bradley, and he is not alone in this, in treating accountability and punishability as convertible notions, is guilty of a major error in moral philosophy, the confusion of "holding responsible" with "a way of holding responsible." (There are types of people other than young children who, though they seem to do things intentionally still are not usually held accountable (at least morally) for what they do, for instance, psychopaths and certain mental defectives. I shall leave discussion of these cases for another occasion.) I regard PPA″ to be defensible against the two objections discussed above.

The only addition to PPA″ we should make in order to account for the often mitigatory and sometimes exculpatory plea, "I was not myself when it happened" (and its many variants), is to emend PPA″ with Locke's point, also emphasized by Bradley, that for an agent to be justifiably held accountable he must be conscious of himself as the person who did perform the act in question. Bradley capsulizes the thesis: "without personal identity responsibility is sheer nonsense."[38]

IV

The life of a person can be distinguished from the biological life of a human being. The biological life of a human being is a sequence of intakes and outputs, of growth and decay, of being born and eventually dying. It is movements and rests, pushes and pulls, actions and reactions. A biological human life begins at conception and ends when the brain ceases to emit waves. Locke drew a distinct line between the identity of a man and the identity of a person. For him the identity of a man was simply the continuous existence of a physical entity through time, while that of a person was self-consciousness and, in large measure, the criterion of re-identification was memory. A necessary but not a sufficient condition of being a person on the persons-as-agents account, however, is having a body. The only acts that exist, after all, are bodily movements. Without the movements of bodies there can be no agents. Nonetheless, there may be agents that operate remote bodies or whose acts are the movements of a consortium of bodies.

I have elsewhere distinguished between two different types of human collectivities[39] (varieties of collections of human beings): what I have called aggregate and conglomerate collectivities. Because my interest here is to provide a basic account of the citizenry of the moral world, it is important to indicate briefly why conglomerate collectivities qualify as persons, whereas aggregates do not.

A collectivity is any collection of persons or any organization primarily composed of persons and to which one normally makes reference in English by the use of a count noun, noun phrase, proper name, or a conjunction of any of these.

I shall call a collectivity an aggregate if the identity of that collectivity consists in the sum of the identities of the persons who comprise the membership of the collectivity. Aggregate collectivities are merely collections or sums of individual persons. In saying that the identity of an aggregate collectivity consists in the sum of the identities of its membership, I mean that any and every change in the collectivity's membership always entails a change in collectivity identity. A particular aggregate collectivity's existence, because it is a particular collection of individual persons, is incompatible with a changing or shifting membership.

The calculus of individuals individuates an aggregate in terms of objects having common parts with member-components of the aggregate. Leonard and Goodman[40] offer the definition, "$x\,\mathrm{Fu}\,\alpha =_{Df} \overline{z|x} \cdot \equiv_z \cdot Y\mathrm{E}\alpha \supset_y \overline{z|y}$" as a partial rendering of their view. The idea is that an individual (x in the definition) stands in what they call the fusion (Fu) relation to a class (α) when everything that is discrete (that predicate symbolized as $\overline{z|x}$) from it is discrete from the class and vice versa. This seems, however, to be somewhat counter-intuitive when we apply it to person-sums. Suppose we are interested in knowing whether the passengers on Flight 549 are the same as the passengers on Flight 548. We would not likely think to do so by determining whether or not the passengers on Flight 548 have common parts with those on Flight 549. We are much more direct. The passengers on Flight 549 are the same as those on Flight 548 when the same passengers are on board each flight. The reidentification of aggregate collectivities over time, then, is accomplished only by reference to their component memberships. Suppose that a statement were made about aggregate collectivity A; if one of the individual persons that are member-components of A had not in fact been a member-component of A, the meaning of the statement would have been different. The nouns, noun phrases, and proper names used to designate aggregate collectivities, "the OxBow lynch mob," "the passengers on Flight 549," "Charlie Company," "the people on the corner," are shorthand devices for referring to conjunctions of proper names or definite descriptions. "Tom, Dick, and

Harry lynched Ralph" and "The mob lynched Ralph" are identical if and only if the mob is composed of only the individuals Tom, Dick, and Harry. Of course the mob, if not Tom and Dick and Harry, is composed of some other enumerable collection of persons.

A collectivity is a conglomerate if the identity of that collectivity does not entirely consist in or is not exhausted by the identities of the persons that are members of it. The continued existence of a conglomerate collectivity is compatible with a varying or constantly changing membership. A change in membership does not entail a corresponding change in the identity of a conglomerate collectivity. If a statement were made about a particular conglomerate (C), then even if one of the individuals belonging to C had not in fact been a member of C, the meaning of the statement would not have been different.

At least four characteristics that conglomerate collectivities evidence are not found in the case of aggregate collectivities. (Undoubtedly there are others, but these seem to me to be particularly important.) (1) Conglomerate collectivities are/have internal organizations and/or established decision procedures by which courses of collective action can be and usually, though not necessarily, are chosen. (2) Members of a conglomerate collectivity generally fill specified differing roles and have different stations by virture of which they exercise certain powers over other members. Simply, conglomerate collectivities tend to have levels of internal power and responsibility invested in positions and not in people. (3) Standards of conduct for collectivity members are internally created and usually differ in some significant ways from the standards applicable in the larger community of persons. (4) Individuals become members of conglomerate collectivities in standardized ways peculiar to each collectivity of this sort.

Although aggregate collectivities may do things that individual component members could not have done alone (e.g., carry a piano), their actions are always redescribable by reducing the act to the component acts of the members (Tom, Dick, and Harry each bearing a certain amount of the weight of the piano). Because conglomerate collectivities have decision structures and basic policy guidelines, they may be treated in and of themselves as having intentions and hence as being agents of their acts. (I have argued this view elsewhere in regard to what I see as the paradigm of conglomerate collectivities, the corporation.[41]) For a conglomerate to be treated as an agent some things that happen must be describable in a way that makes sentences true that say that some of the things the conglomerate does are intended by the conglomerate itself and not just by its individual members.

As we have already seen, attributions of intentionality in the description of any event are referentially opaque with respect to other descriptions of that event. A great deal depends on what aspect of the event is being described. The referential opacity of intentionality attributions aids in driving a wedge between descriptions of certain events as individual intentional acts and as conglomerate intentional acts.

The decision structures of conglomerate collectivities have at least two elements: (1) an organizational chart, and (2) decision recognition rules or policies. These decision structures accomplish a subordination and synthesis of the intentions and acts of various biological persons into a conglomerate decision. Hence, these decision structures license the descriptive transformation of events, seen under another aspect as the acts of biological persons (those who occupy various stations on the organizational chart), into conglomerate acts done for conglomerate reasons. No such structure exists in the case of aggregate collectivities.

To summarize: we can describe many events in terms of certain physical movements of human beings, and we also can sometimes describe those events as done for reasons by those human beings; but further we can sometimes describe those events as conglomerate (corporate) and still further as done for conglomerate reasons qualitatively different from the personal reasons, if any, of component members.

A conglomerate's agency resides in the redescription of events as conglomerate intentional, licensed by its decision structure. But then, as earlier argued, human agency resides, to some degree, in description as well. At any rate I think we may with some confidence say that conglomerate collectivities should be regarded as persons, agents, and, as such, citizens of the moral world. Another way of putting this conclusion would be that "person" is not, though "human being" is, the name of a natural kind.

V

In *A Theory of Justice*, John Rawls lists the following as parties of the initial situation, those parties being roughly equivalent to the population of the moral world:

1. continuing persons (family heads, or genetic lines)
2. single individuals
3. associations (states, churches, or other corporate bodies).[42]

In "Justice as Reciprocity" Rawls writes:

A word about the term "person." This expression is to be construed variously depending on the circumstances. On some occasions it will mean human individuals, but in others it may refer to nations, provinces, business firms, churches, teams, and so on.[43]

I regard the foregoing section as contributing to a delineation of the ambiguity of "person" in moral discourse. Morality is addressed to persons. An entity is a person if and only if it is an actor in the drama of communal life. Persons are neither necessarily single human individuals nor are they necessarily possessed of some quality or characteristic other than the ability to act, by virtue of which they are moral citizens. We understand more about the complexity of the nature of morality when we realize that it is a multifaceted device persons have designed, rather unsystematically, as they have become aware of their own predicament, their own abilities, and their own shortcomings. A morality reflects the realization that persons are complex; that numerous ways, patterns, and habits of acting (and not acting) exist; that human life is not merely a series of choices; that persons to some extent develop character by acting in certain ways and that they then habitually act in character. We *make* the persons we are by the way we act. We form our character traits by replicating actions. For that reason morality, a full-blown morality, is not simply concerned with act or event evaluation. Not all acting is *rationally* motivated, not all acting is the product of "cool" rational self-interest. Insofar as morality has evolved as a defense system against threats to any person from another's acts, we should not expect that morality would be single-tracked, focusing on only one though an important characterisitc of its subjects.

Morality is not, of course, a defense system in the sense that Warwick Castle or the Maginot line were defense systems, but is a collection of guidelines and principles. As such it can be directed only to those members of the ecosystem whose intentions affect their behavior, who are accountable. It is that class of entities about any one of whose members we may say "He could have done otherwise if he had chosen to do so," the only class whose members can make mistakes. Morality is addressed to the members of the only class whose members can commit murder, can steal, can lie.

VI

A number of inferences may be drawn from the agency criterion of moral personhood that should enhance our understanding of morality, but one in particular, of a negative sort, is worth mention at this point. No feature of agency rationally would necessitate treating persons always as ends and never as means only. That an entity is a person does not seem to imply either that the entity has intrinsic worth or inalienable rights.

The principle that all persons are to be respected solely by virtue of their being members of the moral community has played a primary role in recent moral philosophy.[44] (It should be obvious how odd this sounds when we admit conglomerate collectivities into the honored class.) This version of the idea of respect for persons is often traced to certain Kantian precepts. Kant, in *The Doctrine of Virtue*, writes:

Man regarded as a person—that is, as the subject of morally practical reason—is exalted above any price; for as such he is not to be valued as a mere means to the ends of others or even to his own ends, but as an end in himself. . . . And it is just this that comprises his dignity, by virtue of which he assumes superiority over all the other beings in the world which are not mean and can be used—hence over all things. But just as he cannot give himself away for any price . . . so neither can he act contrary to the equally necessary self-esteem in which others, as men, hold themselves. . . . Hence he is subject to a duty based on the respect which he must show every other man.[45]

A major difficulty with Kant's view is that, as Pepita Haezrahi has noted,[46] the cornerstone idea—that all persons *qua* persons have a certain dignity—cannot be deduced from the concept of human dignity itself. Simply, it is not essential to the concept of human dignity that all people have dignity, though Kant does not seem to have acknowledged this. Quite another way of putting matters is to argue that having dignity is an accidental rather than an essential property of any particular person. Surely we can imagine any particular person existing but lacking in dignity. Kant, of course, would reply that although it may be that persons have their price, we cannot in the end imagine any rational being existing and lacking in dignity defined as the quality of worth, irreplaceable by something of equal value. Here, however, one wants to say two things: (1) The issue seems to be one of definition only, and (2) it is not clear at all what kind of property dignity, as defined, is. We talk of someone being dignified, meaning by that that he is disposed to behave in a certain way under certain conditons. But that does not capture what is usually meant by human dignity, i.e., the quality or property of being of worth as a person.

The property of being of worth is a supervenient one; in fact, I would prefer to call it a second-order supervenient property, for reasons that will become apparent in Chapter II. Certainly nothing exhibits the property of "worthness" (whatever that might be). Something is of worth because it exhibits other properties. The key question then in regard to Kant's position is whether if something has the property of rationality it *eo ipso* has the property of worth. The property of being rational, however, is also a supervenient property. Something is rational not because it has the property of "rationalness" but because it has other properties, some no doubt that are dispositional, by virtue of which fact we call it rational. The question then is whether the having of one supervenient property is identical to the having of another or entails or is entailed by the having of another. We might imagine that having the property of being of worth supervenes having the property of rationality or that it is identical (in some unspecified way) to having that property. Clearly, however, these properties cannot be identical. The principle of the indiscernibility of identicals would be violated if that were the case.

We are left with the possibility that the property of being of worth supervenes the property of being rational. That may well be defended, but it would not be necessarily true then that rational beings have the property of being of worth. For example, for the property of being of worth or of having dignity to be properly attributed to something, it might be required to exhibit the property of rationality and the property of being handsome. At the very least Kant's pronouncement that "All persons are possessed of dignity and are hence ends in themselves" is neither obviously analytic nor known to be true *a priori*. The concept of "being a person possessed of dignity" or "being a person of worth" is clearly an important one in moral philosophy. As Kant says, autonomy is the basis of human dignity and the proper attitude to take toward an entity of dignity is respect. But it is not essential to the concept that the property is distributed over the class of persons, that it is a self-evident defining characteristic of class membership. Nonetheless, a frequent course of argument after Kant has been to regard the principle of respect for persons as the underlying or most fundamental justification of our moral obligations and of morality itself. Such a characterization of morality, however, both is woefully simplistic and inverts the role of respect in human commerce.

Respect is a "reactive attitude"[47] generally directed toward some discovered characteristic or known activities of the object of respect. To respect something is to value something it can or does do. (Minnesotans talk of having respect for the weather, meaning not so much that they value it as that they know what it can do and has often done to people unprepared for it. What is valued is one's own life. Having respect for the weather is not, however, to fear it. It is to take precautions.) Respect should not be confused with sympathy or empathy or a willingness to take cognizance of the needs and wants of other people.

For instance, X respects Y *for* something Y does or did or in virtue of Y's action or because X believes Y's action to be evidence of Y's having an admirable character. People earn the respect of other people by their acts. We only really respect those people whom we credit with acting in ways we believe to be right or good. We may treat with deferential regard the people we fear, but that is not to respect them. Respect may be properly seen as dependent on crediting, which is the opposite of blaming. Saying "Y is to be respected" is a way of praising Y; justifiable praise entails that evidence can be cited that Y actually has acted in some creditable or commendable way (given our standards of acting in comparable circumstances). Usually, however, respect is "built up" over time. Hence, to say "Y is to be respected" is to say that Y acts in creditable ways on most occasions or that Y does so generally speaking. We respect persons not because they do act, but because they do or do not act in certain ways.

Another sense of "respect," the legal sense, seems to be often favored by moral philosophers. In the law, for example, we are told that we must respect the boundaries of another person's property. What that means is that we must not do certain things without his permission. Another way of putting the difference between the two senses would be to say that the law tells us we must respect his (property) rights regardless of whether we have any respect for him. Clearly this legal sense of "respect" is what Kant usually intended, for he writes: "The duty of free respect to others is really only a negative one (of not exalting oneself above others) and is thus analogous to the juridical duty of not encroaching on another's possessions."[48]

The juridical duty sense of "respect" is dependent on the existence of rules within an institution, usually legal or political. It is wrong, for example, not to show respect for and pay homage to the Queen—not because she has done so many commendable things, but because she occupies a station defined by the political institution's rules in such and such a way. The law tells us that we must respect a person's right to do y even when or especially when we cannot respect him for doing y, or we will be liable to penalty or suit. If such a principle of respect is dependent for its sense on the existence of certain rules (those in particular that create "negative duties"), then it cannot be the fundamental principle on which the institution is based. It cannot provide the answer to the questions "Why should I respect X?" or "Why should I respect X's property?" "You should respect X simply because he is a person," gets us no further toward an answer to these questions.

We should not forget the admonitions we heard at our grandmothers' knees, "if you want people to respect you, you must be honest (or trustworthy or kind or . . .)." The concepts, principles, and guidelines that, in large measure, constituted that grandmaternal counsel were not, of course, the creation of the dear woman herself. (One could well say that she plays out her role in the moral defense plan.) They have evolved, been created and been nurtured over the centuries by the broader community of persons (of which she is a member) that has, with no little wisdom, concerned itself with seeking general remedy to the problems inherent in the common plight of persons.

In the chapters that follow, my concern will be to offer what I take to be the correct way to understand the nature of morality, that system of act guidelines and character models that has indeed emerged from such reflections, reactions, and anticipations.

2
MORALITY:
Morals and Euergetics

I

The moral conceptual "terrain" is not like a geological one, but not because it is rather more elusive to the dedicated cartographer. Rather, it is because it is not "out there" at all, not a landscape cluttered with objects whose positions can be mapped. Our moral concepts, despite the philosophical metaphor in vogue, are not objects in "conceptual space" that can be plotted, in keeping with some principle of projection, for some purpose. Our moral concepts differ in large measure from our scientific ones in that they create the very world we use them to describe, that is, the world in which there are murders, lies, adulteries, thefts, and vicious acts.

Seán O'Faoláin, master of the Irish short story, some years ago wrote an intriguing tale about an apparently idyllic summer holiday taken by himself, two young nuns, and two young monks, all students, at a mountain retreat in Ireland. The students spent many carefree hours in song as, with childish delight, they undertook learning Gaelic and the traditional dances. Their evening sessions in their rooms and their moonlight cruises on the lake, in point of fact, though boisterous, never overstepped the bounds of laic probity. Nonetheless, they were sternly rebuked by the almost satanic figure of the local curate. "Glory be to God. . . . To think that this kind of thing has been going on under my nose for weeks. . . . To think I cannot go for a summer walk to read my office without hearing this kind of caterwauling! . . . *Only* having a bit of a singsong. . . . Perhaps . . . we think that we are back in the days of the Reformation? . . . Singing? Dancing? Drinking?" Some years later, as O'Faoláin tells it, he met one of the monks who then confessed that he did not in retrospect enjoy that summer, that the wrong kinds of things go on in such mountain retreats. Coincidentally, a few hours later O'Faoláin happened on the curate who confided to him, "They were only children. Such innocents! . . . Of course, I had to frighten them!" The story is aptly entitled, "The Man Who Invented Sin."[1]

O'Faoláin has laid hold of a philosophically important and, as I shall argue, correct thesis: Moral concepts are solely the product of human inventon (usually motivated by the perception of a certain communally oriented need to accomplish a certain end) rather than conventions used to talk about objective, discoverable, and investigatable entities. By inventing the concept of sin (or, for our purposes, the concepts of morality), we invent sin, or the world that is then describable by using "sin vocabulary" is the world of our invention. To invent sin, of course, is to introduce that concept in some propagatively preceptorial fashion into the communal consciousness (neatly accomplished by O'Faoláin's curate by his histrionic pomposity, officiousness, and reverent disdain).

Julius Kovesi puts the thesis quite nicely when he writes: "When we turn to our moral life we do not find that there is some raw material there waiting to be described and evaluated. . . . Our moral notions constitute that world and without our moral life and notions there is nothing there to be described or evaluated."[2]

My thesis may be characterized as the view that our moral concepts are transparent. An early version of this thesis was perceptively argued by John Locke. His account serves as a useful point of departure and a touchstone for my study. For Locke, moral concepts are members of that class of complex ideas he preferred to call "mixed modes." Locke wrote:

> The *Mind* often *exercises an active Power in the making* of *these several Combinations.* For it being once furnished with

simple *Ideas*, it can put them together in several Compositions, and so make a variety of complex *Ideas*, without examining whether they exist so together in Nature. And hence, I think, it is, that these *Ideas* are called *Notions*: as if they had their Original, and constant Existence, more in the Thoughts of Men, than in the reality of things; and to form such *Ideas*, it sufficed, that the Mind put the parts of them together, and that they were consistent in the Understanding without considering whether they had any real Beings though I do not deny, but several of them might be taken from Observation, and the Existence of several simple *Ideas* so combined, as they are put together in the Understanding.[3]

By "transparent" I intend what Locke means when he says that "the Mind put the parts of them together . . . without considering whether they had any real Being." For Locke, these concepts may be contrasted with complex ideas of substance. Ideas of substance are not transparent with regard to nature or "real Being," and hence they are not solely the product of human invention.

On Locke's account the real essence and the nominal essence of a mixed mode are the same. In effect that means that we know all there is to know about murder or lie, and so on, when we understand that concept we have called "murder" or "lie." Mixed modes are combinations of simple ideas of different varieties that arc not offered to us in the combined form by "the real existence of things,"[4] but that we assemble or frame to meet certain of our specific needs. They may be formed in either of at least two ways: (1) from observation of a situation or state of affairs, from which we abstract a type that we anticipate a need to refer to in the future ("the Man who first framed the Idea of Hypocrisy, might have . . . taken it at first from the observation of one, who made shew of good Qualities which he had not"[5]) or (2) from reflection unpatterned by experience.[6] A mixed mode is not an aggregate of its component simple ideas: It has a unity beyond aggregation that is marked, for Locke, by the name given to the concept. (Kovesi prefers to call the unity of the concept, the formal element of the notion.[7]) The act of naming the mixed mode is the act of completing its formation.[8]

Each concept of the mixed mode variety is actually then a combination of simpler ideas that have been arbitrarily united under a name. Every mixed mode concept is an archetype in the mind, because each must be its own prototype, there being no real essence, no substance, that determines the properties of the type or that the name picks out. It is important that a certain confusion not intrude into this account: it might be assumed that the position I am offering is a form of conventionalism, that I am maintaining only that the words we use in moral discourse are arbitrary inventions that are, by agreement, used to talk about moral values. Although I do regard the use of words to be convention-based, that is not at all the point of treating moral concepts as mixed modes. The mixed mode account that I borrow, at least in part, from Locke is more properly seen as a version of nominalism or, better still, a convergence of nominalism and conceptualism. The problem of nominalism is often formulated as being that of trying to determine whether or not essences in nature correspond to our concepts. In answer to the problem, from a Lockean standpoint we should say that, at least with respect to the concepts of morality, there are not such essences, though such essences do seem to exist with respect to our concepts of natural kinds. The issues of nominalism (or conceptualism) should also be distinguished from the question of whether the truths of morality (if it makes sense to talk of such things) are dependent on human invention. This latter issue will be of some concern presently. At this point it will suffice to say that these are separate, if related, concerns. Our focus will be first on the ontic question.

Since moral concepts, if they are mixed modes, are transparent, we cannot reduce the descriptions of our moral life, that is descriptions using our moral vocabulary, to some substantial residue or to some real (or even nominal) objects. A lie, for example, is not reducible simply to the saying of something and hence to sound waves. A lie is not one of a species of sound waves as a pointer is one of a species of dog. When someone has lied he has not just said something. It is not the case that only a certain kind of sound waves has occurred, though that is all that has happened in the world physicist's study. The concept of lie is the genus in which a particular lie is an instance of a species.

The concept of lie, however, is formed, as Locke notes, from a number of disparate sources:

> The *mixed Mode*, which the word *Lye* stands for, is made of these simple *Ideas*: 1. Articulate Sounds. 2. Certain *Ideas* in the Mind of the Speaker. 3. Those words the signs of those *Ideas*. 4. Those signs put together by affirmation or negation, otherwise than the *Ideas* they stand for, are in the mind of the Speaker.[9]

Locke allows that there are probably many other simple and complex ideas in the "lie-complex." The point of import is that, although we might decompose a mixed mode concept into simple ideas and then into the object in nature that caused them, the mixed mode concept is not a species or an aggregate of those simple ideas. Somewhat analogously, we can resolve a business corporation into a list of employees, stockholders, managers, and so forth (each a biological person) and gather all of the persons named on a street corner, but we will not have re-formed the corporation (although we might well have a mob).

The names of mixed modes would seem to pick out what is fashionable, after R. M. Hare, to call supervenient properties.[10] The idea of supervenience recently has come in for a great deal of discussion in areas of philosophy other than moral theory. Because of the role the idea of supervenience plays in my account of moral concepts, it will be useful here to provide a somewhat technical explanation of what it is for a property to be supervenient. (My definition of supervenience owes much to Jaegwon Kim.[11]) We shall say that a property P is supervenient on a property (or a family of properties) Q just in case any object that evidences the property (or properties) Q (at least) nomologically necessarily has the property P. Following Kim: indiscernability with respect to Q#, the closure of the supervenience base, entails indiscernability with respect to P, the supervenient property. Supervenience then logically amounts to a biconditional relationship or a series of biconditional relationships between properties or families of properties. In effect, supervenience is "a relationship of determination or dependence among properties which does not require property-to-property correlations."[12] For example, we do not find the property of murderness in the world, but we find acts that exhibit certain features and characteristics in the world of perception.[13] Our mixed mode concept of murder nomically introduces the property of being a murder to supervene those other properties, and it does so by supplying a rule of language that governs the extension over events of the name of the concept. In this way, the concept of murder makes it possible for us to describe a world in which there are murders by creating that very world.

For Locke, words like "lie" and "murder," the names of mixed modes, label, that is, are firmly annexed to, certain concepts. It might be objected that although "lie" and "murder" are the names of concepts having only nominal essence or being, they are used as well to refer to actual events or to what J. L. Mackie calls socio-psychological phenomena.[14] If that is true, it should be possible to distinguish or separate real and nominal essences in the case of such mixed modes, Locke to the contrary.

Imagine that we decide to treat lies as socio-psychological entities and have developed a theory sufficient to account for their occurrence. Suppose that our theory says that lies occur always and only when an individual is confronted with certain states of affairs and when he believes telling the truth will be detrimental to his interests. Imagine that this theory has been firmly ingrained into our thinking about lies and that it has successfully met confirmation tests. We are tempted to say that a lie is only what occurs when an individual is confronted with that state of affairs and has that belief. But now suppose that someone uttered a sentence he knew to be untrue with the intent to deceive his listener, yet the circumstances did not correspond to our theory's identified states of affairs or the speaker did not believe that by telling the truth he would be damaging his interests. We would not say that the speaker was not lying. Instead we would likely recognize that there are either different kinds of lies or different causes of lying than our theory covers. A similar story can be constructed for murder. Saul Kripke[15] presents an analogous case in regard to heat and the sensitivity of human creatures to heat. If we identify heat with the sensation we feel when in the presence of the motion of molecules, we certainly can imagine a different sort of human biology in which that sensation would be entirely different or nonexistent. If that happened we would have to change our view of heat. But, as Kripke further points out, in the case of heat, such a contingency relationship is an illusion. "Heat is the motion of molecules" and that is going to be the case regardless of *our* biological construction, if it is true at all. In our present concern; the definition "Lie is a mixed mode concept of a certain composition" if true will be true regardless of changes in the causes of lies or in the motives of liars, that is, regardless of changes in nature. This then gives us the sense of the claim that in such concepts the name is affixed firmly to the concept and is only contingently associated with certain occurrences. But there is more to be said about the differences between mixed modes, where real and nominal essences coincide, and substance-terms, where they do not.

As Kripke has shown, we cannot invent a story similar to our "lie-story" for natural kind concepts.[16] For example, if we have a confirmed theory that gold has the atomic structure that we identify with the atomic number 79, then it is not possible that gold should have a different atomic structure (say one that we would now identify with the atomic number 78). It is of course possible that we would not recognize gold at some time in the future, either because we have changed or because some feature of gold by which we now identify it is no longer present (perhaps it no longer appears to have the distinctive color). Now suppose that we found a material that did not have the atomic structure of the element with the atomic number 79 but that appeared to have all of the other properties of gold. We would not conclude that we had found a new variety of gold. Instead we would say that we had discovered something that is remarkably like gold, but not gold. The name, in this case, is used to rigidly designate the substance with a certain atomic structure, just as "heat" rigidly designates the motion of molecules. In the case of moral concepts, however, the name is used to rigidly designate the concept itself and not some entity or class of entities.

Mackie reminds us of the amusing story Locke tells about Adam's invention of the words *kinneah* (jealousy), *niouph* (adultery), and *zahab* (gold).[17] Locke seems to think that the upshot of his tale is that formation of the concept of gold is controlled by the real essences of the substance gold even if we cannot know "what the real Essence is,"[18] whereas the formation of the concepts of jealousy and adultery are purely imaginary. Mackie correctly points out that Locke is mistaken in this conclusion. The difference Locke's story does point out between a mixed mode concept and one of a natural kind is that our intentions in forming them are different; hence the names we use will pick out quite different sorts of things.

> He [*Adam*] intended *zahab* to stand for *that stuff, whatever properties and constitution it may turn out to have*; but he did not intend *kinneah* to stand for *the sort of trouble, whatever it may turn out to be, from which Lamech is suffering*, nor *niouph* for *whatever Adah has been up to lately*.[19]

This way of drawing the distinction, however, will break down if we compare moral concepts to those of things that are not natural kinds, for example, an automobile tire. The name "tire" appears to label a supervenient property, "being a tire," or to pick out things that have that supervenient property (very much like our moral concept names behave), rather than pick out an essence about which we can come to discover certain properties. Our concept of tire determines what a tire is, but the concept of tire is not a mixed mode; tires under other descriptions would seem to be substances. What then should we say? It seems to me that the distinction we want to draw may be stated as follows:

> Our concepts of natural kinds are nontransparent with respect to the world of nature (we pick out the thing and the study of it reveals its properties), while our concepts of artifacts though they are completely formed by our "imagination" (using the rather broad Lockean sense of that term) are still not transparent with respect to the natural world (we can, to some extent, discover the properties of artifacts, and we, in Locke's terms, cannot completely know what their real essence is). Our moral concepts, however, are completely formed by our "imagination" and are transparent in that we do not discover in nature the properties of, for example, lie. *We* determine what a lie is, what murder is, what adultery is.

All moral discourse, then, is about a world that depends for its existence on our moral concepts and hence on rather arbitrary inventions of our intellectual history. Moral discourse primarily consists in description of that world. At this stage of analysis, however, little difference exists between what we say about moral discourse and what we should say about discourse about artifacts.[20] (Except the obvious, that artifacts discourse is not dependent on our moral concepts.)

The treatment of moral concepts as mixed modes has not been a particularly popular one in the Western philosophical tradition. From at least the time of Plato the standard view has been that moral concepts are, though perhaps complex ideas, nonetheless not arbitrary inventions, that they are reflections of objective moral values or that their real essences do not coincide with their nominal ones. For Plato, the Form of the Good is an objective reality. For Kant pure reason reveals the real essence of duty. For others, intuition or revelation acquaints us with moral values that exist somehow either in nature or in the mind of God. Price, for example, claims that right and wrong are "real characters of actions" that are apprehended by our understanding, much as the real essences of natural kind concepts are so apprehended for Locke. Could all of these philosophers (and, as Mackie argues, ordinary moralists as well[21]) have been in error regarding the nature of our moral concepts?

Prima facie, the very existence of so many competitors, each offering not only a different way of apprehending moral values but also pinpointing quite different "objects," is reason to be more than a little skeptical about the enterprise. In his arguments against the theory of innate ideas Locke writes:

> He that will carefully peruse the History of Mankind, and look abroad into the several Tribes of Men, and with indifferency survey their Actions, will be able to satisfy himself, That there is scarce that Principle of Morality to be named or *Rule* of *Virtue* to be thought on . . . which is not somewhere or other *slighted* and condemned by the general Fashion of *whole societies* of Men, governed by practical Opinions, and Rules of living quite opposite to others.[22]

A more telling difficulty with the view that discoverable objective moral values exist is that such a view does not seem to be able to account for the supervenience of moral concepts over natural kind objects. One might think that we could assimilate moral concepts to artifact concepts and say that their names pick out supervenient properties but that we can discover some of their properties by studying the objects included in the extension of the name. To some extent we do this when we study particular murder cases to increase our knowledge of the techniques of murderers. But the discovery of new techniques or uses of murder is not the discovery of new properties previously overlooked in our formulation of the concept of murder, whereas discovery of a previously untried use of a table might lead to or even amount to the discovery of a property of tables that was not originally in our concept. Even so, the property of being a table supervenes the natural properties of the objects that are tables, for example, their being wooden. No one of the natural properties of a particular table has the property of being a table.

If most people regard moral concepts not to be inventions (mixed modes), it is probably owing either to the pervasive identification of morality with religion or to the central role that moral concepts play in our act-descriptions; through frequent usage, we have come to regard them as objective discoveries; the fallacy of objectifying the familiar. In addition, most people may regard the real essences of moral concepts to be other than their nominal ones because they are cognizant of the essential role moral concepts play in our social environment. It is not an unnatural step to regard something that important to have objective reality.

II

We have to this point, following Locke, argued that the nominal essences of our moral concepts are identical to or coincide with their real essences. The paradigm of the concept as its own prototype is, for Locke, the idea of a Triangle. Because we know, as it were, both the real and the nominal essences of the ideas of mathematics we can have real demonstrable knowledge of mathematics.

> Is it true of the *Idea* of a *Triangle*, that its three Angles are equal to two right ones? It is true also of a *Triangle*, where-ever it really exists. Whatever other Figure exists, that is not exactly answerable to that *Idea* of a *Triangle* in his Mind, is not at all concerned in that Proposition. And therefore he is certain all his knowledge concerning such *Ideas*, is real knowledge: because intending Things no farther than they agree with those *Ideas*, he is sure what he knows concerning those Figures, when they have barely *an Ideal Existence* in his Mind, will hold true of them also, when they have a real existence in Matter; his consideration being barely of those Figures, which are the same, where-ever, or however they exist.[23]

The argument is really rather simple: If we formed the idea of a Triangle in such a way that one of its properties is that the sum of its three angles is equal to 180°, then it must be true of the idea of a triangle and of any triangle that the sum of its angles is equal to 180°. And that we know for certain. Analogously, if we formed the idea of lie in such a way that included among its constituents is this idea—saying what one knows to be untrue with the intent to deceive is wrong—then it must be true of lie, and of any particular lie, that it is wrong. In regard to murder Locke writes:

> If it be true in Speculation, i.e. in *Idea*, that *Murther deserves Death*, it will also be true in Reality of any Action that exists conformable to that *Idea of Murther*.[24]

We may then have as certain a knowledge in moral matters as has been generally attributed to mathematics. We don't find out or discover by some experimentation that lying is wrong or that murder is wrong. Insofar as we fully understand the concept of lie or of murder, we know for a certainty that to lie or to murder is wrong. In the sentences that express that knowledge, "Lying is wrong" and "Murder is wrong," *wrong* is what Kovesi calls a reminder.[25] It adds no information, but reminds us of our reasons for forming the notions of lie and murder. Of course, these sentences might serve a teaching function, much as "The sum of the angles of a triangle is equal to 180°" is used to instruct students in elementary Euclidean geometry. Of some further interest, as Locke noted, demonstrations of the truth of the propositions expressed by such statements depends not at all on the existence of triangles or of lies or liars or of murders or murderers. The truth of the propositions depends on our concepts—although in the case of moral concepts we may assume that they are abstracted from our experience with each other.

Although the naming of a moral concept is clearly the focus of formation of the concept, we should not be misled by that fact in such a way that we treat the knowledge we have of moral concepts as contingent on the naming process. Obviously, we might have called the concept of saying what one knows to be untrue with the intent to deceive the listener "loving," and the thing said a "love," just as we might have called the capital of the United States "Burrville" rather than "Washington." Moral discourse is not about names; it is about a certain set of concepts. If we suppose someone to have the concept of lie but to call it "loving kindness," we would think him eccentric (at the least). We may not at first understand his utterances that involve the term "loving kindness," but by finding out what concept he has, we should eventually be able to translate his use of "loving kindness" by our "lie." Admittedly this will be no easy process. "Wrong Names in moral Discourses," Locke says, "breed usually more disorder, because they are not so easily rectified as in Mathematics."[26]

A condition of moral discourse is that it involve our moral concepts (at least one of them) or aim at the formation of moral concepts. It might be supposed that the Lockean approach I am adopting invites a rather relativistic account of morality. That is, morality might appear to be dependent on the arbitrary formation of a certain set of concepts from which certain moral guidelines follow. Surely we might have formed an entirely different set of concepts, and hence we might have quite a different collection of act-guideline statements. We could go further to suggest that, given a number of possible sets of mixed mode concepts, the adoption of one was purely arbitrary and might appear to be a matter of individual choice.

These suppositions contain a germ of what I have in mind, but I do not think that admission commits me to a form of moral relativism. I am not saying that alternative sets of moral concepts might have been, but were not, adopted, if "alternative sets" are sets of concepts entirely different in function from those we have now. Analogously, we might imagine a tribe of people who share none of our mathematical concepts, but who have concepts that are of a roughly geometrical sort (I have no idea what they may be like). Let us say that they do not have the concept of triangle or square or circle but perhaps they work with the concept of amorphous extension, or blob. What we cannot imagine is that they do not have any of our mathematical concepts, having *replaced* them with aesthetic concepts: that is, they work with aesthetic concepts where we work with mathematical ones. (But that is not to say that they calculate with aesthetic concepts.) What we cannot say, under these circumstances, is that aesthetics is their mathematics. Rather we should say that they have no mathematics, though they might have a rather fuller developed aesthetics. What is mathematics is determined by the mathematical concepts we have and what we do with them. We can allow some alterations and even some real differences, say, between Euclidean and Riemannian triangles, but ony insofar as the concepts involved concern the activities of mathematics. Aesthetics is not an alternative geometry, even though aesthetic concepts and geometrical ones can be used in discourse about the same object.

That some concept is a moral one, analogous to the mathematical examples, is not dependent on an arbitrary choice of any individual. To be a moral concept a concept must be, in most respects, like our moral concepts. It must be framed for a certain limited number of specific reasons. Gilbert Harman, in a recent book, writes that our revulsive reaction to cannibals enjoying a meal of human flesh is complicated, "because two moralities are relevant, theirs and ours. In judging the situation we can simply appeal to our own morality: 'Eating people is wrong'. But in judging the cannibals themselves we must take their morality into account."[27] Harman's point seems to be that we are not justified in morally blaming people for doing something we regard as wrong if they do not regard it as wrong. To know what they regard as morally wrong we must be able to identify which of their concepts are their moral ones, even though they may be radically different from our moral concepts.

The identification problem in such a case turns on an understanding of what "radically different" means. If we take it to mean that they (Harman's cannibals) have in their conceptual scheme none of our moral concepts and no concepts that play roles roughly similar to our moral concepts, then we would have to say that they have no morality at all. On the other hand, if "radically different" means that the cannibals do not have our moral concepts, but do have alternative ones, that is, ones that do play roles roughly similar to those played by our moral concepts; then the view is more interesting, but then understanding it involves knowing what we mean by "playing roles roughly similar to those played by our moral concepts."

Let us consider again our analogous case of geometric concepts. Suppose we ask what role they play. It is reasonable, if simplistic, to say that they provide us with ways of calculating various relationships of shape and they allow us to draw distinctions about shapes, often for the purpose of making certain calculations. The concept of triangle not only allows us to pick out triangles, but to calculate size of angles, length of sides, and so on. If the cannibals have some concepts that they formed to allow them to identify and calculate relationships regarding shapes, we should say that they have a geometry. If they don't, then they have no geometry; they get along without it.

To return to the question, "what role do our moral concepts play?" Here we are likely to be led to utter confusion if we do not draw a distinction not often clearly drawn in the philosophical literature. As we have already mentioned in the previous chapter, a rather common method of philosophers of treating ethics has been to discuss theories that primarily focus on determining a person's obligations in certain circumstances and to contrast them with theories that treat morality as primarily concerned with the development of individual character or virtue. If, as I think we should, we regard both sorts of theories as talking about the same thing—morality—it will be more than a little difficult to locate the role of moral concepts, without appearing to be making an *ad hoc* decision. Some theories will provide ways of evaluating character and others will provide ways of describing events and justifying the endorsement of certain choices of action.

Though I think the distinction I shall draw is embedded in our common way of talking and thinking about morality, for heuristic purposes, I want to identify within "the general class" of moral concepts, two distinctly different sorts. The first I shall call *moral concepts* and the second, after Hector-Neri Castañeda,[28] I shall call *euergetical concepts*. For clarity, when referring to the compound class of moral and euergetical concepts, I shall use MORAL or its variants written with capital letters. In the *class* of moral concepts we should find murder, lie, justice, adultery, theft, etc. In the class of euergetical concepts we should find kind, charitable, loyal, loving, benevolent, etc. Now if we ask what role moral concepts play, I think we can say that they were formed because we (a significant portion of the membership of the class of persons) recognized a need to identify certain kinds of actions and events that we wanted to constrain, discourage, or encourage persons to perform. If we go one step further, and ask what principle of selection motivated the recognition, the answer, I think, is: a generally held belief that the minimum set of econo-environmental conditions necessary for anyone to live a worthwhile life should be preserved. In other words, we have moral concepts because, given a generally held belief that we must maintain a certain environment, the absence of which makes human life not worth living, we need to identify specific kinds of acts and other events for the purposes of blaming, praising, encouraging, discouraging, promoting, preventing, guiding. If the cannibals hold such a general belief and recognize such a need, though they identify different types of acts and events, they will properly be described as having a morality and discourse with them might prove morally most enlightening. If they do not hold such a belief and thereby do not recognize such a need, they have no morality and we would be well advised to steer clear of their island, for they are, after all, cannibals.

There are complications, of course. The cannibals might indeed hold such a belief, recognize such a need, but also delimit the class of persons to only those who are full-blooded members of their tribe. If that turned out to be the case, I think we should say that they have a first-order truncated morality. A necessary condition of a full-blown morality is that it consider all members of the class of persons (agents) as its subjects, allowing only essential characteristics of agency to limit membership in that class. (I realize that this implies that persons who have not achieved their majority are included in class of subjects of morality. That seems to me to correspond to common practice. We tend to treat immaturity as a mitigating, and even sometimes as an exculpating, excuse, but we still regard children as proper subjects of moral judgments and of full-blooded praising, crediting, and blaming sentences.) First-order truncated moralities apparently abound. The primary error they commit is embedded in a myopian view of the econo-environment; they cannot see far enough to appreciate that isolated utopias can only exist in the ecosystem for relatively short time spans.

If the cannibal's morality is not first-order truncated, if they do admit to moral citizenship all members of the class of agents, but if they have only a limited number of moral concepts (perhaps they exclude murder and lie), then their morality will be second-order truncated. Second-order truncated moralities simply are not as rich in moral concepts as our morality. Our morality, however, is not necessarily ideal. We can imagine a morality much richer in concepts than ours. Indeed our morality is evolving: New concepts are invented or assimilated to morality as we learn more about the conditions necessary for anyone to live a good life and how to maintain those conditions. (I shall say more of this process in a later chapter.)

Euergetical concepts do not seem to have been formed because of a general belief that certain specifiable econo-environmental conditions need to be maintained. Rather, they seem to emerge from generally held views about ideal human commerce. Castañeda characterizes them as "general direct injunctions not to cause unhappiness to others," that are "imprecise and vague . . . yet precise enough so that conflicts between the euergetic requirements and institutional duties are possible."[29] Castañeda's most perceptive characterization of the euergetical aspect of morality is that it "attempts to internalize in everybody a direct concern for others."[30]

Again, various truncated versions of euergetics might exist from one community to another.

The distinction *within* MORALITY between morals and euergetics that I am trying to draw, of course, may be profitably characterized as the distinction between concerns for the rightness of acts and concerns for the goodness of agents. It is the distinction between doing what is right and doing what is good.

My inquiry should not be confused, however, with a study of the meaning of the words "right" and "good."[31] I am not specifically interested in the meaning of words at all. I am interested in MORAL concepts, though it is not accidental in the formation of such concepts that we give them names, it is a purely contingent matter that we give them the names we do. Furthermore, I do not regard "right" and "wrong," "good" and "bad" as peculiarly moral concepts. Instead I view those words either as didactic reminders or as discriminators used to promote conceptual reformation.[32]

III

MORALITY should not be identified with what Mackie calls "a general, all-inclusive theory of conduct."[33] For reasons that will become clearer in the last chapter, MORALITY must be kept distinct from practical reasoning. As I shall argue in that chapter, the sense of reasonableness that is relevant to practical conduct (rational self-interest) may often endorse actions that are not morally correct. We should conceive of MORALITY as a somewhat restricted system of guidelines that is meant to apply to persons without respect to their particular professions, vocations, or indeed their economic status. MORALITY is blind to the idiosyncracies that mark particular endeavors, or as it is often put: MORALITY is directed towards persons *qua* persons, rather than persons *qua* businessmen, and so on. Euergetics will be treated as that dimension of MORALITY that is aimed at the achievement of ideal relationships between people of disparate means, by providing standards of human excellence against which individual conduct may be measured. Morality, on the other hand, my primary interest, is a mechanism of constraint and encouragement invented with the aim of maintaining an environment in which anyone could achieve "the good life."

There is nothing particularly original in this account of what morality does. G. J. Warnock, for example, has written: "The 'general object' of morality . . . is to contribute to betterment—or non-deterioration—of the human predicament. . . ."[34] But, of course, this conception of the aim of morality is not new with Warnock either. Hobbes certainly held a related view and Plato ascribes such a view to Protagoras.[35]

By and large, the general idea is that we are confronted with two facts about our world that we need to consider if we are to foster the desired environment: (1) the supply of natural resources is limited, what Rawls calls "the condition of moderate scarcity," and (2) despite certain natural affections for each other, our concept of rationality in light of (1) militates against sympathetic benevolent behavior (we are rationally selfish and not always short-sightedly so).

The Hobbesian account of the state of nature and the ensuing civil state, with its laws and sovereign powers, has had a profound effect upon much of our thinking about the object of morality. Although I fancy much of the Hobbesian view, I think it is skewed with respect to its account of the state of war. Hobbes, as is well known maintains that in the state of nature all persons exist in a state of war against each other and that they are driven by fear of death and a desire to secure "such things as are necessary for commodius living"[36] (in other words, by rational self-interest) to associate in the civil state. To so associate is for each to relinquish his "right to every thing," in exchange for peace. The power of the sovereign to enforce covenants provides the backbone of the basic morality of the state: that "the nature of justice, consisteth in keeping of valid convenants."[37] Morality, according to this view, is then virtually indistinct from the mechanism of the law of the civil state, and its object is to preserve the state of peace which, on Hobbes' account, can only exist in the civil state.

Montesquieu offered a somewhat different account of the state of nature and the state of war, but it is one that I find both more attractive and one that seems to me to have a higher probability than Hobbes' account of corresponding to events as they might have unfolded in prehistory. (I do not, however, subscribe to Montesquieu's natural law theory, that is, his view that justice exists eternally and is not the product human invention. It is arguable that Montesquieu did not regard many of his natural laws to be normative, that they were, for him, descriptive of the state of nature, but he frequently does refer to moral concepts as objective. "We must . . . acknowledge relations of justice antecedent to the positive law by which they are established."[38]) Montesquieu maintains that a man alone in nature thinking first and foremost about his preservation would feel, to excess, "nothing in himself at first but impotency and weakness."[39] Rather than feeling belligerent, he would feel inferior. Rather than seeking dominion over others, he would shrink from the adventure and the others likewise. Peace would reign.

This hypothetical savage would, however, Montesquieu continues, recognize his basic needs, for example, for nourishment, and he would be driven to satisfy them. Furthermore, fear, though it at first induces men to avoid each other's company, because it is reciprocal soon leads them to associate. In such an association, each realizes his natural affection for the members of his species (a version of what some current sociobiologists refer to as the primary motive of species association[40]). Having thus associated, each realizes the advantages of acquiring knowledge from each other and hence the state of society is born.

> As soon as man enters into a state of society he loses the sense of his weakness; equality ceases, and then commences the state of war. . . . the principal advantages of this society they endeavor to convert to their own emolument, which constitutes a state of war between individuals.[41]

Montesquieu identifies the law as the primary force that is devised to maintain a modicum of social tranquility. I think, we can add, however, in a more Hobbesian vein, that MORALITY was invented to further the preservation of the conditions necessary for a good life in the society of others, conditions that are liable to deterioration during the unchecked combat. Law is used to ward off what are perceived to be immanent internal threats to the "civilized combat" within each state. Montesquieu himself recognizes and encourages a relativistic view of the civil law. He writes that civil laws "should be adapted . . . to the people for whom they are framed that it should be a great chance if those of one nation suit another."[42]

The major advantage of taking a Montesquieuian rather than a Hobbesian view of the state of war is that one is not quite so tempted to identify MORALITY with binding rules or positive laws that make civil associations possible. One can, though Montesquieu was not concerned to do so, more easily distinguish the institution of the law from the conceptual system of MORALITY, which as we have seen includes more than conduct rules. To assume a Montesquieuian stance concerning the state of war rather than a Hobbesian one, is to regard Warnock's "uncontroversial liability of things to go badly for people"[43] not so much a product of the "limitedness of human sympathies"—the Hobbesian natural propensity to be actively hostile to the welfare of others—as a result of the sense of power that our social association confers upon persons and that blinds them to their natural weaknesses, needs, and affections. Montesquieu (and Rousseau as well) can be read as providing us with a conception of ourselves as something more than creatures driven by self-interest to develop a mechanism of constraint and encouragement, and also as providing a basis within our nature on which to rest the euergetically desirable habits, that is, the virtues of good character.

The preservation and the betterment of the society to which persons are drawn by reciprocal fear, and held by natural affection and advantage rather than by pure self-interest, and only in which can they hope to achieve a sense of worth (or the good life), is MORALITY's *raison d'etre*. The point of our having moral concepts and euergetical concepts is, in the end, just that. The reasons we have specific moral concepts rather than others is that we are convinced that we have identified certain environmental (socioeconomic and ecological) conditions as causally crucial to the good life.

3
An Extension of the Montesquieu Conjecture

In the previous chapter, I utilized Montesquieu's idea that the entry of persons into the civil state is the beginning rather than the end of the state of war among them. Contrary to Hobbes' view, man in the state of nature is regarded as weak and possessed of an overwhelming inferiority complex. Civil association, to which he is driven by fear and his natural affection for the members of his species (as well, we might imagine, as by natural familial ties), transforms his sense of impotency into one of power. He realizes that his strength is founded on the fruits of his industry secured by the association, but he, for self-interested reasons, naturally then attempts to convert all of the "advantages of society" to his own profit, to expand his sphere of influence. As each individual attempts to do likewise, the state of war begins. The point of law, we could now maintain, is to restrain the combatants; to exact *civil* peace (but not to restore what Montesquieu took to be the peace of the state of nature, for that must only be transitory because it is alien to human nature). The civil state (as opposed to civil association) we could then characterize as the state of controlled combat. If we extend this account further, and certainly well beyond what Montesquieu was inclined to do, we should say that legal regulation converts the war within the civil association into the marketplace. The civil law (including the criminal code) establishes definite boundaries on strategy-choice by the combatants and enforces its restriction with penalties that are, supposedly, greater than the expectable return for playing the proscribed strategy. Of course, such an account of civil law only goes a part of the way to capturing its multifarious purposes. Clearly some laws were made with the intent of enforcing moral judgments and principles in a very broad sense. Others are designed to regulate primarily noncombatant behavior: traffic laws, etc. Law alone, however, cannot insure that the conditions necessary for anyone to achieve a good life will not deteriorate in the heat of the "civilized" battle. This is true for a number of reasons, but primarily these: First, many of the conditions in question depend on the adoption of certain attitudes on the part of the combatants that are not legislatable; second, law is an institution (to be discussed in Chapter 6) with rules that generate obligations for an individual, which obligations at times will be in conflict with other institutional obligations that, seen from the point of view of the maintenance or betterment of the human condition, may not always be paramount; third (an elaboration on the second) most of us recognize the potential danger to society of allowing to pass unchallenged the corporate executive's retort, "Is it legal?" to the question "Is it ethical?"

Given the Montesquieuian Conjecture we might imagine a society, a civil association, prior to having established laws and hence in a legally unrestrained state of civil war, where, nonetheless, members had framed a number of MORAL concepts; some of these concepts, the moral ones, would likely constitute the principles to be codified in civil legislation. In the interim between association and legislation we could say that they had a MORALITY. The formation of their MORAL concepts is, as Mackie has argued, "the first line of defense."[1] That it is not always a successful defense and needs to be enforced and augmented by law is, as I would prefer to think of it, a testament to the sense of strength civil association arouses in and imparts to individuals, rather than a testament to an inherently selfish human nature. Civil association, in so far as it makes the marketplace possible, makes the concept of economic rationality possible as well. The great problem that MORALITY was invented to solve (even if it has been only partially successful, hence in need of legal augmentation) is how to produce coordinated and associated actions that do not destroy the point of individual means-to-ends reasoning (that characterizes the marketplace) while constraining behavior damaging to persons, to society, or to the human condition. The practicality of MORALITY is just that its concepts are the product of the recognized need to solve this problem. If we cannot work a successful solution, the unconstrained marketplace will devour its participants and civil association will be its own destruction. The natural drive to association lends an air of the Sisyphean to the enterprise.

The Montesquieu Conjecture leads us to view ourselves not as by nature selfish, though we are by nature rational (though that is not necessarily our defining characteristic). Both prudence and our proclivity to association are important elements in our MORAL invention. In effect, MORALITY often reminds us of our individual frailties as well as the tenuousness of the association wherein the sense of security is the stimulus for our aggrandizing endeavors. In recent years, the focus of discussion on the age-old question "Why should I be moral?" has settled on certain game theory examples, in particular the Prisoner's Dilemma. That game demonstrates rather dramatically that prudence, the virtue of the marketplace, of itself, even if formulated in terms of long-run rather than short-run outcomes, is never sufficient to assure the preservation of the very marketplace in which it is the prime principle of strategy. The market's own virtue destroys the market; there is no way internally to counter the marketplace's tendency to entropy.

Hobbes, of course, recognized this fact and hence the social contract converts individual long-term prudence into an agreement to abide by the rule of a sovereign, whose motives were (supposed) to be (exclusively?) self-interested. The sovereign's power, secured by the self-interested agreement of each citizen to obey, is the coercive force external to the controlled combat of the marketplace; its theoretical purpose is to preserve the conditions necessary for individual action by putting constraints on individual self-interest. Hobbes writes:

> so also have they made artificial chains, called *civil* laws, which they themselves, by mutual covenants, have fastened at one

end to the lips of that man or assembly to whom they have given the sovereign power, and at the other end to their own ears. These bonds, in their own nature weak, may nevertheless be made to hold by the danger, though not by the difficulty, of breaking them.[2]

Hobbes' solution, and that which seems to follow from the game theory studies, is single-tracked with respect to basic motives. The bond between an individual and any other individual and all individuals and the state is prudence. Montesquieu's Conjecture directs us to other considerations, even if Montesquieu did not follow them out. Fear of deprivation of the fruits of labor is not the sole motive. Natural affection and affinity is of equal importance and it happens to be a fact of our MORALITY that a number of its admonitions are directed at behavior that simply cannot be assimilated to any form of prudence, short- or long-term.

The primary difference between Hobbes' and Montesquieu's account of MORALITY does not lie in the acknowledged object of the creation of the artifact (to counteract Warnock's "tendency of things to go badly"); the difference is that for Hobbes MORALITY is sheer artifice, the embedding of a fictional bond, while for Montesquieu the bond is not a fictional but a genuine proclivity to species association. For both, however, the creation of or the strengthening of the bond alters the dictates of prudence in favor of the maintenance of the general conditions, by inducing individuals to regard sacrifice as not necessarily counterproductive. Such an outlook, especially when augmented by law, solves both the problems of assurance and coordination that are highlighted by the study of games like Prisoner's Dilemma.[3] Whether such an approach to an answer to the question "Why should I be MORAL?" may be expected to be successful will be discussed in a later chapter, Chapter 8.

4
The Role of Model Building: Lifeboats, the Spaceship, and the System

Our moral concepts are mixed modes; they are arbitrary inventions, transparent with respect to nature. That does not mean that they are created in a vacuum, or that no objective requirements can be brought to bear on the framing of our moral concepts. Quite the opposite is the case. Because the point of having moral concepts is to discourage or encourage certain choices, in order to maintain or better the human condition, the understanding we have of our environment is essential to the framing of such concepts. The moral concepts we do have, as their longevity testifies, have in large measure met the requirement of relevancy to the environment. That environment is, however, subject to change, and it is to those contingent features of the environment that some moral concepts are pitched. Shifts in the balance of the elements of that environment can cause correlative changes in the conditions requisite for a good life. I shall not attempt to fully elaborate on what constitutes "the good life" or "a life of worth" (I shall use those terms interchangeably), other than to suggest that to live such a life is to realize a majority of one's realistic goals (some philosophers[1] and economists[2] would call this a "minimum standard of decency"). If I had to specify, I would reluctantly use the social-indicator approach to

58

economic welfare developed by recent sociologists. In their account, a minimum standard of decency is achieved only when a person receives or has available those goods and services necessary for him to maintain his self-respect in exercising his abilities toward the acquisition of his goals. Contrary to the standard philosophical treatment, however, I shall not argue that persons have a right to a minimum standard of decency, as so defined, or assume that standard to be the end state toward which morality ought to be patterned. The notion for me is not so much normative as it is an explication of an underlying assumption of all morality. Simply, insofar as our moral judgments aim at the preservation or betterment of our environment, they presuppose such a notion as the "minimum standard of decency." If the particulars of a social-indicator approach are offensive, I would gladly substitute any other explication of "the good life" or "the life worth living." Actually I believe that common morality, the morality Alan Donagan identifies with the Hebrew-Christian tradition,[3] recognizes such a notion as at least quasi-normative and that recognition combined with a generally adequate assessment of "the human predicament," accounts for the measure of its popularity and success over the centuries. My interest is not either in creating a morality or in defending an existing competitor in the sweepstakes. I am concerned with understanding the object, scope, and function of morality.

Insofar as adequacy of assessment of the human environment is the prime factor in establishing or grounding a morality, and as environment is prone to changes of some magnitude, we should expect those changes to be registered in an adequate moral conceptual scheme. In other words, a minimum set of econo-environmental conditions (hereafter MEC) is necessary for persons to have a chance of living a good life and provides the justification for the formation and retention of moral concepts; the discovery of this minimum set is relative to some conception of the general human environment. The more adequate that conception, the more likely the morality to achieve its object. The problem may be construed as trying to find a satisfactory fundamental model of the human condition. In the recent literature of ethics, economics, and ecology, a good deal of space has been devoted to discussing various versions of two currently popular models: the lifeboat (or lifeboats) and the spaceship.

Generally, these two models are regarded as incompatible. I think both models are inadequate for reasons that I will sketch below. As an alternative I shall offer, but only as a suggestion in need of refinement and elaboration, what I should like to call "the system model." (I wish I had a catchier name for it and in fact that name is somewhat misleading.)

Insofar as our moral beliefs do rest on factual beliefs about the MEC, they are prone to a certain degree of alteration owing to errors of fact or changes in the econo-environment. It is an important fact of our moral history that what Kovesi has called "diluting redescription"[4] has served as a narrowing device on the scope over action of moral concepts. In recent years, moral debate has focused on such issues as whether abortion is murder or whether euthanasia is murder or whether saying things that are not true but are in the national interest is lying. On the other hand, more specific act-descriptions occasionally are separated from broader categories and assimilated in the moral lexicon. Also, moral terms are broadened in scope by a sort of "expanding redescription" exercise. In all of these cases, however, there is a common factor: justification. Simply, if someone maintains that abortion is not murder, then it is incumbent on that person to justify his view by drawing attention to certain key features of murder that are not features of abortion. The person may then go further by arguing that abortions when properly described, do not cause the human environment to deteriorate; that is, they are not events that threaten the MEC, and hence that it should not be wrong to perform them. Of course, to be successful in such a justificatory enterprise one needs to know about the factors external to human beings that have probable causal relations with the MEC.

A moral conceptual system rests on (1) our concept of "the good life" and (2) our understanding (or vision) of the impact of both natural factors and human behavior on the econo-environment in which we live. If (1) is to be realistic, then it will be dependent on a correct account of (2). Our understanding of the impact of variable factors on a system is, as we have learned in the physical and biological sciences, aided by the development and testing of basic models.

There has surfaced a wide-spread dissatisfaction with the abundant, God-provided and sustained, post-Eden model of the human condition, or what some economists call the "cowboy model," that has characterized our conception of the human environment for centuries. This dissatisfaction primarily has been due to the recent general awareness of the far-reaching effects of pollution, overpopulation, and natural calamity. The traditional model was fostered, rather like Hobbes' political theory, by a rather limited vision of community, a nonglobal perspective that has proved dangerous in the twentieth century. The new models, or in some cases old models in new apparel, offered as replacements are defended not in terms of their moral impact but, as they should be, on grounds of representational accuracy and ability to explain and predict.

Ecologist Garrett Hardin has propounded the lifeboats model of the human condition, according to which we are to imagine all living people as adrift in a number of lifeboats of various sizes on an (apparently) endless expanse of ocean.[5] The number of lifeboats corresponds to the number of nations. Each lifeboat varies in regard to on-board supplies: Some of the boats are adequately equipped for their passengers, some are well-equipped, and some are not adequately equipped. The lifeboats are thereby limited in passenger capacity by size and on-board supplies. Some lifeboats, however, are already overflowing with passengers whom they cannot support, and people are constantly being thrown or swept into the ocean to begin frantically swimming toward other lifeboats, seeking admission or, at least, handouts.

Given the lifeboats model of the human condition, we are led to equate the MEC with the state of those lifeboats that are at least adequately provisioned for their actual passengers. By "adequately provisioned," we would include having sufficient space, sufficient nutritious food, and consequently sufficient time for the pursuit of personal goals. Preservation of the ratio of adequate provisions to passengers on such lifeboats would seem to be the primary object of morality. In other words, morality, by and large, is reduced to a question of distributive justice. The maintenance of an adequately provisioned lifeboat obviously would demand that a certain general course of action be practiced by its passengers when, for example, they are beset by pleas of swimmers who have lost their berths on other boats and seek entry. We are encouraged by Hardin to expect that despite altruistic training, ingraining of the religious principle of being "one's brother's keeper," the realities of the lifeboats' world would restrain passenger benevolence. Each boat will only hold so many passengers. More than that number would sink it, and all would be forced to swim and most likely would perish.

The lifeboats model of the human condition forces focus on the self-survival of each person on a particular lifeboat, *vis a vis* the swimmers. Suppose, the standard example, 20 people swim to a 40-passenger lifeboat that already has 30 passengers and plead for entry. The addition of 10 passengers will alter that lifeboat from an affluent to a barely adequate state. Certain choices are open to the passengers. They can: (1) allow none of the 20 entry, maintaining affluence; (2) allow some (but a limit of 10), settling for survival adequacy; (3) allow all entry. If the passengers decide (recognizing that arriving at a decision is not unproblematic) to do 3, they are all doomed; 3 is, for all practical purposes, identical to all abandoning the boat. Without an agreed-on discrimination procedure, 2 will be difficult to engineer (unless they abide by a "first come-first serve" principle). 1 is recommended by such proponents of the model as Hardin. Choosing 1 and enforcing it will mean that all 20 swimmers will likely die. No matter what choice is made, the death of human beings will probably ensue; we can stipulate that choice 1 = 20 deaths, choice 2 = 10 deaths (and, if conditions slightly alter, the likely death of some of the other 40), choice 3 = the likely deaths of all 50. Obviously choice 2 will result in the least number of highly probable deaths. But choice 2 also destroys the conditions for a comfortable life for the remaining passengers. They all must live at mere adequacy levels without a cushion against the proverbial rainy day. Choice 1 is clearly the optimal choice for the passengers taken as an aggregate of self-interested persons. Choice 3 would seem to have nothing in its favor from the point of view of the passengers.

If the lifeboats model is a good representation of the human condition, a number of renovations in moral concepts would seem to be required. For example, killing persons or allowing them to die by refusing them entry or handouts when doing so would deteriorate the MEC on a lifeboat would not be murder; it would not seem to be wrong. This might demand a reformation of the concept of murder through diluting redescription. This type of analysis has led moralists to attack the lifeboats model as having built-in antimoral aspects. They argue, for example, that:

> We *should* share all food equally, at least until everyone is well-nourished. Besides food, *all* the necessities of life should be shared, at least until everyone is adequately supplied with a humane minimum. The hard conclusion remains that we should share all food equally even if this means that everyone starves and the human species becomes extinct.[6]

It is no wonder that some people regard moralists as totally out of touch with the realities of life. Nothing seems more absurd than to argue that we are morally obligated to do something that makes morality a farce by eliminating its subjects. Although philosophers making such "moral" pronouncements tend to adopt a Kantian rather than a utilitarian stance, they seem to have forgotten Kant's arguments, e.g., against suicide. Kant writes:

> One immediately sees a contradiction in a system of nature whose law would be to destroy life by the feeling whose special office is to impel the improvement of life.[7]

They miss the central issue of the model. The question is not whether, in terms of current morality, we can justify the distribution decisions that are likely to occur. The question is whether the model is an adequate representation of the human condition. If it is, some of our moral concepts may be anachronisms.

If the lifeboats model is ajudged to bear a strong resemblance to the human condition, an enormous number of interesting subtleties could well occupy a legion of moral philosophers. We should probably regard the history of acquisition of a seat on a lifeboat as a pertinent moral datum. If acquisition was gained by certain means, we might not regard the claims that go with passenger status to be justified; hence actions taken to retain passenger status might not take the same descriptions as do those of "entitled" passengers. Also, perplexing moral concerns would be present if we could make status distinctions among the passengers: first class and steerage.[8]

The popular alternative model to that of the lifeboats is that of the spaceship, "Spaceship Earth." The term was apparently coined by economist Kenneth Boulding.[9] On this model we are to view the human condition as if we are all crew members of a space craft on a lengthy voyage amongst the stars. Spaceship Earth has limited reservoirs of everything. The MEC on this model appears to be that state of the spaceship in which crewmembers share the resources without markedly depleting the capital stock.

The spaceship model incorporates a view about the "rights" of passengers to the resources that is quite different from that of the proponents of the lifeboats model. Survival depends on the frugal use by all of a finite stock of resources not easily renewable and never renewable without significant energy losses from the system. The idea of common ownership of or a shared right to those resources is generally promulgated. The crew's realization that the vehicle is a closed system, according to Boulding, should foster the idea that "stock" instead of "flow" must be the prime indicator of economic well-being. The relative homeostasis of the resources bank, rather than mining, production, and consumption, is the mark of a successfully operating craft. Maintenance of the MEC on board depends on the parsimonious use of resources. We may suppose that the MEC on this model is a series of linear programs with objective functions of the form:

A.
$$Ts = \sum_{i=1}^{N} Pi\Delta ri$$

where Ts is the value of the output from N resources, pi is the price and ri is the change (positive for an increase) in that stock resource commodity i and can be defined by an equation in which a generalized structure coefficient is conjoined with the production commodities, Qj:

B.
$$ri \equiv -\sum_{j=1}^{M} cijQj, i = 1, 1, \ldots N$$

The accounting procedures for N and c will have to be such as to include all resources and commodities necessary for the maintenance of the spaceship ecosystem. Certain commodities must, however, be manufactured or the minimum standard of decency will be irreversibly deteriorated. Hence a constraint on the spaceship's econo-environmental homeostatic maintenance will be:

C. $$\sum_{j=1}^{M} Pj \ Qj \geq c_o$$

where c_o is the required commodity level. And a further restriction is that such production cannot ever exceed the resource stock, ri. This constraint is renderable as:

D. $$ri^o \geq -\Delta ri, \ i = 1, \ldots N$$

The problem of spaceship economics may then be defined as one of trying to optimize equation A as defined by B and constrained by C and D.[10]

The lifeboats and spaceship models differ in certain crucial ways, contrary to Onora O'Neill's view that "The current metaphor suggests more drama and less danger."[11] The spaceship model, to be sure, does not lead us to think immediately in terms of imminent life and death choices. People are not, for example, located in space outside our spaceship begging entry. The idea of the common resources usually associated with the spaceship model avoids the unequal initial acquisition state that generates (in part) many of the lifeboats passengers' decision-making difficulties. It is usually suggested that each crew member has an equal "right" to the stock on the spaceship. But that is not really the idea of the more astute model-proponents. In Boulding's account, for example, each person does not have an individual right to the stock of resources in the spaceship. Individual persons do not seem to have any rights to that stock at all. Undoubtedly this is a recognition of the Hobbesian implication that if everyone has the right to everything, a state of war would always exist among all of the crewmembers on the ship. "As long as this . . . right of every man to everything endureth, there can be no security to any man."[12] If anything can be said to have a right to the commons in the spaceship model, for model proponents, it would seem to be humanity, taken as a whole. Individuals are viewed as having the use of the resources only insofar as necessary to support the minimum standard of decency on the ship. The criticism that the spaceship model is suicidal because it inevitably leads to the "tragedy of the commons"[13] is a product, I think, of a misconception of the general principles of ownership. The modellers are not arguing that individuals have inalienable rights to the commons without corresponding responsibilities for its upkeep. Instead, they offer the picture of persons who do not have Hobbes' second natural right at all, though they have responsibilities for maintaining the reservoir in a fairly stable state. In the spaceship model, the encouragement of events that preserve or replenish the capital stock of the spaceship is identified with the object of morality.

A number of difficulties occur with the spaceship model, not the least of which surely is that it is far from having a strong positive analogy to current political conditions on earth. The lack of and the low probability for the future of any sort of global sovereign control may throw serious doubt on the utility of the model. The model seems to be incomplete without a Hobbesian sovereign. Perhaps of somewhat lesser concern, no class of acts seems morally neutral on the spaceship. Every event on the spaceship is translatable into either a relative maintenance of the homeostasis of the capital stock or a nontrivial consumption without replenishment of that stock. The model-proponents may be committed to holding the view that if "X ought to do a" is false, then "X ought not to do a" is true. Even a "minimum morality" on the spaceship would be, in Carolyn Morillo's terms, "very strenuous indeed,"[14] Again, however, if the spaceship model is by and large a correct picture of the human condition, we should expect a reformation of our moral concepts that would expand their scope over human events. We will probably find it necessary to reframe such concepts as theft and to add to our moral conceptual mechanism more exacting concepts that will cover various kinds of consumption without replenishment.

A fundamental difference between these two models, one on which a decision in favor of one or the other might be based, is that they incorporate radically different views of humanity. The lifeboats model implies that humanity is to be treated as an individual of what in Chapter 1 was called an aggregate type. The spaceship model treats humanity as if it were a conglomerate collectivity. The spaceship is not merely a more dramatic and less dangerous-sounding metaphor for a lifeboat, at least given the way it is usually propounded.

Each passenger in a lifeboat is to be viewed as governed by his own conception of self-interest; each is said to be entitled by virtue of his having a place in the original lifeboat position, to a certain piece of its provisions. Corresponding responsibilities then arise for each in regard to the upkeep and distribution of his "piece of the pie" and, supposedly, for the general maintenance of the safety of the other passengers: the Lifeboat Lockean proviso.[15] No one else in the boat can really have serious concerns over who, in fact, occupies the other seats so long as the boat is safe and no one is made worse off by the actions of any passenger or the aggregate. Should one of the passengers, when the boat is full, decide to give up his seat to a swimmer, it is all the same to the other passengers, so long as the new passenger is not a dangerous person, for example, a known murderer or thief; and the former passenger takes his place in the ocean with the sharks.

The spaceship model would have us imagine that the totality of persons has an indivisible right to the resources of the ship. What I have called conglomerate collectivities can have such rights because they are actually metaphysical persons *qua* moral persons.[16] But the totality of persons, the class of persons, simply cannot be a conglomerate collectivity. The class of persons cannot be a member of itself. "Personhood" designates the sum total of all persons at any one time and that is an aggregate. Aggregates cannot have rights or responsibilities that are not reducible to the individual rights and responsibilities of their constituent members. Hence, if the right to the spaceship resources resides in the collective spaceship crew, as the model-builders would have it, the ascription of that right will be reducible to ascriptions of individual rights to those resources to each member of the crew. If we all have a claim to the resources of the Earth, then each of us has some claim to those resources or to some of them. But then to the dismay of the modellers, the spaceship is revealed to be a disguised solitary lifeboat. The real difference between the spaceship and the lifeboats models is numerical; the spaceship is the only vessel on "the sea." This would account for O'Neill's intuition that "if we are feeling sober about the situation, lifeboat Earth may be more suggestive."[17]

There will be a number of objections to the above claim. Certainly the lifeboats model supposes more than one lifeboat, and secondly it supposes that not everyone is in a lifeboat, that there are swimmers. The spaceship modellers cannot make either supposition. But neither supposition is essential to the lifeboats model. No damage is done to its basic conception of the MEC if only one boat is on the sea. The amount of supplies and the amount of room on board are the primary dictators. Although there are no swimmers in space, the swimmers are only convenient for raising questions about population and goods distribution, questions that could be asked in terms of passenger reproduction.

The lifeboat modellers' reliance solely on self-interest, means/ ends motives underlying passengers' actions to preserve the MEC has a devastating catch, possibly a variant on the Prisoner's Dilemma. Self-interest, where a limited stock is involved, would dictate the attempt to "cut the odds" on depletion to the critical stage, and hence increase personal luxuries by throwing overboard as many of the other passengers as possible. The hedge against personal disaster can be appreciably improved if there are only 20, or 10, or 5, or 2, or 1 ("as long as I am that sole survivor."). In the absence of some form of coercive force to deter greed, some "insurance," the passengers are each and always at the mercy of each other. Dare any prudent one among them nod off to sleep expecting to awake anywhere but in Davey Jones' locker?

Both of these competitor models of the human condition offer important insights, despite some lack of positive analogy to the world as we know it and some consequential difficulties due to economic conceptions. I have said that the spaceship must, in the end, be viewed as a solitary lifeboat. We can remedy the difficulty noted above with the lifeboat by altering its conception of the gauge of the MEC; we borrow the idea of capital stock fundamental to the spaceship. We must, however, make one more serious alteration. The result, I think, will be a third model that I hope will be recognized as a worthy opponent in the battle of the model builders.

Despite their origins in the literature of ecology, both popular models take insufficient cognizance of that most important of ecological principles, the idea of system. Both models emphasize an artificial dichotomy between persons and the world of resources persons need to survive. The lifeboat model probably introduces this duality into the idea of system more than the spaceship does, but even the spaceship modellers usually fail to pay sufficient heed to the place of persons *in* and not *in relation to* the ecosystem. Both models concentrate on determining the amount of resources necessary for maintaining a minimum standard of decency of individual persons, based on a traditional analysis of that concept, rather than on treating the MEC as a function of a *system* in which consumer/producer persons are only one of the elements. In other words, both models tend to impose cowboy economics on a nonabundant world, with only minor modifications. They still uphold the traditional economic distinctions.

Persons, however, are parts of the ecosystem; they are to be counted among its resources, not just as its consumers. We are not just in the spaceship trying to survive, *we are a part of* the spaceship. The calculation of whether the system is maintaining relative homeostasis has to involve reference to whether the persons in it are maintaining their own relative homeostasis. This calls for adjustments in the basic economic determiners. The same linear program used for the spaceship economy can be modified to capture the system conception. The calculation of changes in resources will have to be adjusted to include calculated changes in the physical and mental states of the persons in the system. Environmental impact will then not be restricted to altered nonhuman resource states. We can treat constraint D as including in "ri" (resource stock) what usually are called "externalities" and what may be imperfectly labeled "the human factor."

This is not to suggest that the system's homeostasis demands that all persons achieve or maintain homeostasis. The system can, no doubt, remain relatively stable despite the unstable state of some of its elements. What it does suggest is that the MEC in a system like our human environment depends on the maintenance of the homeostasis of the econo-environmental system as a whole, in which each of us is an operative part. The well-being of the system is ultimately a limit on each of our own. It is only, to borrow a term from pathology, metastatic disturbances that truly threaten the system. Morality then can be conceived as our forward guard against metastasizing disturbances to the human ecosystem. A person would be acting morally if his actions are compatible with the maintenance of the homeostasis of the human ecosystem. The idea of maintaining personal physical and mental stock is admittedly in need of a good deal of explication. (It may indeed, prove to be an economic analog of Plato's doctrine of the justice of the soul.) But no useful purpose would be served here by attempting either to articulate the system model or continue a comparison of it to its two more famous competitors. Indeed, a number of other competitors may be worthy of consideration.

The evaluation of conceptual paramorphs[18] of the human condition in terms of their positive analogy, explanatory versatility, and predictive success should not be unlike the kind of evaluation commonplace in the physical sciences. Explanation in science often proceeds from the description of some fact (some anomaly) to the invention of a conceptual paramorphic model that, when articulated and conjoined with a series of transformation rules linking the model to the facts, subsumes the anomaly under a general theory that makes it intelligible.[19] (This is obviously a complex business, and this is not the place to attempt a full account of the role of models in explanation.)

A number of major developments in technology, biological science, and medicine have so dramatically altered the world of human experience in recent years as to suggest that our traditional assessments of the human predicament, indeed of what is a human being, may be inadequate. We have the power to sustain life by a number of exotic devices. We can transplant vital organs. By recombining DNA we can create new life forms. By genetic engineering we may be able to create human beings with radically different genetic structures, and hence with interests quite different from our own and whose conditions of welfare will not necessarily correspond to ours. Traditionally we have viewed ourselves as a relatively stable lot with basic needs, desires, abilities, and interests not unlike our distant forefathers, and the environment as an external something to be mastered to suit those needs. One has but to recall the Biblical admonition to grasp the pervasiveness of this belief:

> and God said to them, "Be fruitful and multiply, and fill the earth and subdue it; and have dominion over the fish of the sea and over the birds of the air and over every living thing that moves upon the earth."[20]

Suppose, however, we look at matters in quite the opposite way. Suppose we consider the advisability of fabricating human beings to fit the environment that has emerged because of our excesses of the past. The idea of clonal reproduction to replicate existing persons, already adjudged to be better suited to the environment, for example, has been seriously proposed by genetists and molecular biologists.[21] To ask if we morally ought to do such things raises serious difficulties, because we are asking for a moral assessment that if followed would determine the nature of human welfare, of the MEC that it is morality's task to protect. For example, if we say that we ought not morally to genetically engineer human beings so that they will have no need for unbefouled air or pure water, or that we ought not to establish clonal reproduction banks so that at death a replicate can be manufactured to replace the deceased, we are implying that human interests as they now are should not be altered and that the constituency of the class of persons is not to be increased by, for example, clonal reproduction. But this tends to make morality a circular business. Morality would be both determining what constitutes the MEC (or human welfare) and the class of its subjects (what constitutes a person) and establishing the primary control device to insure the welfare of those persons. Morality then begins to sound very much like the rules of a game like chess. Joseph Fletcher has written:

> If we try to cope with the morality of birth technology and genetic engineering by simply applying the right-wrong rules of an inherited and "time-tested" value system we will most likely be . . . unable to make constructive judgments because our evaluations are already determined, preset.[22]

Any attempt to legislate by morality against the investigations and experiments of scientists in these areas is fundamentally antiintellectual, antiscientific, and doomed to failure because we are, after all, inquisitive creatures. The discovery of new human capabilities and (consequentially) different elements in the MEC is just not a task of morality. Morality was invented to suit our needs, not to dictate them; it follows that morality can be readjusted when we become cognizant of environmental shifts or system alterations, whether in terms of conditions or constituents, that antiquate the traditional conception of the MEC, of the human predicament. That is the truly morally significant role of human condition model building.

Warnock has put this point, though without specific reference to model building, most perceptively:

> It is the proper business of morality . . . not of course to add to our available resources, nor . . . to our knowledge of how to make advantageous use of them, nor . . . to make us more rational in the judicious pursuit of our interests and ends. . . .[23]

The treatment of morality as a defense system, however, is prone to a certain overextension of the metaphor that may account for the popular attempt on supposed moral grounds to shackle scientific experimentaion. In political parlance, defense follows acquisition—conquest then defense. However, it is a maxim of politics and war that one ought not to acquire more than one can defend. That is reasonable when understood to mean that one must continually update and reevaluate one's defense system to guarantee maintenance of one's conquests; in that sense the metaphor fits what I am saying about morality. However, if the maxim is understood to mean that one dare only venture where one has a defense system already in place, then the maxim is but a slogan of a dangerous isolationism that is not simply overcautious or conservative: it is so bound to the past and blind to the present and the future as to be virtually no defense at all.

5

Moral Concepts and Their Function in Discourse: Contemplating Murder

In the next two chapters I shall concentrate on the moral aspect of a MORALITY. In Chapter 7, I shall examine certain features of the euergetical aspect. My focus in the present chapter may appear to be of limited scope, but I hope to suggest why it should be taken as representative of moral concepts and their associated names in moral discourse generally. Suppose we consider the following two questions: (1) Is euthanasia murder? and (2) Even if it is not murder, is it wrong (that is, morally wrong)? The term "euthanasia" should be viewed only as a place-keeper. I would replace it with "assassination," "abortion," or "capital punishment," if that is preferred. My discussion will not be directed toward anything peculiar to euthanasia; my concern is to show why sentences like "Murder is wrong" and "Euthanasia is wrong" are of entirely different types.

Undoubtedly there are a great many ways to commit murder. Agatha Christie entertained millions of us with myriads of plausible plots of the deed. The following three Christie accounts will be useful examples:

Case 1: The window was open. It was a bit of a scramble, but she found no real difficulty. Then she substituted a bottle of hat paint for Amy Gibbs' cough lictus. Hoping Amy'd do exactly what she did do—wake up, drink it off and then everyone would say she'd made a mistake or committed suicide.

Case 2: Tommy Pierce sat on the third story window ledge whistling and occasionally rubbing a pane of glass vigorously when he heard anyone coming. Somebody came in. Tommy showed his zeal, sitting half out of the window and polishing with zest. Then that somebody came up to him, and, while talking, gave him a sudden sharp push.

Case 3: They swayed to and fro still Bridget strove to wrest the knife away from her, and still Honoria Waynflete hung on to it. And then, little by little, the mad woman's strength began to prevail. Bridget cried out "Help! Help!" but she had no hope of help coming. She and Honoria were alone. With a supreme effort, she wrenched the other's wrist back, and at last she heard the knife fall. The next minute Honoria Waynflete's two hands had fastened round her neck in a maniac's grasp, squeezing the life out of her. She gave one last choked cry.[1]

Although further elaboration of the details in each case is wanted, everyone I think will agree that each of these cases is a murder, or simply that despite dissimilarities, "this is a murder" aptly describes (whatever else it does or does not do) each of them. Of course someone might claim that "this is a murder" does not *describe* these cases at all because "murder" is not a descriptive term, that it has *no* descriptive content. Rather it is purely a "prescriptive term," to use R. M. Hare's terminology[2] (but not his account of "murder"—he regards "murder" as "secondarily evaluative," to be discussed below). According to this claim, it has primarily or purely a (commending or) condemning force. But that it is merely prescriptive simply cannot be the case. Surely, whatever else "the murder of Amy" does, it picks out an event via a description. The proper use of the word "murder," as Hare will agree, is governed by rules that define its extension over the class of events, and it does so in terms of the presence of certain event-characteristics or properties (those that were chosen for emphasis at the time the concept was formed).

Hare's secondary evaluative analysis of the meaning and force of words like "murder" gains a foothold because a sentence like "Honoria murdered Bridget," if emended to Agatha Christie's account of Case 3, strikes us as adding a dimension not found in the original narrative. It sounds as if a speaker who calls an event a murder has pronounced something more than a descriptive judgment on the event, that he could not be evaluatively neutral regarding it. He is, after all, condemning its perpetrator, may be expressing his disdain, displeasure, and so on, at its occurrence. Hare calls this multi-illocutionary element of words like "murder" their prescriptive meaning, and any term in a certain context that has both descriptive and prescriptive meaning, an evaluative term.[3] "An evaluative judgment is a judgment in which such a term is used,"[4] with the proviso that the speaker be sincere or not using the evaluative term in some insulated way.

All genuine evaluative judgments, for Hare, as a matter of definition entail imperatives that guide choices. It is not obvious that Hare is right in this assertion, that in sincere use terms such as "murder," even if they are evaluative, must by *definition* entail imperatives that guide choices. Oddly, Hare maintains, in *Freedom and Reason*, that,

> The human word 'ought', unlike its counterpart in an angelic moral language, not only faces both ways [is a Janus-word to use Nowell-Smith's terminology—PAF] in the sense of having both descriptive and prescriptive meaning—for the angelic word does that—but can sometimes look in the direction that suits its user's interests and bury its other face in the sand.[5]

Suppose that it is the prescriptive aspect that has been "buried" in some usage of an evaluative word like "murder," then although the word still is, indeed by definition it must be, used evaluatively, it cannot imply an imperative. (Hare makes it quite explicit that, although we may emphasize one or the other aspect of the meaning of a word, the words used in moral discourse are not ambiguous. They do not have "a series of distinct senses." [In fairness to Hare, his example is "ought" rather than the moral concept words such as "murder" and "lie" with which I am concerned. As regards words like "ought," "good," and "right," however, I shall argue in the next chapter that he is mistaken as well.]) After all, it is the buried prescriptive element that Hare defines in terms of that imperative implication. The result would be an unassertive evaluative judgment, but Hare does not allow for such judgments. For Hare's account to be consistent, it would seem that he must imagine that aspects of a word's meaning have after-internment powers. The metaphor here becomes so muddled as to obscure sense.

What we should say is that imperatives are but categorical ways of telling someone to do something. They differ dramatically from prescriptives and descriptives. Further, we can define prescriptives in terms that do not depend on the entailment of imperatives. Imperatives can be conditioned, for example, "If Bill arrives, close the door," but they can never be the condition of anything, though descriptives, prescriptives, and evaluatives can. Evaluative judgments are, but imperatives are not, propositional; they can be used to formulate alternative behavioral choices from which an agent might select a course of action. Imperatives cannot so function. Castañeda nicely summarizes the difference between imperatives and evaluative judgments (what he calls "normatives"). He writes: "Imperatives can be used only assertively while normatives can be used both assertively and unassertively."[6] It seems highly dubious that an assertive categorical command always entails an unassertive use of an evaluative judgment (one with its prescriptive head in the sand). We should, I think, grant that Hare is correct in saying that ordinary evaluations such as "This is a good knife," although they do not direct the behavior of persons, do have a strong suggestive or recommending aspect. But that is not to say that they imply an imperative. "This is a good knife" does not entail "Buy this knife," though it may be read as counseling, "If you need a knife for cutting bread, this one is a good choice." What Hare actually seems to want us to say is that the prescriptive aspect of evaluative judgments is revealed in that their makers are committing themselves to specific choices in the future, on pain of self-contradiction.

Two of Hare's claims are important to our study. The first is that evaluative judgments entail that their speakers are committed to certain choices and hence have certain pro or con attitudes regarding the objects of evaluation; and the second is that "murder" is an evaluative term (or secondary evaluative term), so makers of judgments containing the word "murder" necessarily make evaluative judgments, hence are committed to certain choices, because they have certain attitudes regarding events of which certain descriptions are true. I think Hare is wrong in both claims.

Let us say that if a judgment commits its maker to certain attitudes or beliefs and to certain choices, it has the feature of "Harean implication." Simply, a Harean implication is nondetachable and noncancellable, that is, it is a hard and fast logical implication (in Hare's example, between the making of a judgment and the having of an attitude and the commitment to the making of a choice). We will say that a judgment p has the feature of Harean implication if and only if X makes the judgment p only if X has the attitude A and a belief B, and commits himself to making choice C if certain conditions arise in the future. (We will stipulate that a judgment can have the feature of Harean implication in a truncated or mongrel form if X makes that judgment only if X has the attitude A or the belief B.) By "nondetachable" is meant that we cannot find a way of saying just what judgment X made so that the implication that X has the attitude A (or holds the belief B) and has committed himself to doing C when certain circumstances arise is absent. By "noncancellable" is meant that we cannot find a way of saying just what judgment X made and then append a clause to the effect that it is not the case that X has attitude A (or holds belief B) and has not committed himself to doing C when certain circumstances arise. Let us contrast Harean implication with what I shall call Gricean implication. An implication is Gricean (1) if one can restate the judgment (without loss of sense) so that the purported implication is absent, and (2) one can add a further clause to the conjunction of the judgment and the purported implication that annuls the implication without annulling the judgment. Simply, a judgment has the feature of Gricean implication if what one generally or conventionally implies about the attitudes, beliefs, or commitments of its maker is detachable and cancellable. Grice provides the following example:

> "She was poor but she was honest," where what is implied is (very roughly) that there is some contrast between poverty and honesty, or between her poverty and her honesty.[7]

If someone says "She was poor *and* she was honest," he would be asserting the same thing as "She was poor but she was honest," but no implied contrast between poverty and honesty is to be found in the substituted sentence. Second, if someone were to say "She was poor but she was honest, though I do not wish to imply that there is any contrast between poverty and honesty," he would not be uttering a contradiction or an unintelligible remark. We would no doubt think him a bit eccentric for using such a peculiar locution to say only that she was poor and honest, but that is because we conventionally associate certain beliefs, attitudes, and commitments with the way certain judgments are made. That is not, however, a matter of logic.

I want to argue that if there is an implication from the making of an evaluative judgment to an attitude (a belief) and a commitment of the maker, as Hare argues there is, that it is a Gricean and not a Harean implication. On the other hand, I do want to argue that the implication from "Honoria murdered Bridget" (when sincerely spoken) to "The speaker believes that what Honoria did to Bridget was wrong" is at least a truncated Harean implication, and that is one of the reasons why "Honoria murdered Bridget" is not an evaluative judgment.

If the shopkeeper says "This is a good knife but I do not mean to imply that I am committing myself to using it when whittling," we might well wonder why he uttered the locution at all, but we cannot say that what he said was unintelligible. All he need be saying is that this knife meets some generally accepted criteria for knives or for knives of a certain type. I take the shopkeeper's judgment to be paradigmatic of evaluative judgments, and hence to indicate that such judgments evidence Gricean and not Harean implication to attitudes, beliefs, and commitments.

A confusion perpetrates the misunderstanding of the function of words like "murder," and encourages thinking of all evaluative judgments about the events described by those words as having the Harean implication feature; that confusion is rooted in a failure to appreciate that evaluation is always done according to a criterion of goodness given a description. In fact it is just that feature of evaluations that ensures that the implication to an evaluator's attitudes and commitments is Gricean. A particularly pertinent way of exposing this fact is to consider the possibility of evaluating murders themselves. Simply, evaluation may be worked on murders (or thefts or lies or adulteries) as well as on knives and poisons.

In 1863 Thomas de Quincey made use of this discovery with remarkably entertaining results. He writes in "On Murder Considered as One of the Fine Arts":

> Immoral! Jupiter protect me, gentlemen, what is it that people mean? I am for morality, and always shall be, and for virtue, and all that; and I do affirm, and always shall (let what will come of it), that murder is an improper line of conduct, highly improper; and I do not stick to assert, that any man who deals in murder, must have very incorrect ways of thinking, and truly inaccurate principles; and so far from aiding and abetting him by pointing out his victim's hiding-place, as a great moralist of Germany declared it to be every good man's duty to do, I would subscribe one shilling and sixpence to have him apprehended, which is more by eighteenpence than the most eminent moralists have hitherto subscribed for that purpose. But what then? . . . Murder . . . may be treated *aesthetically*, as the Germans call it—that is, in relation to good taste. . . . When a murder is in the paulo-post-futurum tense —not done, not even (according to modern purism) *being* done, but only going to be done—and a rumor of it comes to our ears, by all means let us treat it morally. But suppose it over, done, It is finished, or (in that adamantine molossus of Medea) Done it is: it is a *fait accompli*; suppose the poor murdered man to be out of his pain, and the rascal that did it off like a shot, nobody knows whither; suppose, lastly, that we have done our best, by putting out our legs, to trip up the fellow in his flight, but all to no purpose—why, then, I say, what's the use of any more virtue? Enough has been given to morality; now comes the turn of Taste and the Fine Arts. A sad thing it was, no doubt, very sad; but *we* can't mend it. Therefore let us make the best of a bad matter; and, as it is impossible to hammer anything out of it for moral purposes, let us treat it aesthetically, and see if it will turn to account in that way. Such is the logic of a sensible man, and what follows? We dry up our tears, and have the satisfaction, perhaps, to discover that a transaction, which was shocking, when tried by principles of Taste, turns out to be a very meritorious performance.

Thus all the world is pleased; the old proverb is justified, that it is an ill wind which blows nobody good; the amateur, from looking bilious and sulky, by too close an attention to virtue, begins to pick up his crumbs; and general hilarity prevails. Virtue has her day; and henceforward, *Virtù*, so nearly the same thing as to differ only by a single letter (which surely is not worth haggling or higgling about)—*Virtù*, I repeat, and Connoisseurship, have leave to provide for themselves.

What de Quincey has put his finger on is that often underestimated fact that evaluating implies accepting standards of *goodness* regarding the object being evaluated, but that use of such standards is only a conventional adoption, that is, there is only a Gricean implication to the having of attitudes of a certain sort about the object under evaluation. Perhaps we are a bit disturbed by the idea of a club that treats murder as a fine art, a club of murder connoisseurs, but we may rest comfortably in the assurance that none of the members of de Quincey's club would ever think of doing the deed himself. They know a murder when they see one, but they also know a *murder* from a murder. (For those with some fascination in regard to these matters, de Quincey expends the bulk of the essay on the honing of criteria of goodness for murders. Not unexpectedly these passages read rather like Aristotle's *Poetics*.)

An upshot of our analysis so far is that either "murder" cannot be an evaluative term, even a secondary evaluative term, *or* the speaker of the sentence "Murdering Amy by poisoning her with the hat paint is a good murder" would have to be saying something unintelligible, something like "Poisoning Amy with the hat paint was a good not-good or good bad thing to do." Clearly the latter sentence is not a proper translation of the former, though the speaker is not saying something unintelligible.

If we apply the Gricean implication test that we have found works for evaluation to a sentence like "Honoria murdered Bridget," we get rather quizzical results. Surely the speaker could restate this locution in a way that does not imply that the speaker has a negative attitude toward what Honoria did to Bridget and that he was committing himself to not doing something similar to someone else if the occasion were to arise. He could simply use the Case 3 narrative. And he could seemingly annul the implication that Hare would assign to him without annulling the judgment. But at least two things here are quite different from our previous examples of evaluation. First, the speaker is not invoking any criteria of goodness on which his judgment is based. Second, it does not matter to us or his judgment that he could or would annul the implication Hare would assign him, because the implication to his attitude and commitment is irrelevant to the judgment both logically and conventionally. What he cannot annul is the implication from "Honoria murdered Bridget" to "What Honoria did to Bridget was wrong." He cannot sincerely and sensibly say "Honoria murdered Bridget and that does not imply that I believe that what Honoria did to Bridget was wrong." But that is not because "murder" is an evaluative term. It is because when someone says "Honoria murdered Bridget," he *is* saying that what Honoria did to Bridget was wrong. That will be the case regardless of the attitudes or commitments of speakers.

We should probably conclude that "murder" is not an evaluative term, but what I hope has been suggested is that little reason exists to persist in drawing the ritual distinction between evaluative and descriptive terms. Instead, we should concentrate on evaluating and describing as two of the things we do. I have identified two key features of evaluating: dependence on standards of goodness of type and Gricean implication to the evaluator's attitudes and commitments. Judgments of the sort "_____ is murder" do not evidence the first feature and if they can be shown to have the second it is irrelevant to understanding their meaning and function. Hence, judgments and questions using "murder" are not, just because they use that term, evaluative nor do they call for evaluations. Of course if someone were to say "Poisoning in this way (citing Case 1) is a good murder," or alternatively, "Now that's a murder!" then he would be evaluating; but it is important that he can do so only after the description of the event in question as a murder is settled. The difference between moral judgments and evaluative judgments is that in moral judgments, we are concerned about the proper description of what we do or might do, rather than about identifying the absence or presence of qualities that would justify our claim that one of two things falling under the same description is better or worse than the other. In morality we are interested, as aptly put by Julius Kovesi, "in the relevant facts that justify us in regarding our acts as falling under one rather than another description."[8] It is with this concern in mind that we look at our first question: Is euthanasia murder? We need not be concerned with speaker attitudes or commitments. Question 1 deals only with the rules that define the extension of "murder" over the class of events and that are an articulation of the concept of murder. Nonetheless, in accounting for those rules we can, I think, account as well for the intuitive force of Hare's secondary evaluative analysis of moral terms such as "murder." There is no Harean implication in evaluation though there may be a kind of Harean implication feature involved in the making of moral judgments.

II

Murder involves killing a person, but we all know that killing a person is not always murder; for example, killing under legal orders in war and in self-defense. What then distinguishes murders in the broader class of killings? Or, what do cases 1, 2, and 3 have in common that makes us confident that each is properly described as a murder? When the question is put in that way it invites, among some recent philosophers, a response in terms of Wittgenstein's "family resemblance" doctrine.[9] What makes it possible for us to use the same word to describe a number of apparently different things or events is that, although no single feature or trait is to be found in all those things or events, on inspection, a pattern of similarities in features is discernible.

Related to this family resemblance view is the notion that all word usage is not governed by firm boundary distinctions, that boundaries are drawn arbitrarily for specific reasons at specific times. The problem of whether or not euthanasia is murder appears to reduce to one of seeking out empirical similarities between events; that is, of first establishing that our three cases, for example, can be related in some way and then that euthanasia has some *significant* features in common with one of those cases. I emphasize *significant* because the decision as to the applicational scope of a word obviously should not rest on a minor or unimportant feature of one of the three cases or of euthanasia. The program in simplified form would be something like this: We would show that the poison case shares some significant characteristic with the pushing and that the pushing shares some characteristic with the strangling and then that pulling the plug on a medical support system of a person who cannot live without it has a significant feature in common with the strangling.

There are, however, compelling reasons for not adopting the family resemblance theory, at least in the case of moral concept words. In light of my discussion of moral concepts as mixed modes, what some of those reasons are should be fairly obvious. The family resemblance view would have it that we can discover new things about, for example, murder by an empirical comparison of events. In effect, the theory confuses discovery of instances or techniques with the learning of a concept. The names of moral concepts are not family names. They are the names of mixed modes invented for our special reasons. They do, of course allow us to pick out a family of events but they do not do so in the way "Jones" allows us to pick out a family of persons. To be a murder is to exemplify the concept of murder, not to be related to a poisoning as Mary Jones is related to her daughter Elizabeth Jones. We learn nothing more about what murder is by reading a dozen Agatha Christie novels or what a lie is by studying the speeches of Richard Nixon. We learn how (perhaps), but we don't learn what. Family resemblance theorists confuse the open texture of exemplification with conceptual open texture.[10] Moral concepts are open-textured only insofar as they admit to a variety, possibly an inexhaustible number, of ways of murdering or of lying. They are not open-textured if that means that they are indeterminate with respect to meaning.

If we imagine, as I think J. L. Austin did, that the specific collection of words we have in our language is the result of an "invisible hand" sorting process, a kind of natural (or sociological) selection, then we may expect that the primary reason why we have the words, expressions, and concepts we do is to be found in certain biological, sociological, and historical facts about us. Should we want to provide a complete account of why we have the word "table" in our language, to borrow an example from Julius Kovesi,[11] and why it has a certain use, we would need to supply a certain amount of sociohistorical data. The data would include how we came to have the need to distinguish types of furnishings in our homes, why we wanted to do so, and where it is important in our lives to do so; in addition, we would have to consider the physiological facts that necessitate that tables be a certain height, etc. The concept of table emerged from such a sociohistory and the extension of "table" is governed by that concept (or intension), that complex idea.

An understanding of our sociohistory contributes to our understanding of the point of our having specific words that are used to do certain things. Comparative sociohistory reveals that other communities have hosts of other words that are used (get their point) for other sorts of activities than we practice. The language used by a community is rich or poor in certain kinds of words because members of that community, in trying to manage their experiences, have specific needs to form concepts to help them describe or refer to certain events or acts.

Stuart Hampshire attributed to Austin the view that "for every distinction of word and idiom that we find in common speech, there is a reason to be found, if we look far enough, to explain why this distinction exists."[12] This "Principle of Sufficient Linguistic Reason" is, of course, hueristic. It is most suggestive, for it invites, I think, the view that I want to hold, that the applicational scope of such non-natural kind terms as moral terms is governed by concepts (intensions) that emerge with the life-style of a people. Concept governance of the extension of such terms accounts for the reason we don't have to wait until after an event has occurred and then compare its characteristics with those of other events to describe it appropriately as murder. We don't discover that an event is a murder by discovering that it is like the poisoning of Amy. Instead, to be a murder, an event must evidence in some way that set of characteristics or features we have associated in the complex that is our concept of murder. All murders evidence, though in different ways, all of these features. Nothing is a murder that fails to do so, no matter how much it resembles, for example, the poisoning of Amy. Of course, we do not look for the property of murderness to be exemplified in the event, just as we did not look for tableness in the object. We look for properties that exemplify the concept of murder. To claim that Honoria murdered Bridget is to imply that, without violating the scope rules set by our concept of murder, one could cite features of the event in question that would be relevant to its inclusion in the extension of "murder" rather than, for example, within the extension of "self-defensive killing." Certainly that is not at all like ordinary evaluating; it involves no standard of goodness of kind.

What then is our concept of murder? What set of event features makes up the complex? As we know murder to be a moral concept, we can expect that, because it would have been formed for either the purpose of encouraging or of discouraging a type of behavior, the event features associated in the concept are believed to have a positive or a negative effect on the MEC. Imagine Adam inventing not *kinneah* or *niouph* but *laharog*. He learns that Cain has killed Abel by, let us stipulate, hitting him over the head with a heavy rock. He realizes that such actions would if generally practiced destroy the hope of most people to realize a full and rewarding life and, if he needs it, he sees the evidence of God's anger to support his belief that Cain has done something wrong. He wants to admonish Seth and his other children not to do as Cain did, but he realizes almost immediately that there is a major difference between this injunction and telling his wife and children not to eat of the fruit of a particular tree, when all he has to do is point to the specific tree and say, "Don't eat of its fruit." In this case he clearly does not mean to convey or not *only* to convey that he does not want them to hit each other over the head with large rocks. What he intends is to identify any acts that have certain features, that are exemplified in Cain's act, the presence of which he believes makes such acts threats to the human condition. Cain's act was, of course, the hitting of his brother on the head with a heavy rock and it was the killing of a brother, but neither of those features exhausted the notion Adam wanted to convey. Had Cain strangled Abel or had the victim been not Abel but the neighbor Lamech, Adam still would have wanted to admonish Seth and the others not to do that sort of thing. He forms the concept of murder by associating the ideas, that he also finds as features of Cain's act, of an act being (1) an intentional killing of any human being (2) who is innocent and not an immediate threat to the life of the agent, (3) in part, at least, because of the agent's expectation of personal satisfaction or aggrandizement as a direct outcome of his act.[13]

This particular rendering of the concept of murder is likely to be controversial, but I think it can withstand most of the purported counterexamples. Two were suggested to me: (1) Suppose someone intentionally kills a legally innocent person who is no immediate threat, not for personal satisfaction but for political reasons; and (2) suppose the legal system of a country permits certain killings of innocents, as in dueling or in gladiatorial contests. Are we not inclined to say that both cases would be murders? I think we would, on the contrary, say that (2) is definitely not a murder as long as the fight is fair and the parties consented to do battle. (1) may appear to be more problematic, but we have a somewhat simple way of dealing with it. It is a murder because political reasons are generally thought to be subsumed under personal ones. However, "assassination" perhaps better describes the case. Terrorists and other violent political activists have been urging in their rhetoric a retrenchment of the concept of murder to exclude political assassination; they are also urging that under certain circumstances, commission of the act, an assassination, would not be wrong or blameworthy. Indeed it might even be praiseworthy. It will be recalled that at the beginning of this chapter I said that I was going to use "euthanasia" as a place-keeper and could as well have chosen "assassination" or "abortion." What I shall say of the possible evolution of "euthanasia" could as well have been said of "assassination."

Our three original cases from Agatha Christie in their more complete telling all satisfy the requirements for inclusion under the concept of murder. Again, it may be useful to remind that they do so in quite different ways, evidencing the open texture of exemplification of moral concepts.

Insofar as the reason we have the concept of murder is to identify deeds for which one is liable to be blamed, reproached, or punished, the idea that murder is wrong is a part of the concept of murder. The same can be said of lying, cheating, committing adultery, and so on. In the case of some of our act modifier concepts such as inadvertence (excuse words), the reason we have them is because we have recognized that blame, reproach, and punishment are meaningless or ineffectual if, for example, the event was brought about by sheer accident. We have other act modifier concepts, that Austin called "words of aggravation,"[14] such as intentional, deliberate, and purposeful because we want to blame or reproach certain acts at certain times, even though we do not recognize a need to form a moral concept to capture the particular instance. It is of some interest that these moral modifier concepts tend to function in the grey areas of act-description where no moral concept clearly has staked the extension of its name. If "Smith murdered his brother" is true, it will not be wondered whether he did so inadvertently nor intentionally. But if it is true that what he did was to pull the plug on his brother's life support system while his brother was in a coma, it might well be asked if he did so inadvertently or intentionally.

The point of our having the word "murder" is that we want to prevent the occurrence of certain events. The very concept, murder, as we have seen, contains the idea that acting so as to cause an event properly described as a murder is wrong. Indeed it was formed for just that reason. "Murder is wrong" is therefore necessarily true. This accounts for the fact that "Murder is wrong" is uninformative to mature speakers of the language. The very point of having the word renders it unnecessary for anyone to decide rightness or wrongness when an event occurs that is properly described by it. To imagine a world in which we (our language-using community) did not have the concept of murder is to imagine a world in which the rightness or wrongness of every killing has to be decided afresh. If such decisions, as they are likely to, slur into type-decisions ("killings of this sort are wrong"), the formulation of the concept of murder would be in its nativity.

We are now in a position to find out whether euthanasia is murder. The answer calls for no evaluations or, even, valuing on our part. It calls only for inspection, but not to see if euthanasia has some feature in common with strangling. Rather it is to see if euthanasias have the characteristics of being intentional killings of human beings who are innocent and not immediate threats to the agents and which are done, at least in part, because of the agent's expectations of personal satisfaction or aggrandizement. Certainly an involuntary euthanasia is an intentional killing of a human being (though questions may be raised as to whether the "victim" in some of the publicized cases is a person, he is a human being) and the "victim" is usually innocent under the law and not an immediate threat to the agent. We may I think safely assume, however, that no one perpetrating the act does so for personal satisfaction or gain. It is likely an act performed in torment, and even against its perpetrator's deepest hopes and desires. Acts of involuntary euthanasia, then, are not murders. They are killings, but the question of their rightness or wrongness is still open. If we ask for the point of the concept of euthanasia, we would probably learn that it was formed to allow the drawing of a distinction between inducing a painful and inducing a painless death. Reasons why we might need to draw such a distinction are multifarious, but no grounds seem to exist for the belief that the primary need for doing so was to prevent the occurrence or to encourage the occurrence of certain events or to render liable to blame or worthy of praise those who perform acts appropriately described as euthanasias. I think that the same may be said of abortions, assassinations, and capital punishments.

Someone might say "Euthanasia is murder," as a way of proposing that although euthanasia lacks at least one of the characteristics or features of murder, that particular characteristic or feature is inessential to the concept. In so arguing he would be trying to reform the concept of murder. Alternatively, saying "Euthanasia is murder" might be a move in a kind of analogical argument from which the speaker wants to derive the conclusion "Euthanasia is wrong." In many respects, what I shall say about deciding the question "Is euthanasia wrong?" incorporates a place for such analogical arguments.

III

Let us turn to the second of the two questions with which I began the chapter: Even though euthanasia is not murder, is it nonetheless wrong? Euthanasia, as we have seen, is not like fratricide, a species of murder, but the concept of euthanasia might still have been formed because of a generally perceived need to deter certain acts, and hence euthanasias would be wrong. Murder is not the only thing that is wrong. We have formed the concepts of lying and stealing, etc., for similar behavioral constraint reasons. If euthanasia had been so formed, then there would be at least two kinds of killing that are wrong, murder and euthanasia. But euthanasia does not seem to have been formed for such reasons. It is a medical concept, as is abortion. That reasonable dispute occurs over the rightness or wrongness of euthanasia signals that it is not at base a moral concept like murder. When someone says "Euthanasia is wrong" or "People ought not to perform acts of euthanasia," he is not using the words "wrong" or "ought not" in the same uninformative way that they were used in the sentences "Murder is wrong" and "People ought not to commit murder," but he is making what can be properly called a moral judgment, and doing so is quite a different matter from deciding whether euthanasia is murder.

Making moral judgments involves consideration of values and possibly even, the formation, though usually primitive, of a moral theory. When we make a moral judgment we do not evaluate something of a certain kind against a standard of goodness for that kind. Saying that something is wrong is to imply disapproval of it and if that disapproval is moral, it will be because the speaker believes that thing to have a deteriorative effect on the human condition. As long as a non-inverted comma use of "wrong" is involved (and "wrong" is intended morally) the implication to that belief will be Harean (in the truncated sense), not cancellable or detachable from the judgment.

Moral judgments come in many forms:

1. descriptive judgments using moral concepts, e.g., "This is murder." or "Richard Nixon lied."

2. discriminatory judgments that are used to identify certain obligations or duties as paramount over others, e.g., "You ought to care for your children," and to encourage their fulfillment.

3. discriminatory judgments to identify acts or events that are not clearly captured by a moral concept but that are believed by the speaker to be causually significant with respect to the maintenance of the human condition. The acts in question either fall under a broad concept that encompasses from the moral point of view a mixed bag, or they are captured by a concept not formed for moral reasons and not clearly included or excluded by a moral concept, if one had been invented to cover other acts or events of the broader class. As an example of the first type, consider "Saying something that you know to be false, in order to protect a friend from a violent person bent on doing him grievous bodily harm, is right" (or "wrong," if you're Immanuel Kant). As an example of the second, consider "Euthanasia is wrong."

If we imagine that the concept of killing of persons to be the broad class concept from which, for moral reasons, we have distilled murder, and we have clearly conceptually distinguished murder from killing in self-defense, we are still left with other sorts of killings that do not neatly fit in either the class of murders or self-defensive killings. An example of one such type is Mr. Jones' pulling of the plug on the life support system of his comatose daughter, that is, euthanasia. If someone says "Euthanasia is (morally) wrong" he is saying that because of their deteriorative effect on the human condition (as the speaker understands it) euthanasias are morally quite different from self-defensive killings, that they are to be discouraged, that perpetrators should be blamed and possibly punished for them. He is probably saying that, in the class of killings, euthanasias are more like murders than self-defensive killings, or killings in war, or legal executions. Indeed, he may emphatically say, "Euthanasia is murder!" not literally saying that euthanasias are murders. His use of analogy is directed at exposing a common feature of euthanasias and murders (other than that they are killings).

It is of importance in the evolution of moral concepts that such judgments are tested against the common perception of the human condition. If the idea that it is wrong to perform acts of euthanasia is to be assimilated into the concept of euthanasia, the effects of euthanasias on the human condition will have to be generally believed to be damaging. General acceptance of a moral judgment of this type, then, fosters the birth of a moral concept. If euthanasia were to become a moral concept in this way, if it were to incorporate the idea that it is wrong to do it, the debate over euthanasia would cease. There is no debating over whether or not murder is wrong or lying is wrong or theft is wrong. Debates that involve those concepts turn out on inspection to be disputes either about whether some particular act falls within the extention of the name, "murder" or "lie" or about whether other acts that fall under the broader class concept of which a moral concept is a member are really, in effect, disguised instances of the very thing the moral concept was invented to cover. For example, in the broader class concept of telling of untruths we find both lies and deceivings of villians who seek to harm friends. Kant seems to be arguing that deceiving the villian *is* lying, whereas someone might, I think rightly, object that it is not at all lying to do so. In the debate over euthanasia, some argue that euthanasias are a sort of disguised murder while others counter that they are no kind of murder at all.

Even if euthanasias are not murders they might, of course, prove to be another kind of killing that we should discourage if we are about the business of preserving the human condition or the MEC. If the evidence were to show that, then we would have at least two moral concepts in the broader class concept of killings. It is unlikely that many people are aware that when they make moral judgments of the third type distinguished above, they participate in a process that could lead to the evolutionary alteration of our moral conceptual scheme. (Their general lack of cognizance of that fact is, perhaps, a part of what distinguishes the alteration as evolutionary rather than revolutionary.)

It is no secret that arguments by analogy serve as prime justificatory tools for speakers who make moral judgments of the second and third type. Hence the force of "Euthanasia is (like) murder" or "Abortion is murder." "Euthanasia is an act of mercy," on the other side of the debate, takes quite another approach to justification. The implication is supposed to be drawn that acts of mercy are essential to preserving the conditions necessary for anyone to have a good life and hence there is a need to encourage them, euthanasias being a subclass of that sort of act. Such a justificatory route assumes that one of the reasons for our having invented the concept of mercy was that we wanted to encourage merciful acts because of our perception that they contribute to the preservation or betterment of the human condition. That does not, however, seem to be indisputable. It is often noted that not harming persons is generally thought to be more important than helping or showing mercy to them.[15] Perhaps the justification of the moral judgment "Euthanasia is not wrong" should be mounted on the idea that *not* doing the deed is harming the "victim," that life itself, in some cases, is a great injury militating against, if not making impossible, having a worthwhile life. It should come as no surprise that this tack is now being explored by defenders of the practice of euthanasia.

Usually the maker of a moral judgment (at least *ante eventum*) is attempting primarily to guide choices, to advocate behavior, but he is often also doing something else, something of which he is likely unaware. He is sometimes, in effect, nominating or "seconding" a candidate moral concept.

6

Institutional
and Moral Obligations,
or Merels and Morals

In this chapter my primary concern will be with fixing the role of institutions with regard to questions about morality and obligation. Much that has been written on the significance of institutions in understanding obligations and moral issues has shown misunderstanding of the role of institutions *vis-à-vis* moral-"ought" judgments. I hope to exhibit and remedy certain aspects of that misunderstanding, first, by clarifying the concept of institutional obligation, and then by showing that moral-"ought" judgments, though in one sense sometimes parasitic, are yet in important ways independent of institutional obligation-creating rules.

I

I use the word "institution" generally in the same way as John Rawls when he writes: "by institution I shall understand a public system of rules which defines offices and positions with their rights and duties, powers and immunities, and the like."[1] The term need not exclusively refer to such paradigmatic "social institutions" as penal systems, universities, banking and legal systems, but could cover any well-established social arrangements and practices within a community. Institutions are recognized by their more or less for-

92

mal character and by the fact that they impose order on participant behavior through rule and regulation. In the language popular in philosophy today, institutional rules, regulations, and customs define certain kinds of behavior; that is, they make possible certain kinds of descriptions of experience. Indeed, they make possible certain experiences. Familiar games have proved to be useful paradigms for examining intra-institutional relationships and behavior.[2] Some major difficulties with the game model have been demonstrated, but as long as the temptation simply to equate institutions with games is avoided, the model is serviceable, and I shall avail myself of it.

An institution's set of rules (broadly defined to include regulations and customs) is not merely a collection of devices that regulate antecedently existing behavior patterns. Rather the rules define, or in Searle's terms are constitutive of,[3] new kinds of activity; that is, they identify the performance of certain actions as "counting as" the performance of an institutional act (for example, from Searle, "A touchdown is scored when a player crosses the opponents' goal line in possession of the ball while play is in progress"). We may say that a rule is constitutive if and only if it is a member of a system of rules, so that behavior that accords with at least a large subset of the rules of that system can receive descriptions that could not be given if the system did not exist.[4]

This account of constitutive rules may sound unfamiliar and even unnecessarily imprecise. Searle maintains that a rule is constitutive if and only if behavior that accords with it can receive descriptions that it could not receive if there were no such rule. But Searle also speaks of constitutive rules "on the fringe" of some system of constitutive rules.[5] He talks of degrees of centrality in such a system. According to Searle's account, every constitutive rule, including all fringe rules, would have to make new descriptions possible. In my version, a rule would still be constitutive, even though in itself it does not make a new description of behavior possible, as long as it is a non-dispensable member of a system of rules some of which do make new descriptions possible.

The following are plausible ways of construing the relationship within an institution between its constitutive rules and the behavior that they prohibit, permit, and require of participants.

1. Within institution I, X (a person) has the right to do y in circumstance C if and only if a rule in I specifically gives permission to X to do y when circumstances of the sort C arise.[6]

2. Within I, X has an obligation to do y in circumstance C if and only if a rule in I specifically requires the doing of y when circumstances of the sort C arise.

3. Within I, X has an obligation not to do y in circumstance C if and only if a rule in I specifically prohibits the doing of y when circumstances of the sort C arise.

4. Within I, if doing y is not specifically prohibited by any rules in I, then X is at liberty to do y in I. Obviously then X is at liberty to do what X has a right to do and also X is at liberty to do what he is not prohibited from doing. It is a misuse of "liberty" to say that he is at liberty to do what he is required to do.

1–4 above are indeed controversial. I want to extract from them a great deal, some of which will fly in the face of certain standard treatments of deontic logic and many moral theories. I would argue:

(a) that the proper understanding of a right is as a permission given to someone to do something within an institution. This removes any temptation to treat "rights" as special properties of agents. After all we did not find any such properties in our investigation of agency. To have a right to do something is not to be in possession of some property or other, but to be in a position to do something when one chooses without penalty and with justification.[7]

(b) that rights are always intra-institutional (or, if you will, institution-specific). There are no such things as natural rights, because the mechanism of permission granting simply does not exist out of the context of institutions. I do not have, for example, the right to life by virtue of the fact of my birth or because of my nature as an agent, but I may have that right by virtue of the rules of the legal institution of my country. The "state of nature" is not only a state without obligations, as Hobbes allowed; it is a state without rights as well.

That the granting of permissions is a purely institutional affair is made especially clear in the sentences used to grant permission, which often contain act-descriptions that would not be possible if the institution that provided their context had not a specific subset of constitutive rules. That is, the description of those acts are made possible by the introduction of terms created by or given their special sense by a sub-set of the constitutive rules of that institution. For example: chess players are given permission by the rules of the game to castle if neither king nor rook has previously moved and the intervening spaces on the back line are clear. All chess players whose circumstances are properly described in that way have the right to castle. The expression of that right in fact is impossible (is totally senseless) outside the game's context; the act properly described as castling and the right to do so are completely bound to chess. (One ought not, however, pay excessive heed to this particular example.)

Often the descriptions of the acts permitted by an institutional rule, or in an institutional context by a person, are not bound to the institutions in the way castling is bound to chess: that is, their descriptions are independent of the institutional context. For example: on an airplane the pilot at certain times gives passengers the right to smoke cigarettes. Or, another example: the teacher in the classroom gives a student permission to leave the room. What we should say is that permission granting is institution-specific and that sometimes the descriptions of the acts permitted are institution-dependent and sometimes they are not. In the latter case, only the authority to give permission is bound to the institutional setting. In those cases the institutions do not make the acts possible; they make the performing of them possible under certain conditions. The due process clause in the legal institution, for example, cannot make life possible; and the airplane pilot does not make smoking cigarettes possible (in the same sense of "possible").

(c) that the sentence, "X has the right to do something," is a description of X's institutional situation. It should be understood as equivalent to the sentence, "X has been granted permission by or given the rules of I to do something." The latter sentence is clearly either true or false. Settling whether or not X has a right to castle is in principle no different from determining that the object on which the chess board is resting is a yellow table.

(d) that what I have said of rights (that is, permissions) is also true of obligations (so-called positive and negative duties). Hence, the sentence, "X has an obligation to do something," is a description of X's institutional situation. It should be understood as equivalent to, "X is required by or given the rules of some institution to do something." This point will be of greater concern momentarily.

II

The remark "X has the right to do z but ought not to do z," made in an institutional setting is usually a prudential or tactical remark, though under certain circumstances it might be the expression of a moral judgment. In order to explore the relationship between institutional rules and various uses of "ought" I shall use as an example a relatively primitive game (with a minimum of rules). It was originally associated with the shepherds of the Salisbury Plain and was popular in Elizabethan England and has held a degree of popularity even to this day. It is the game variously called "Merels,"[8] "Morelia," or "Nine Men's Morris."[9]

The game is played on a layout conforming to this pattern:

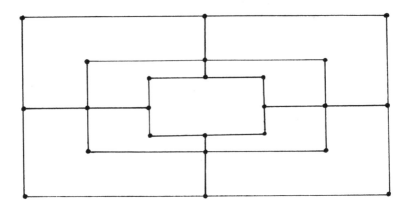

The entire set of rules for the two-person game of "Merels" is as follows:

Each player is provided with nine men of distinguishable colors, and each in turn places one man upon the layout at any intersection, corner, or meeting of the lines, hereafter called spaces. (a) Turns alternate after each move throughout the game. The object is to get three men in a line. (b) A player who succeeds in getting a line of three men has the right to remove from the layout any one of his adversary's men, except that he cannot take one from a line of three unless there are not others remaining on the layout. After all nine men are entered, turns are taken by moving any man to any adjoining space, provided it is vacant. (c) When a new line of three is formed in this way, the player has the right to remove an adversary's man from the layout. (d) It is advantageous for a player to place his men in a position to form and reform two lines alternately several times. Play continues in this way until one player has only three men left. Any of the three men can then hop over to any vacant space on the layout. (e) When either player is reduced to two men, his game is lost.[10]

Let us suppose that two shepherds, having etched the layout in the turf of the Salisbury Plain, reach the point where Shepherd X forms the first line of three. Shepherd X has the right (see 1-4 above) to remove one of Y's pieces: he certainly is not obliged to do so. The game will not stop nor even be corrupted if X does not exercise his right.[11] But suppose it is said that he *ought* to remove the piece if he intends to disadvantage Y and hence ultimately win the game. "Ought" would have either a prudential or tactical use and does not derive from the rules of Merels, although those rules make it ("X ought to remove the piece,") an intelligible remark.

Imagine now that the game has progressed to endgame and that if X exercises his right of removal (earned in the appropriate way), Y will lose the game. Furthermore, suppose that Y had struck a bet with X that the loser would forfeit five of his best sheep to the winner, and X is well aware that his victory will cause great personal and family hardship, Y's children will starve, for example, and that he (X) could absorb a similar loss without difficulty. (Moral philosophers may be intrigued.) It may seem appropriate in such circumstances to say that X has the right to do something (remove Y's piece from the layout), but he ought not do so, and that is clearly not a tactical remark. The force of that "ought not" as in the case of the prudential "ought" falls outside of the game of Merels. It is what I prefer to call a moral use of "ought not." If X removes the piece, X might be blamed for ruining Y or for making such a bet with Y in the first place, but X will not be penalized within the game of Merels for exercising his right of removal. The rules of the game of Merels have nothing at all to say about sheep, or the financial status of participants, or about wagers.

Let us take a closer look at the tactical and prudential uses of "ought" just exemplified. (I shall return to moral uses of "ought" in section III.) When ought statements are made in institutional contexts (and when their force is not moral), they are not obligation stating. *Institutional obligations*, that is, those obligations created by an individual for himself by his participation in a particular institution, cannot *characteristically* and *best* be expressed by using "ought;" rather they can be best expressed by using "must." Let us see why this is so. While, in the first example above, X *ought to* (as a matter of tactics) remove Y's piece, Y *must* (is *obliged* to) allow his piece to be removed, that is, he has an institutional obligation (he is required) to do so.[12] Or to use an example from chess, a player *must* (not "ought to") move his king out of check. "Ought," in settings like these, signals or at least allows for the presence of option or choice available to the addressee. The speaker of an "ought" sentence of these sorts is expressing the belief that the course of action stipulated is not absolutely binding upon the person to whom it is directed. "Must," however, forecloses the possibility of choice; it conveys the sense that the course of action is inescapable (insofar, at least, as the participation-status in the institution of the addressee is to be maintained.) Of course, one can always escape the requirement to move the king out of check by simply ceasing to play chess when one's opponent places one's king in check. This might suggest that the institutional obligation could best be expressed by "Y ought to move his king out of check if he wants to continue playing chess"; but such a conditional directs attention away from the moves in the game towards Y's state of mind or to Y's "wants." However, the main information still conveyed by such a sentence is that Y's moving the king is necessary if the game is to continue. Talking about Y's wants is only a way of introducing that institutional information, so the "ought" there does collapse into "must." Even if the intent to participate is assumed in the rules, it is not assumed in sentences that state the obligations that derive from those rules. If we were to ask a chess player, participant *qua* participant, why he moved his king out of check when certain game situations occur, his answer will most likely not be that he recognized that he ought to do so insofar as he wanted to continue playing; he will state that the rules of chess dictate that he must do so, that the set of his possible institutional moves has been greatly limited and that the effect of his next move will be a particular kind of modification of his status in the game. We should say that Y's situation is best described by the sentence "Y is required to move his king out of check," in conjunction with a set of sentences that describe the placement of the pieces on the gameboard and that that conjunction entails (stipulated for simplicity) that Y's next move is *a* if and only if it is not *b* (where *a* and *b* are move-descriptions such as "K to K3"). The question "Ought Y's next move be *a* or *b*?" from the point of view of economic rationality can be completely and satisfactorily answered intra-institutionally by applying game-theoretic methods (in the cases of chess and Merels) for zero-sum non-negotiable games. It will be solely a question of strategy, consequences, and preferences. Y would be in a classic game theory choice situation in a perfect information game so that a "best-play" strategy easily could be devised for him. Acting on "best play" strategy in standard accounts of game theory is often, and I think correctly, counterposed to acting "ethically," which for my purposes can be described as ignoring "the possibility of the other's taking advantage of one's good intentions [and] . . . carrying out these intentions any way."[13] The tactical use of "ought" can always be given a game theoretic analysis. Hence it always can be reduced to sentences describing a "best play" strategy. "Y ought (tactical remark) to move the king to K3" will be true if that move occurs in a "best play" strategy devisable for Y at that juncture of game play.

If the standard modal deontic logicians and other moral philosophers remain insistent on using "ought" to render institutional obligations, then that "ought" will have to be understood as a very special "ought." We could call it an institutional use of "ought," but it will convey what the ordinary "must" conveys.[14] My own inclination is to leave "must" to do the institutional obligation-stating work for which it is suited: its ordinary use in institutional and noninstitutional contexts straightforwardly signals the binding requirement or prohibition. Moreover, the use of "ought" in statements of institutional obligation is apt to be misleading. If the constitutive rules of Merels or any institution do define what it is to play Merels, in the sense that they make it possible for behavior that accords with them to be described as Merels playing, they have to exclude the possibility that someone may be playing Merels and not acting in accord with a large subset of those rules. That possibility is not excluded if the statements of institutional obligations do not convey the sense of a binding requirement on participant behavior; that is, if they convey a concessive or optional "requirement" as "ought" usually does.

Statements of institutional obligation then *must* report binding requirements of action for participants *qua* participants within the institution and *ought* to be formulated as, e.g., "Y must do *z*." Whether or not someone must do something is, in the end, a question of fact, of finding the correct description of his institutional situation. Such a description is made possible by institutional rules.

III

Returning to the other uses of "ought," our shepherds on the Salisbury Plain, and their game of Merels: suppose that Shepherd X has Shepherd Y in a bad way. On making one move, he will end Y's game. Further, Y and X have struck up a wager which will, in the circumstances of his defeat, make it impossible for Y to meet his legal obligation to provide for his children's welfare. In simplified fashion, let us say that at least three institutions are involved in the situation: (1) the game of Merels, (2) wagering, and (3) the legal institution (especially that part of the law concerning parental obligations). The rules of Merels grant the right of removal to X and also force on Y the obligation to (he must) cease his play (do *s*) in this circumstance; he has lost. The rules of wagering create an obligation for the loser of the wager to (he must) pay in full the amount of the wager (Y must do *p*).

The legal institution admittedly is much more complex than two-person games such as Merels or wagering, but that complexity does not appreciably alter the types of obligations (in this case, parental duties) that arise therein. For the sake of simplicity, let us stipulate that one legal rule of the community of our shepherds is that parents are obliged to provide the necessities of survival for their growing children. Shepherd Y, a father *must* then provide for the sustenance of his young children (he must do *c*). We may say then that Y has institutional obligations with respect to *s*, *p* and *c*.

Y cannot, of course, do *s*, *p* and *c*. In particular, doing *p* precludes doing *c*, and *vice versa*. Naturally we are presented with the interesting question: "Ought Y fulfill *p* or *c* since he cannot do both?" A definitive answer to that question, if certain other important conditions are met, is what I shall take to be *paradigmatic* of a moral-"ought" judgment. The logic of institutions can in no way settle the issue. Richard Brandt has set up the situation nicely when he writes: "If there are two conflicting obligations . . . and a decision must be made as to what should be done, we do not normally say, 'What is then really my obligation?' To ask this is somewhat odd, since it is already clear that there are two obligations, which conflict. . . . the preferred phrasing in the situation is 'What ought I to do?' "[15]

As previously mentioned, "ought" has a myriad of uses, for example, tactical, prudential, and institutional. It is used morally when it either identifies one obligation as paramount in a conflict of institutional obligations or reminds (generally as a teaching device) that one obligation in such conflicts is paramount because it is generally believed to have a more positive effect on the human condition. This is not meant to suggest that every moral-"ought" judgmental use is bound to occur in situations of obligational conflict or that each judgment makes some oblique reference to such conflicts. The notion of (moral) paramountcy obviously rests on some structure of priorities; a kind of hierarchy of institutions and activities is created in view of morality's primary task, given the shared perception of a community as to the conditions necessary for anyone to live a worthwhile life. We should expect that as more is learned about the conditions necessary for persons to live worthwhile lives and as beliefs change regarding those conditions, an elevating of the obligations of certain institutions and a corresponding lowering of those of others will occur. Most of the time persons are able to fulfill all of their obligations, although on occasion circumstances are such that people cannot fulfill two or more obligations that fall due at approximately the same time (that is what I understand to be an obligational conflict situation). In those cases, moral-"ought" judgments and what I shall call "moral principles" have a key role to play. In just those situations, aptly described by Brandt's comment, the notion of a moral obligation does arise.

I understand by "moral principle" any member of that set of beliefs a community shares about the kinds of behavior that need to be encouraged or discouraged given its perception of the conditons necessary for the possibility of persons living lives of worth. In the Oxford English Dictionary's seventh definition of "principle" we find the helpful "a general law . . . adopted or professed as a guide to action: a settled ground or basis of conduct or practice. . . ." A moral principle is a former discriminatory moral judgment that has ceased to serve a judgmental role for members of a community but nonetheless would likely be cited by members as a guide to their actions if they were pressed to explain them; also, importantly, it provides analogical support for the other moral judgments they do make. Community members at certain times in their socio-history cease making certain discriminatory judgments regarding certain actions and the fulfillment of certain obligations rather than others in genuine conflicts, although they continue to guide their lives by what once were the dictates of those judgments; that is, they start acting on principle in those cases. Usually, as we have seen in the previous chapter, they have framed a moral concept that eliminates the need to make discriminatory judgments. To adopt a term Wittgenstein used in another context, in *On Certainty*, we may describe moral principles as "hardened"[16] moral judgments. They are no longer judgments insofar as no one in the community actually judges them, for example, no one judges that he ought not to commit murder. If he is convinced, or can be convinced, that the act he contemplates is an act of murder, the "ought" in "I ought not to do it (commit murder)" is truly redundant (for reasons developed in the previous chapter). It withers away.

Because two rather different kinds of redundancy might be called to mind regarding my claim that the "ought" in the statement of a moral principle is redundant, it will be important to distinguish them. The first kind would be the tautological sense. One wouldn't call an event a murder if he thought himself to be morally justified in perpetrating it, unless he does not understand murder to be a moral concept, that is, unless he is ignorant. A second redundancy does creep into my account, especially because of the communal reference point I emphasize. One might say there is no conversational point in certain communities in saying "You ought not to do this," because it is known that everyone addressed already stands in agreement. Although I have in mind the first kind of redundancy for moral principles, I believe that the second often is a prelude to the first. Moral concepts, as we have seen, are not formed out of the blue. They are a product of "agreements in judgment." Conversationally redundant "oughts" are, however, not going to be eliminatable in the statement of principles, so a candidate moral principle that contains a conversationally redundant "ought" will not be a pure moral principle. Pure moral principles will be only those in which "ought" is tautologically redundant. We might imagine then two levels of moral principles in a community: emerging principles and pure principles, and the difference between the two will be that pure principles involve only moral concepts.

Community moral beliefs, as discussed earlier, can and do alter over time. That certain beliefs about the moral paramountcy of one institutional obligation *vis-à-vis* another are no longer thought to be subject to question, or are only extraordinarily so subject, is not a logical matter. It is a function of community history that some things are done on principle and others need to be decided.

It might be convenient if all the moral-"ought" judgments supportable in a community could be logically derived from its moral principles, as the obligations of an institution can be derived from its rules in conjunction with true sentences describing someone's state of affairs within that institution. But unfortunately that is not the way it works! Moral principles may form a part of the framework in which moral-"ought" judgments are made, but the maker of a moral-"ought" judgment does not infer his judgments from those principles, even if he will often justify his moral judgments either by citing a moral principle or by trying to identify them by analogy with a moral principle.

Futher considerations tell against the translating of sentences that say that someone ought to do something into sentences that say that he has an obligation, or, in other words, that support my contention that "ought" and "has an obligation" or "is obligatory" or "is obliged" are not intertranslatable.

Two views that continually crop up in the literature may provide a focus for this aspect of our discussion: (A) Everything obligatory for someone is something he morally ought to do, and (B) What someone morally ought to do in certain circumstances is *one* of the things that he is obligated to do. There are at least two popular interpretations of the first view: [A¹] There is, on final analysis, really only one obligatory act in any circumstance and that is what a person morally ought to do. On this account, conflicts of obligations actually never arise, on some sort of careful analysis they melt away. Kant seems to hold a similar view. [A²] Often we have an obligation to do many things and we morally ought to do them all, but the simple physical fact that we cannot do them all limits us from meeting all our obligations and hence from doing everything we morally ought to do. Ross, in his earlier writings, held a version of this view.

My own position is a revision of [B], a revision because I am not arguing that every conflict of obligations has a moral arbitrator. Morality may well be disinterested in certain conflicts; its response to those conflicts might be "Do whatever you please" or "Do what pleases you." Also an important point, from the moral point of view, neither or none of the institutional obligations in a conflict may be endorsable. (A pox then on both or on all of your houses!) Such a moral judgment might be put in the form "you have an obligation to do *a* and one to do *b*, but you ought to do neither." It may not necessarily add "you ought to do *c*." In any case such a sentence does not say that you have a third obligation to do neither *a* nor *b*.

What I am trying to show is the desirability of not translating obligation claims into sentences using "ought." If the Shepherd's conflict is not an apparent but a real one, and unless I have fouled up the story telling it is a real one (not dissolvable even if more information comes to light, etc.), then the (A¹) view is inadequate. Shepherd Y *has* at least two obligations and cannot fulfill both. What we are left with then is (A²) or (B) (as revised) and the question is, which is to be preferred as a characterization of what we want to say about the function of moral-"ought" judgments? Do we want to say that Y ought to do both of the things he is obliged to do, but as a matter of fact he simply cannot, but whichever he does he is morally justified? Or, do we want, apropos of Brandt's comment, to say that it would be nice if Y could meet both, but in so far as he, as a matter of fact, cannot, then he morally ought to do c rather than p? If we take the first alternative, we are saying that morality is either, with respect to this matter, disinterested or impotent. But it does seem reasonable to assume that morality will not be disinterested in every conflict of obligations (and we can tell the story in any way necessary to meet that requirement), so we seem to be left with the distasteful conclusion that morality is impotent to advise, despite interest, on such difficult conflicts as confronts Y. But that is an untenable view of morality, as I think most of us will agree, for it destroys the very *raison d'etre* of morality, a guidelight to choice of action to maintain or better the human condition.

I must emphasize that I am *not* saying that only in conflict situations do we make moral judgments. Clearly the desirability, from the moral point of view, of doing certain things and refraining from doing others, is decided or decidable prior to the advent of conflicts, in practice, though, we just do not often so decide, which is to say that we do not have moral principles that suit every occasion. If I am right that "ought" does not translate "obligatory," that "must" (with some attached condition) does, and that moral judgments are generally speaking "ought" judgments, then they just do not state obligations. In some cases, they endorse obligations; in other cases they advise action choice without reference to obligations. Putting this point somewhat differently: insofar as a law exists that forbids murder I have, as a citizen under that law, an obligation not to commit murder and, as it happens, also a moral obligation. If no institution in which I am involved forbade murder, I would not have an obligation not to murder, but morally I still ought not to murder. It would not, however, be correct to say that in those circumstances I have a moral obligation not to commit murder. Similarly, as things now stand, we cannot without change of sense substitute a form of "to oblige" or "is obligatory" for ought in a sentence like "One ought not to lie." "One ought not to lie" certainly does not say the same thing as "One is obliged not to lie" or "One is under an obligation not to lie" or "One must not ever lie."

Of course, it seems natural to talk of acts as being "morally required" or "morally obligatory," and sometimes we say that something is a "moral duty." (We less frequently say that someone "morally must" do something.) The reason we use those expressions in that way is that we are aware of the idiomatic nature of such utterances and let the word "moral" function as a sort of indication of aberrational usage. If I say that doing something is "morally required" of you and it is not required of you by some institution, then I may be saying in an empathic way that your doing it will be consistent with or is essential to the preservation of the conditions I believe to be requisite for human well-being. Should you ask what penalty *you* will pay for not doing so, I will generally be silenced. I can try to convince you that it is in your interest to maintain those conditions, but you do not lose any game, go to jail, or pay a fine if you do not do it.

The idea that many people, and not just moral philosophers, may find disturbing in my account is that moral judgments and principles are not ever obligation-stating or creating. The cursory reader might be led to the conclusion that I have eliminated from moral concern a large number of traditional "moral obligations." That is not, however, the case. Take for example the parent's oft-cited moral obligation to care for his offspring by supplying sufficient food, clothing, and shelter. As matters currently stand the legal institution of country and state requires that parents provide those necessities. Morality generally but not always endorses that obligation in specific conflictual cases. But suppose the legislators of the state were tomorrow to rescind all parental obligation-creating laws. Would parents not still have a moral obligation to succor their offspring? I think the answer is yes, but not because a moral rule exists that creates that obligation. I think the answer is yes because the family is more than a biological unit, it is, in our society, an institution itself and it creates for its members familial responsibilities. However, suppose that by some social upheaval the family as a unit is abandoned by all members of society. Suppose in its stead all men and women are free to cohabitate when and where they please and do so, and all offspring of such unions are raised from birth in communal farms. (If you wish, suppose further that a billionaire has endowed a trust with sufficient funding to maintain the communal nurseries into the forseeable future.) If such an arrangement were to come about, it would be at least odd, indeed silly, for a biological parent in the society to believe that he or she had a moral obligation to provide for the care of his or her offspring. They have no obligation to provide anything for their children. No institutional rules and no laws say they should do so.

It may prove helpful to further elaborate on this point. We are commonly told[17] that a person ought to go to the aid of another person when the other is in danger. If I were to discover that a woman is being attacked on the street corner near my home, I ought to go to her aid. But do I then and thereby have an obligation to go to her aid? Ewing,[18] for example (but he is not unique in this), equates believing (on moral grounds) that one ought to do something with having a duty to do it. It sounds most odd, however, for me to say that I have an obligation to go to the woman's aid. Should I go to her assistance and drive off her attacker I will no doubt be praised in the public media. I will, and I think rightly, be hailed as a hero. A hero for doing what I had an obligation to do! That is what does not ring true. I am a hero precisely because I did *not* have an obligation to go to her aid, although going to her aid was the right thing to do.

My discussion of moral judgments and obligations might leave the impression that all moral judgments are concerned with situations of obligational conflict. Such a view would be patently false, but neither is it implied by my account. In a common use to which moral-"ought" judgments are put, the speaker is not addressing himself to a conflict of obligations, but instead is offering advice to someone (or himself) regarding a course of action. A rather dramatic example, one concerning euthanasia, would be when someone says to the distraught father of a comatose patient, "You ought to (or ought not to) remove his life support systems and let nature take its course." Of course, we might discover on filling in the facts of the circumstances that occasioned the utterance that the father in question did see himself in an institutional obligational conflict, but that need not be the case. We could by stipulation remove all institutional restraints and obligations while not removing the fact that a person feels a need to choose a course of action regarding a comatose human being.

"You ought to do *x*" often is uttered as a guide to action long before and not even in anticipation of a conflict of obligations. When a moral judgment (as above) is uttered, the speaker is saying (or doing) the following: (1) claiming that he believes that the addressee's doing *x* is of paramount importance because the features of *x* in some way are likely to contribute to maintaining conditions prerequisite for the well-being of anyone and (2) informing the addressee that he believes that a failure to do *x*, in the absence of an exculpatory excuse, will be a ground for blaming the addressee.

To reiterate a point I have been trying to make throughout: if I have an institutional obligation to do *x* and no conflict exists, then "I must do *x*" is true. Whether or not I morally ought to do *x*, whether *x* is a moral obligation, depends upon other considerations. What I argued is that we do not have moral obligations in the *absence* of institutional ones, simply because we cannot have obligations without institutions. But that does not imply that morality has nothing to say regarding our choices of action when institutions are not involved.

IV

A moral judgment when it is made seriously (and when it is not used in the "inverted comma" sense as a report of social norms) is always an expression of the speaker's belief that the course of action is to be regarded as paramount among whatever options the addressee might have, because it is consistent with the maintenance of those conditions the speaker also believes or are generally acknowledged to be necessary for anyone to lead a worthwhile life. A moral judgment made in the absence of institutional obligations does not state an obligation or a requirement. It is one thing to say that doing *a* is advised because it will have a salutary effect on the well-being of persons, and another to say that because it will have such an effect, it is required, obligatory.

There is a way that has been used to generate what appears to be a moral, with the logical force of an inescapable, requirement on the acts of persons. In brief, it is argued, for example by Alan Gewirth,[19] that there is a basic principle of morality, the principle that one always act in accord with the generic rights (defined as freedom and well-being) of all persons. That principle is said to emerge from the generic features of action. If an agent were to act in a way that would violate the generic rights of himself, it is maintained, he would not be acting rationally; he would be acting in a self-contradictory manner. Gewirth writes that "since it is necessarily true of the agent that he wants to achieve his purposes and since his having the generic rights is *logically* necessary to such achievement, the rational agent, being aware of this *logical* necessity, wants to have and act in accord with his generic rights."[20] Furthermore, violating anyone else's generic rights casts doubts on one's own possession of them; "if he violates or denies the *Principle of Generic Consistency* he contradicts himself."[21] Another way of putting Gewirth's point would be that to violate another agent's generic rights is to deny agency of that person, but one cannot both believe that the recipient of my actions is a person and that he is not a person hence to violate his generic rights is to contradict myself and to do so is to behave irrationally. What we appear to have then is a *logical* necessity for being moral that is based on the contingent fact that to be an active agent and hence a person, one must be free and enjoy a certain level of "well-being."

Suppose it is suggested, consistent with the account of persons presented in the first chapter, that freedom and well-being are not both generic features of action. Perhaps only freedom is and, in fact, only a modicum of freedom, within the bounds of some type of determinism. At the very least it would not be irrational to dispute the inclusion or exclusion of essential generic features. But more important the attempt to create a logical necessity for being moral, if it did convert moral judgments into assertions of requirements that one can only fail to meet on pain of irrationality, would in the end make a sham of choice and hence of the very freedom morality is meant to protect. If I must do x or I am irrational and I do not do x, then I certainly cannot be held blameworthy for not doing x, for I am irrational. But I must be held blameworthy for those of my irrational acts that violate the generic rights of others, or Gewirth's formulation of morality has no point. What he would seem to need is an independent criterion for settling the question of when I am and when I am not blameworthy for my irrational acts. But that would then be a morality.

Suppose we formulate Gewirth's view as follows:

> It is necessary that X not do *a* if *a* is a violation or a denial of the generic rights of any person (including X).

First, this is incomplete, because we lack a reference to the source of the requirement or rule that limits the alternative ways of acting by excluding *a*. In other words, a clause of the sort "in order to . . ." or "because of . . ." is needed. Gewirth would probably have us append the clause "in order to avoid self-contradiction" and hence locate the source of the requirement in "neutral" logic instead of in some normative principle.

Returning to the above formulation and assuming the addition of the appended clause, we are still left with a puzzle as to how we are to understand the necessity claim. That puzzle may be put, in the currently popular form, by asking whether the nature of the necessity here involved is *de dicto* or *de re*? It seems to me that because the necessity is clearly laid on the truth of a proposition that the necessity is *de dicto*. We may read the formulation as saying "The proposition 'if X does *a* and *a* is a violation or a denial of the generic rights of any person, then X contradicts himself' is necessarily true." It is regarding the truth of a proposition that necessity is claimed, and not that X refrain from doing *a*. So much and no more can be gained from an appeal to "neutral" logic. Saying that a proposition is necessarily true is to say that there can be no possible world in which its contradictory is true. That does not state the desired requirement of action. Its contradictory is, "It is not the case that the proposition 'If X does *a* and *a* is a violation or a denial of the generic rights of any person, then X contradicts himself' is necessarily true." If we suppose a possible world in which that is true, we are supposing a world in which agency is believed to have essential elements that do not include the aiming, as Aristotle would have said, "at some good," for it is from that element of agency that Gewirth draws the notion that well-being and freedom are essential to the concept of agency. Suppose in such a world that the question arises for X, "Should I do *a*?" Suppose further that not doing *a* is not required by the rules of some institution in which X is a participant. I take it that nothing specifically about *a* will, in the possible world as described, render the proposition "It is necessary that X not do *a*" true. The "must" so generated is totally dependent on the way the concept of agency is explicated. (Gewirth, we should say, has unnecessarily cluttered the concept.) An analogy to the ontological "proof" of the existence of God should also be evident. The only retort that would seem mountable is that in this possible world there simply is no agency. But all that has been shown is that the *de dicto* necessity of a moral requirement of action is a product of semantic analysis and the law of contradiction (logic). Gewirth's necessity, his moral-"must" is only apparently one of acting. It is actually the necessity of a proposition being true, given that he has properly analyzed the concept of agency. It does not express a *requirement* of action.

In games, as we have seen, we can obtain a requirement of action. Suppose we render the chess rule "The King *must* get out of check" as "It is necessary (in chess) that the King get out of check." The second statement says that in chess, if the game is to continue, the King cannot be left in check. What is said to be necessary is not the truth of a proposition, it is clearly the doing of some act, moving the King. It is of further interest, in terms of iterated modalities, that the proper account should be that it is necessary, if it is possible, that the King be moved out of check. If it is not possible, the King is in checkmate. If the King has only one possible move to escape check, then the King is required by the rules of the game to make that move; it is necessary that the King make that move. That necessity is the necessity of acting within the institutional parameters of possibility, it is not the necessity of a proposition's being true. The use of logical rules to generate a sentence like the second statement, however, fails to produce a result similar to the above.

The logical necessity generated by the law of contradiction is concerned with propositions, not with acting. The law of contradiction is about the conditions for propositions being undeniably true or false. To say that a proposition is necessary, in this sense, is only to say that it is necessarily true, not that it is necessary that someone do something. When we use the institutional "must" in regard to an act we are not, or not just, maintaining that a proposition with a certain content must be true. We are maintaining that a certain act, taking a certain description, is the one that someone is *required* to perform and that requirement is dependent on there being a specific rule or rules in the institution. We should conclude that the attempt to generate a moral requirement of action cannot be solely dependent on the laws of logic (self-contradiction being the favorite). But it cannot either rest on the existence of a moral institution with rules analogous to chess rules, to provide the desired sense of requirement of action, because there is no such moral institution.

No class of obligations is the moral one; we do not have on the one hand institutional obligations and on the other, moral obligations. Saying that someone has a moral obligation to do something is to characterize his institutional obligation to do that something as paramount (for moral reasons) in a conflict situation. We do not have obligations and moral obligations as Farmer Jones has cows and pigs. We have institutional obligations, some of which are moral in certain circumstances. There are no moral rules of a constitutive type. That is the reason we cannot say that there is "the moral institution." In fact, if the moral institution did exist, its rules would no doubt at times create obligations that would conflict with those incurred from participation in some other institution. The resulting conflict could only be resolved by appeal to a paramountcy principle that could not be derived internally from either of the institutions party to the dispute.

V

I have argued that changes in moral principles are dependent on a general acceptance of some moral judgments by a community over a period of time. The implication might be drawn that I am maintaining here, contrary to what was suggested in chapter 2, that the community's moral principles are addressed only to the constituent membership of that community. Although moral principles develop within a community, they are, unless that morality is first-order truncated, addressed to the membership of the class of persons, not solely to community members. Moral principles do not carry unwritten or unspoken addressee limitations. The subject of the moral principle "You ought not to commit murder" refers not to that collectivity designated by "members of the English-speaking community of the United States of America and the United Kingdom." It refers to all members of the class of persons regardless of their communal associations, language, and so on.

That moral judgments are made within a communal framework, and that the privileged status of moral principles is a function of communal history, places no restrictions on the class of persons to whom such principles are directed. Regardless whether someone accepts certain moral principles, and hence identifies himself with the community in which they are principles, there is a reason, what I shall in chapter 8 call "the moral reason," for him to act consistently with those principles when they apply to his circumstances. One way of interpreting the sense of universality, which so often in the literature is cited as a distinguishing feature of moral judgments and principles, is thereby provided.

VI

The justification of moral-"ought" judgments is an indicator of the relative status of the moral beliefs of a speaker and in a community. If a speaker is asked to justify his expression of the judgment that (1) "X ought not to do a," he might respond by uttering a sentence of the form (2) "X ought not to do b." When asked for a reason why (2) should be the case, he might again offer an "ought" or "ought not" judgment, but if he does, he will still be vulnerable to another "Why?" question. The chain of reasons cannot end with a sentence containing an "ought" or "ought not," if these words are used in a discriminatory way. Discriminations are always subject to further justification. A justifier's chain can terminate only either in a sentence of the form, "b is paramount to c" or in one of the form "That would be (moral term)." It can also terminate in a sentence that contains "ought" if "ought" is not functioning as a discriminator in that sentence. For example, "One ought not to commit murder." If a "why?" question were asked of any of those responses the justifier can only assume that either the questioner is ignorant of the language or that he is questioning the applicability of the moral concept, for example, "murder," to the case in question.

"Why would that be murder?" is quite a different question from "Why ought I to refrain from pulling the plug of the support system of a comatose human being for whom there is virtually no hope of recovery?"

Moral principles, including those stated in "ought" sentence forms, do serve as final answers, "bedrock" responses, to questions of justification. Moral-"ought" judgments cannot play such a role. In fact, most moral-"ought" judgments cannot be nonanalogically related to moral principles in a justificatory process. That should come as no surprise, for if a direct (say implication) relationship always could be drawn from moral principles to appropriate moral-"ought" judgments, the discriminatory feature of those judgments would be a facade. If, as I have argued, "ought" sometimes does have a discriminatory (judgmental) moral use, then a major justificatory avenue open to the maker of such judgments is an analogical appeal to a principle, for example, euthanasia is murder. The success or failure of such an appeal, or of the attempt to show directly that euthanasia is incompatible with the maintenance of the conditions necessary for persons to live the good life, when broadcast generally across the membership of the community is an indicator of whether or not the moral-"ought" judgment ("Persons ought not to pull the plug of the support system of a comatose human being for whom there is virtually no hope of recovery" or "Euthanasia is wrong") will eventually harden into a moral principle itself. If it were to "harden," a chain of justificatory reasons in the future might then be successfully terminated with "That would be euthanasia!" This process I take to be the moral corollary, or exemplification, of the process suggested by Wittgenstein's "river metaphor" in *On Certainty*.[22]

7

"He wos wery good to me, he wos!": Euergetical Concepts

Thou art not quite in outer darkness.
There is something like a distant ray of light
in thy muttered reason for this:
"He wos wery good to me, he wos!"

Charles Dickens
Bleak House, Chapter XI

I

Those familiar with Charles Dickens' masterpiece, *Bleak House*, will recognize my title as a poignant utterance of little, pathetic Jo, the street sweeper. I shall not be offering a critical analysis of *Bleak House* or of the character of poor Jo (not that that would not be an edifying endeavor for a moral philosopher). I borrow Jo's words because they epitomize a certain kind of evaluation of human behavior. I want to talk about goodness, about what it is to be a good person. In this chapter I hope to expose basic intuitions about interpersonal behavior and about human excellence of character. I shall argue that doing what morality demands, fulfilling one's moral obligations, is not sufficient to insure that one is a good person, is not a mark in and of itself of excellence of character. Someone may both be moral and not a good person and hence liable to blame (though not moral blame) for his behavior, paradoxical as that may sound.

MORALITY's primary function, I have argued, is to constrain and encourage certain kinds of acts. MORALITY does not provide goals for living nor is being moral a goal to be achieved by living.

115

MORALITY, except in certain extreme cases (paid executioner for an organized crime syndicate), has, for example, little to say about vocational choice.[1] Briefly, insofar as a person meets his moral obligations and refrains from acting in ways forbidden by moral principle (stealing, murdering, or lying), he is moral.[2]

Richard Taylor, writing under the *nom de plume* "Diodorus Cronus," published a fable, "The Governance of the Kingdom of Darkness,"[3] that crystallizes the problem with which I am concerned in this chapter. Taylor's story is that the office of Prince of Darkness has been vacated owing to a sudden act of God's grace: the pardoning of Lucifer. A new administrator of Hell must be selected, and four candidates are nominated. Suffice it to say that three of them are despicable types of one description or another; the fourth is a character named "Deprov," who on first inspection has no apparent credentials for the office. He has led, we are told, a law-abiding and blameless life. He has a dreadful fear of the law and "felt a deep shame at the mere thought of his integrity being challenged in any way." When alive, Deprov was a cruel man, even though he met his moral and legal obligations. He is a dedicated Kantian truth-teller. One day, for instance, upon finding a disconsolate girl in the park and discovering one side of her face to be horribly discolored and disfigured, Deprov took several polaroid pictures of her and with a smile of satisfaction presented them to her. "He had, he later said, only taken pictures, and had not tried to make anything seem different from what it really was, thus displaying a respect for truth."[4] When asked why he seemed to enjoy tormenting the lonely, the sick, and the brokenhearted, Deprov "protested that he could never enjoy anything of the sort. . . . on the contrary, he had often foregone genuine pleasure and enjoyments in pressing his crusade for truth, law, and morality."[5] When informed of the 'honor' he could not understand why he had been nominated to sit on the Throne of Hell. Our intuitions are not, however, offended if he is chosen to succeed Lucifer in the "Unholy Chair." Granted that our intuitions beckon in that direction, it seems plausible for us to say of someone, without fear of contradiction, that he behaves in a morally correct way, that is, he does what he morally ought to do, and that his doing so or doing it just so contributes to his being or doing evil. Simply, what we seem to be endorsing is the view that a person can be doing both evil and right when, for example, fulfilling a moral obligation. (That is not to be confused with the view that a person may be good or be doing good, but not being moral at all, in fact being immoral.[6])

Virtue or goodness of character, I shall argue, has less to do with meeting obligations or requirements or with acting on moral principle than it does with the manner in which acts are performed and their result in terms of happiness promoted, it has to do with whether persons exhibit in their actions any of a number of specific qualities or attitudes gathered under the umbrella of the term "kindness." The judgment that what someone did was good and the judgment that what he did was moral are quite different, if related, kinds of judgments. Judgments about the morality of an act, as earlier discussed,[7] are a variety of paramountcy decisions, that is, those based on beliefs about the conditions necessary for, and the preservation of, that minimal human environment in which anyone can achieve the good life. On the other hand, the statement "X is a good person" is I want to argue here, a commendation of X more for the *way* he does the various things he does (usually when other people are involved) rather than what he does, and only *implies* that he generally does what morality endorses. I want to show this, in part, by showing that the roots of the concepts used when we make these judgments are distinct from those of moral concepts.

The moral judgment that Jones ought to do x puts forth the claim that doing x is more important from the moral point of view than doing any of the other things that Jones might do at the time. But what does Jones have to do to satisfy the moral judgment that he ought to do x? He merely has to do x. How should he do x? The moral judgment does not usually dictate the manner of his doing x, even if it dictates his intention, for example, that Jones must have as his sole or primary motive for doing x that doing x is right. Suppose that x is "Pay your $5 debt to Smith." Morality is satisfied when the debt is paid. There are, however, many ways in which the payment can be made and morality does not appear to rule all but one of them out of order; for example, morality does not dictate to Jones that when he pays his debt to Smith, he should do so with a certain degree of gratefulness.

A complete divorce of questions of goodness from those of morality is not, I think, possible; morality, as I have characterized it, and virtue, or what Castañeda quite rightly calls "the euergetical dimension," are the dual aspects of what I have called MORALITY. (I am most impressed with Castañeda's account of the euergetic dimension as "the arm of morality that attempts to internalize in everybody a direct concern for others."[8]) Suppose that Jo, who believes that "Nemo" is a good person, were to learn that "Nemo" has children whom he often beats and a wife whom he brutalizes and that he never keeps his promises to his business associates. Jo would likely then feel constrained to vitiate his judgment of Nemo's character. He might, of course, still say that Nemo was good to him, but he would not likely say that Nemo was (in some unqualified way) a good man. Ross says of actions, "no action will have the utmost *moral* excellence which an action in the circumstances can have, unless it is also the right action."[9] (My italics indicate that "moral" is being used here in the larger sense.) No person can be excellent of character (good) unless he does what he morally ought to do. Nonetheless, though we should, with Ross, regard doing the right thing (the morally endorsed thing) as the limiting case on goodness, we still may look to independent criteria for judgments of human goodness. Putting the point in another way, euergetical concepts are not moral concepts, though their scope over actions is limited by our understanding of what constitutes morally right action.

II

Though I do not think it to be of much consequence, it is hard to ignore that the words "good" and "moral" in their most common uses play quite different roles. They are, in revealing ways, not interchangeable. Consider especially adverbial use. Compare "He acted morally in the time of crisis," with "He acted goodly in the time of crisis." The latter sentence may not even sound like proper English. However, one neither obscure nor rare usage of "goodly" exists that the *Oxford English Dictionary* defines with the terms "favourably," "graciously," "kindly," "courteously," and "in a proper or becoming manner." Even so, if we wanted to substitute a sentence using some form of "good" for a sentence using "morally" we have to convert the sentence to read, "He acted in the time of crisis in a way that was a good way to act." "Good" is primarily an adjective; all of its other forms pale to near obscurity. "Moral" has a very active adverbial use as well as an adjectival one. However, the point I want to draw, though surely numerous other lessons are to be learned, is that "moral" does not change its sense from adjective to adverb ("It was a moral act," "He acted morally.") If "good" were a synonym for "moral" in adjectival use, one might reasonably expect it to function similarly in adverbial usage, but clearly the adverbial "good" says something quite different from the adverbial "moral." It says that the actor behaved graciously or courteously or kindly or befittingly. It does not say that he did what he morally ought to do.

"Good" and "moral" obviously do not exclude each other; being moral contributes to being good, to having a good character, to being virtuous. One can, however, usually and sensibly ask of a person: (1) whether or not he is moral or behaved morally, and (2) whether or not he is a good person or if what he did was good or a good thing to do. Evidence supporting a positive or negative response to either question does not necessarily support an answer to the other question.

III

As previously suggested, I shall treat "kindness" as a sort of umbrella euergetical concept; that is, my proposal is that goodness, when we are talking about persons, is kindness. A person is good if his acts toward others (and himself) are properly describable both as morally right and as kind.

Obviously there are many ways to be kind and many words can be used to describe acts of kindness. For examples, think of "considerate," "forgiving," "merciful," "loving," "gentle," "benevolent," and "charitable." I use the term "kind" to cover them all. For my purposes in this chapter, I do not use it as the name of our concept of one virtue among others.

The *Oxford English Dictionary* (*OED*) cites as one of its definitions of "kind:"

> 5. (of person) Naturally well-disposed; having a gentle, sympathetic, or benevolent nature; ready to assist, or show consideration for others; generous, liberal, courteous. . . .

I have chosen "kind" rather than, for example, "loving" as the umbrella concept mainly because it is open to fewer varied and indeed contrary interpretations than its rivals. "Love" has frequently been characterized as having at least two totally different senses, *agape* and *eros,* and more recently George Nakhnikian has distilled three different senses, "unconditional love," "transactional love" and "undemanding love."[10] Although we may argue over what way of doing something is really the kind way, for example, telling an employee he is fired, we all share essentially the same notion of what kindness is. That cannot be said of love. The other reason for using kindness as the umbrella-concept is that it has a somewhat broader scope than the other possible competitors: sympathy, benevolence, charity, mercy, and so on. It is suited more naturally to the umbrella function, and it does not, even in its narrow interpretation, exclude the other traditional virtues from the description of the acts in question.

There are intriguing things to be learned about "kindness" from the links that have been drawn between its various usages. One such link bears directly on the present discussion. The *OED* lists the first set of definitions of the word "kind" (1–3) under the heading "I. Natural, native." In regard to persons the usage, now obsolete, is cited (3c) "Having a specified character by nature or a specified status by birth." The second set of definitions (4–9) is grouped under the general heading "Of good birth, kind, nature or disposition." The fourth definition is said to be the link between the first and second sets. It is "4. a. Well-born, well-bred, of generous or gentle birth, gentle (obs.) b. Of a good kind; hence, good of its kind. . . ." The link is forged in the notion of noble lineage, of being well-bred. The Latin is *"generousus."* The root is *"genus,"* which returns us to "kind," not the "kind" of "kindness" but of type or class. "Kindness" was conceived, in the case of persons, as the way the best of the human kind behaved and the best of the human kind were the well-bred and gentle folk.

The not so disguised apparition of Aristotelean *areté* emerges in the etymology. The kind person is the best of his kind. The etymological evidence is, however, only a convenient hook on which to hang my contention that goodness can be identified with kindness (taken in the "umbrella" sense).

IV

Often in specific cases, that an act is/was kind is disputable. Sometimes it is kind to tell someone the truth, so that he will no longer delude himself with visions of grandeur; sometimes it is kind not to tell him the truth so that he may enjoy a few happy moments. The variations may be virtually endless and thereby retard any attempt to locate a mark of "kindness." But even if an act is dissimilar from any others, we would surely be able to modify its description with "kind" or "unkind," if we had or could obtain certain information. Understanding the concept of kindness is not dependent on our knowing the multitudinous ways persons may be kind.

When we are interested in determining whether or not someone has been kind when, for example, he did a, we are usually drawn to question what he intended. Clearly, we believe that no one can be kind unintentionally. But kindness must involve more than motives, or someone could be kind only by intending to be kind, even when his actions have unhappy results. Unperceptive, well-intentioned do-gooders abound, but the world seems no better a place because of their motives than if they had had no motives or had evil intents. No matter what my intentions, if I am not cognizant of the various aspects of the situation in which I act, I may perform the most unkind of deeds. We cannot avoid the fact that acts are viewed as kind because of the difference their being done one way and not another makes to the persons for whom they are performed. On the other hand, it seems counter-intuitive to say that I may be kind only insofar as my acts have certain consequences despite my intentions. How do we resolve the difficulty? Consider the following:

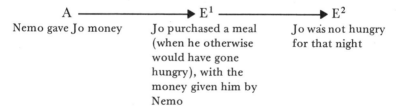

A   → E^1 → E^2

Nemo gave Jo money	Jo purchased a meal (when he otherwise would have gone hungry), with the money given him by Nemo	Jo was not hungry for that night

As a first approximation, we might say that an act is kind if its effects include an event that under some description makes true a sentence that says that its having occurred made life easier for the person to whom, for whom, with whom, or about whom the act was performed. Nemo's act, on this account, is a kind act if it has an effect of the sort E^2. But this will not do. A judge, for example, can be kind to someone even when condemning him to death. One of the determinants of a kind act cannot simply be, if it is at all, that the outcome event makes life easier. What we should say is that the manner in which an act is done makes its being done less rather than more difficult, more rather than less bearable, for the person directly affected. But, as suggested above, this is insufficient.

Traditional deontologists will offer a further complication. Suppose that Nemo's sole intention in (his reason for) giving Jo money was to get rid of him, to silence a begging nuisance. Would that information not also materially alter the description of the act as kind?

$$R^1 \dashrightarrow A \longrightarrow E^1 \longrightarrow E^2$$

Nemo's desire to
get rid of Jo

There is clearly a difficulty in representing R^1 on a simple causal path to A because R^1 is neither an act nor an event. I acknowledge the problem, but for the sake of simplicity I shall sidestep the issue and adopt the convention of treating the reasons one has for doing something as causes. Let us grant that the *primary* reason for Nemo's giving Jo money is R^1. R^1 need not be, however, the only reason that Nemo gives Jo money. Undoubtedly, if Nemo's sole reason for giving Jo money was to get rid of him, we would be reluctant to characterize Nemo's act as kind. Let us suppose then that Nemo has at least one other reason for giving Jo money (rather than, for example, throwing a rock at him), though it may be only an ancillary reason to his wanting to be rid of Jo. We have a new diagram:

$$[R^1 \ \& \ R^2] \dashrightarrow B \longrightarrow E^1 \longrightarrow E^2$$

Nemo's desire to do what he
does to Jo in a way that makes
its being done less rather than
more difficult, more rather than
less bearable for Jo, given the circumstances

I call the act "B" rather than, as before, "A," because they are quite different acts. First of all, B has a different causal ancestry and in the second place (granted that R^2 is *a* cause of B) it will be true of B but not necessarily true of A that Nemo did *not intentionally* mock Jo's condition when giving him the money, or intentionally throw the money on the ground in order to watch Jo grovel for it or hand it to him while (intentionally) uttering a sentence like "Take this you little beggar and get out of here" or. . . . To put this in another way, at least one true description (that is not simply about causal ancestry) of B will be substantially different from all of the descriptions true of A in that it will contain an expression like "with an intentional pat on the back" or "with an intended sympathetic nod."

Two further qualifications are necessary to complete this sketch of what distinguishes a kind of act from one that, though in many outward respects similar, is not kind (if not unkind). An act cannot be kind if the agent has, as yet another reason for performing the act, the desire to heighten the disappointment of the recipient when the agent refuses to do it, or does not do it in a kindly fashion, in the future. Surely if we discover that one of Nemo's reasons for giving Jo money in a kindly way today is to dash his expectations tomorrow, or to win his confidence in order to use him in the perpetration of some crime, we will have to modify our original description of his act. There is nothing odd about that, however. We often find that the present forces us to modify our descriptions of the past; that is just because the accordion effect of events, that is, the subsumption of effects into event-descriptions, is a basic convention of our use of language. Furthermore, recognition of this point is a clear indication that we generally believe that kind acts are not to be instrumental or means to some other end, whether kind or not. Another way of putting this might be to say that we are at least reluctant to call an act a kind one if the agent has a reason for being kind other than what might be called the basic euergetical reason: a recognition that it is important to human commerce that we treat each other with compassion, etc. This noninstrumental requirement seems to me to capture certain Kantian intuitions.

The second qualification is more an elaboration than a qualification. We are creatures of habit and training. We do many of the things we do as "second nature." We replicate not only the acts we perform, but the manner of their performance. Hence being kind can become habitual. But questions have been raised as to whether a replicated kind act is really a kind act. If Nemo were in the habit of being kind, so that at the time he gave Jo money it is not true that one of his active reasons for doing so was of the R^2 sort, that his only active reason was to rid himself of Jo's company, is the act properly described as a kind one? In framing the question, of course, I have made use of a distinction not earlier involved in the analysis: I have put the question in terms of active reasons, implying that something called "passive" reasons might exist. That would be, I think, rather misleading. I use "active" here in a less mysterious way, only to pick out the reasons that would be given by an agent if asked why he was doing what he was doing in the way he was doing it. To know that an agent is habitually kind is, however, to know that a causal path can be constructed to account for the agent's coming to have such a habit; the causal path will terminate in an act or series of acts whose description(s) makes true a sentence that says that one of the reasons the agent had for behaving in the manner he did was something like R^2. In other words, if it is true of someone that he habitually acts in a certain manner, then it will be true of him that at some time he intentionally acted in that manner. Aristotle, it will be remembered, tells us that "goodness . . . is the child of habit, from which it has got its very name, ethics being derived from *ethos*, 'habit' . . . ."[11] One may be naturally disposed to be kind and yet in a specific case not be kind; but when one is in the habit of being kind, one can be counted on to behave accordingly. Habit is the offspring of intention, even if in the case of a particular habitual act one cannot identify the reason (desire and belief) that was the cause of its being performed.

Clearly, the habitually kind person will find it easier to be kind than the person who has not been in the habit. The latter may well have to wrestle with his desires and his beliefs about his interests before acting in a kindly fashion and, on my account, that is surely not a fault. But it is also no fault of the habitually kind that they do not have to struggle to the formation of the "kind intention." The problem with habitual kindness is not that it militates against goodness. Not at all! The problem is to provide an acceptable account of how a habit with so broad a focus can be established at all. Obviously, one forms the habit of smoking a pipe after dinner by smoking a pipe after dinner. There are, however, innumerable ways of being kind, and it is sometimes difficult to say in any particular instance what constitutes being kind. Sometimes just to speak to the Jos of this world can be a great act of kindness. On some occasions, simply to acknowledge another's presence can be a kind act; sometimes it will be the greatest kindness not to do so. It probably is not true that every act performed to, for, or with another person can be a kind act. Yet most such acts can be kind: even the executioner can do his task in a considerate, even compassionate way. Certain acts, of course, can never be tempered with kindness, e.g., the willful torture of a child. (Analogously, Aristotle pointed out that certain acts are never susceptible to the mean, for example, murder and adultery.) Their very nature as base and immoral excludes them from being done in a kindly fashion. But that is because they transgress the limiting case; they are immoral. I acknowledge that giving a proper account of the formation of the habit of kindness is a difficult task, but I cannot see any reason that it cannot be done. Thankfully, however, I leave the task for another occasion.

In summary: an act is kind not simply because of its effects nor simply because of its causes. We recognize an act to be kind if when performed it does not exaggerate the difficulty (though it might prove to have most unwanted consequences for its recipient), that is, that it does not make its being done more unbearable than it has to be for the recipient. We recognize an act as kind when we are confident that it was done in such a manner because the agent had as a reason (a desire coupled with a belief) for his act that he did not want to make its being done more unbearable (etc.) for the recipient,[12] or because he is in the habit of so tempering his actions. My account of what constitutes an act of kindness is a synthesis of consequentialist and intentionalist theses; it avoids the counterintuitive results of holding either thesis exclusively.

Having said what a kind act is, we may say that a kind person is an agent who usually acts in a kindly manner. In accord with the etymological data, it seems proper to say that such a person is the best of "human kind" and that, of course, is another way of saying that he is a good person. Being *good to* people is to be *a good* person. The evaluation of persons has its locus in the determination of purely factual matters.

IV

I have argued[13] that our moral concepts spring from particular beliefs roughly characterizable as being about the need and the way to preserve a certain human environment; that is to say, they are beliefs about the importance of maintaining a community in which certain things are done and other things are not done. Our moral concepts (such as murder, stealing, and lying) facilitate the incorporation of those beliefs in our descriptions of events. The problem here is to identify the source of the euergetical concepts, such as kind, benevolent, and charitable.

Clearly, a value element is inherent in our moral and euergetical concepts; that is, we have the moral and euergetical vocabularies we do because of the specific concepts framed by the community of language-users. In fact, by "concept" I intend what some sociobiologists call "secondary values."[14] I suggest that we represent these secondary or invented values as a collection of a subset of the community's beliefs and associated behavior patterns. In my account, its moral concepts are a product of a community's beliefs about the environment necessary for any member to live the "good life" or a "life of worth." Our moral vocabulary provides a shorthand way of referring to certain events or acts (whether actual or contemplated) that otherwise could be picked out by lengthier descriptions characterizing those events as desirable or undesirable in light of the general preservational concern. "That is murder," for example, is more than a description of an event; it expresses displeasure about the event's occurrence and in *post-eventum* use usually blames the perpetrator. This multifaceted or economical nature of moral terms reflects their lineage, of our having created them to satisfy a number of related needs. Euergetical terms are economical mongrels of a different lineage; they owe their existence in the language to a different, if associated, kind of recognized need.[15]

Pinpointing the need that is the progenitor of the euergetical concepts is facilitated by a consideration of the concept of "human nature" developed by the Scottish philosopher Dugald Stewart.[16] Stewart, in a fashion characteristic of his age, distinguishes five "active principles" in the human constitution, divided into two classes: instinctive or implanted propensities and governing principles of actions. In the latter group he places self-love and "the moral faculty," while in the former he locates (1) appetites, (2) desires, and (3) affections. Our interest in euergetics, if Stewart is right, should not be in understanding self-love or the moral faculty but in instinctive desires and appetites.

In particular, Stewart maintains, not unlike Montesquieu, that among our basic desires is the desire of society; we are all led by a "natural and instinctive desire to associate with our species."[17] Stewart argues, as opposed to Hobbes, that the history of mankind reveals that human beings have always been found in a social state; even in those societies in which the advantages (from a purely self-interested point of view) of social union would seem to be small, the desire for association is strong. He further argues that as societies become more complex, social relationships become more, rather than less, important to each individual. Stewart, with so many others, is quick to point out that the family is the basic unit in which this desire is cemented and nurtured, and that the family is itself a natural union necessary for the continuity of the species. "The social union does not take its rise from views of self-interest, . . . it forms a necessary part of the condition of man from the constitution of his nature."[18]

Stewart's (and Montesquieu's) observations, confirmed or reaffirmed recently by a legion of sociobiologists,[19] were that human beings naturally feel a delight in the society of their fellows that cannot be explained solely by appeal to principles of rational self-interest.[20] Stewart and the sociobiologist would seem to part company only in that he was not fully prepared to argue that satisfaction of the desire for society is essential to well-being or that frustration is tantamount to a breakdown in the integrated system that motivates the cooperative behavior essential for adaptation to the physical and technological environment.[21] That is not to say that Stewart would not have agreed with the sociobiologists, only that he had not sufficient background in the field (indeed, no such area of study existed at his time) to allow him to make such a claim.

In regard to human natural affections, Stewart makes another and, I think, telling point, one that is neutral regarding sociobiological theory. He argues that we all have certain benevolent affections, non-self-interested agreeable feelings toward our kin and those we consider our friends, and a desire for their happiness;

these affections are quite natural in origin. He further argues that we have similar affections towards the unfortunate. In defense of this conjecture he endorses a point made by Butler in the second sermon on *Compassion*: Our constitution and that of the world are such that the sources of our suffering are more in the hands of other persons than those of our pleasure. Quite simply, each of us has a greater power, whether under the influence of anger, reason, or duty, to make life miserable for our fellow human beings than we have to make happy those with whom we associate. By a similar token, we have it more within our province to relieve or mitigate the suffering of other's than to increase their enjoyment. A recognition of this fact, coupled with the aforementioned natural desires for society, amount to a recognized need to encourage kindness.

That the presence of the natural affection for the suffering cannot be subsumed into a general self-interest account of human nature is seen if we, with Stewart, distinguish three ingredients in our reaction to a distressed person. First we experience, Stewart tells us, a painful emotion. (It is of no consequence to my account to provide an explanation of why we feel pained at the sight of another's distress.) Second, we have a selfish desire to rid ourselves of the cause of our discomfort. Third, we are inclined to, if possible, relieve the other's distress from a disinterested concern about his welfare. If all we naturally had when confronted with the suffering of others were the first and second ingredients of the reaction, then, as Stewart argues, our actions invariably would be to run away from the sight. Kindness, compassion, pity, and love cannot be explained solely as the progeny of rational self-interest, no matter how enlightened.

Stewart's analysis and, as I understand it, the upshot of many sociobiological theories may be fairly summarized by saying that certain primary motives (or "values"[22]) essential for the preservation and the flourishing of the species and the individual are implanted in human nature and are hence a product of evolution. These primary values provide the basis on which "second-level values" (includes moral and euergetical concepts) are developed within a community. Given the experience of the community and its rational abilities, a specific set of "second-level values" are created to function as guidelines for act-decision making. The invention of a related vocabulary is, as earlier discussed, a necessary aspect of the formation of such mixed-mode concepts, facilitating incorporation of those concepts into descriptions of events and actions.

I have then, in agreement with Stewart and many sociobiologists, located in human nature a certain set of primary social needs or motives that give rise within the community to the invention of euergetical concepts; these concepts embody our beliefs about the need to be kind, compassionate, benevolent, charitable, the need to act in a certain manner. These may be contrasted with our beliefs about the need to maintain a certain econo-environmental support system, our moral beliefs, but, as I have suggested, these are not totally distinct concerns. They are two aspects of our MORALITY. The evaluative "X is a moral person" is associated with beliefs and concepts of the first sort while "X is a good person" primarily depends for its sense upon beliefs and concepts of the euergetical sort.

V

It should not be concluded that, by my account, it is better to be a good person than a moral one, or that being kind is better than doing right. Instead, the position I am defending is that moral concepts and euergetical concepts in judgments of human behavior are invoked for different reasons. Somewhat analogously, we can describe a building in terms of its creation of livable space or in terms of its thematic unity within a neighborhood. Different things are relevant to these different judgments and one does not exclude the other. But that analogy does not quite hold, for being moral is the limiting case on being good; one cannot be good and not be moral. Human excellence of character is the achievement of a synergistic unity of morality and kindness, of doing right and of being kind. This point is not missed by Ross, who in his famous book *The Right and The Good* had all but driven a wedge between the two notions. In his later work, *Foundations of Ethics*, he writes:

> No action will have the utmost . . . excellence which an action in the circumstances can have, unless it is also the right action. But . . . a right act need not be a completely or even a partially good act. . . . The doing of the right action will be the best action only if it is done from the best motive of which the circumstances could give rise. . . .[23]

However, Ross still maintains that, "an act may have a high degree of . . . goodness and yet be entirely different from the right act."[24] In my account an act might be viewed as kind without being morally right; but it could not be good, and someone's doing it could not contribute to his being a good person.

It may be a fact of life that we have more occasions to be kind than to be moral. That does not mean that it is harder to be kind than moral or that it is more important to be kind than moral. Moral decisions are among the hardest, if not the hardest, people ever have to make. That people in general are moral at the crucial times is essential to the preservation of the environment necessary for the possibility of the good life for any of us. Nothing is seemingly more important in those instances; being kind may not seem to be very relevant to the situation. The Ik of Northern Uganda, anthropologist Colin Turnbull has argued, have shown us that when environmental conditions are so altered as to threaten the survival of a community, kindness is a luxury.[25] Certainly the Ik ceased to be kind to each other almost from the advent of their troubles. But early in their plight, most of the Ik seem to have ceased to think of their acts as constrained by moral principles. Nothing was more important than individual survival, even if that could only be, at best, bare subsistence without hope. Their fate as a viable community was thereupon sealed. The "end of goodness," an expression for which Turnbull has a fondness, precedes the end of morality in their tribal history, but it is a close race. The Ik have shown us, I think, that both goodness and morality are luxuries, if all that is desired is short-term individual animal survival. They have not shown that they are luxuries to human survival, providing in fact, evidence of the opposite. Human beings can exist without morality and in a world without goodness, but the lives they then lead are neither of worth nor very long.

A further complication: often actions have multiple effects, so that being kind to one person may do an unkindness to another or to a group of people. Rawls has written that "benevolence is at sea as long as its many loves are in opposition in the persons of its many objects."[26] How multiple effects, with different euergetical "ratings," are to be calculated into a determination of whether an act was kind is a difficult problem. It is one that I do not believe a philosopher can solve alone, and I am suspicious of algorithms for such matters. Perhaps at this point we need to turn to the novelist, the dramatist, or the film director for exemplars. One suggestion does seem intuitively to recommend itself—that there are two limiting cases on goodness. One, and the absolute limiting case, is morality. An act cannot be good if it is morally wrong. The second, and possibly weaker limit, is that an act cannot be good, regardless of whether it is performed in a kindly fashion to the person that is its primary object, if an effect of its being done is the making of life more difficult or more unbearable for some third party. To attest to this limitation principle is to reject Polemarchus' dictum that the good (just) person benefits his friends and harms his enemies. It affirms the Socratic conviction, "It is never right to harm anyone."[27]

8

Faint Hearts
and Fair Ladies

I

In Chapter 3 the question "Why should I be MORAL?" was discussed in relation to Hobbes' and Montesquieu's accounts of the object of law and morality. The suggestion was that MORALITY provides a way of reformulating the concept of prudence so that individuals in civil association might be described as having prudential reasons for being MORAL. It was, however, also suggested in that chapter that such a way of answering the question was inadequate, that MORALITY incorporates more assumptions about human nature than that persons are motived primarily by self-interest. In Chapter 7 I have characterized that aspect of MORALITY as euergetics. The question "Why should I be MORAL?" may now be seen as two questions: "Why should I fulfill my moral obligations, and not do those things that are morally wrong?" and "Why should I be kind to other persons?" Still, these questions may be taken in two quite different ways: as a request for the justification of a MORALITY given the human condition, a challenge of rational and scientific criticism to our inventions; and second, as it is usually interpreted, a challenge to give a rational person acceptable reasons to do what MORALITY endorses, despite personal inclinations to do otherwise. With regard to the first interpretation, I hope that most of the chapters of this book provide the outline of how such a justification should proceed. This task, it seems to me, is important, the very basis of MORAL evolution. The second interpretation is more of a mixed bag, mainly because a number of distinctions are not drawn by those attempting to respond to it. Of first importance is that we distinguish between providing an answer rational persons will recognize as cogent and providing an answer that will motivate those persons to behave MORALLY.[1]

Plato and, more recently, nonphilosopher Karl Menninger[2] argue that immoral (or illegal) acts are irrational acts or (in Plato's case) acts committed out of ignorance. But clearly something is wrong with such an equation, for it is commonplace to hear of rational people choosing to do perfectly terrible things for perfectly good reasons. One thinks immediately of the Master Criminal. Russell Grice writes:

> The Master Criminal's . . . peculiar talents have no bearing at all upon the question of whether there is a reason better than any in terms of independent interest for doing actions of certain classes; and they have no bearing upon the question whether there is such a reason for his doing them. The difference between the Master Criminal and his less talented fellows is that [MORALITY] does not succeed in ensuring that there is a reason in terms of his independent interest for his doing them.[3]

There are at hand what I shall call "first-order reasons" for a person to do what he does to, for, or with another person in a kindly way, for him to fulfill his moral obligations and for him generally to behave morally. Let us consider, again, obligations. Every "ought" or "must" judgment implies a proposition that takes the form "There is a good reason for (the subject of the judgment) to do a rather than b." (I): "X ought to do a" does not, however, imply (II): "X has a reason (good or not) to do a." (II) is implied by (III): "X believes or is convinced or agrees that he ought to do a." I have a reason for doing something if I believe that I ought to do it. On the other hand, there may be a good reason for me to do something even when I am ignorant of it. (There is no reason to discuss here the goals, beliefs, perceptions, and so on, that I might have and that cause my belief that I ought to do something.)

I shall identify "X has a first-order reason to do *a*," with *"There is* a good reason for X to do *a."* The latter sentence will be true under a wide variety of descriptions of X's circumstances, but none of those descriptions necessarily makes true the sentence, "X *has a reason* to do *a."* Suppose, for example, that X is playing chess and in the course of the game his opponent places his king in check. The rules of chess demand that when a player's king is in check he must manage to get out of check or lose the game. There is, then, a good reason for X to move his king out of check (to do *a*), supplied by the chess rules. It does not matter that X may want to lose the game. Regardless of his "wants" or his beliefs, there is a good reason for X to move the king. The chess example may be generalized to any institutional situation and to any station (with its related duties) within any institution by saying that for any obligation or duty incurred by participation, a good reason always exists to fulfill that obligation or to do that duty.

If our MORALITY is justifiable, if it suits its object given the human condition, then there is a good reason to do what it endorses. But obviously, more must be said about that.

I want to contrast "There is a good reason for X to do *a*" with "X has a good reason to do *a."* I shall refer to this second sentence as expressing the proposition that X has a second-order reason, or a motive for doing *a.* If X were to be asked why he moved his king out of check, he would likely cite the chess rules. But the skeptic is not silenced by rule recitation. He retorts: "Yes, but why should you, X, move *your* king out of check?" Suppose X offers: "Because I do not want to lose the game." By that answer, X identifies his motives (given his understanding of his institutional circumstances) with the reasons he has for doing something. The skeptic still may ask why X wants to win the game, but effectively the issue has been converted from one of citing a reason one has to do something to one of explaining why one desires, wants, or hopes. The skeptic may pursue, but not on his original ground.

I showed in Chapter 6 how a justificatory path can dead end in a moral concept or in drawing an analogy to a moral concept. In justification, deontic language sooner or later disappears and when it does the limits of the language specific to the activity in question are touched. First-order reasons run out when the "bedrock" of a moral concept or an institutional rule is struck. I do not, however, want to say that one answers the skeptic's question, "Why not commit murder?" by saying something like, "Murders have a deteriorative effect on the human environment. . . . .": I have two reasons:

1. The skeptic would then likely counter with the "Not everyone will commit murders" argument, or its kin the "Surely one little murder is not going to matter" argument. But both these arguments are irrelevant because they depend for their sense upon our treating as intelligible the unintelligible question, "What's the matter with this murder?"

2. All that I do by saying that "Murders have a deteriorative effect on the human environment" is to verbalize the belief that is generative of the very moral concept used in the sentence. That may, of course, serve as a persuasive educational move, but not as a final step in a justificatory battle.

Euergetical concepts perform in a justificatory chain in ways similar to moral concepts. They terminate the reason-giving enterprise. Suppose the skeptic asks Nemo why he gave the money to Jo, and Nemo responds, "Basically I wanted to get rid of him, I suppose." To this the skeptic retorts: "You could have done so by throwing a rock at the little beggar." "But that," Nemo answers, "would not have been kind." Does the skeptic's next ploy, "But why be kind?" hit the target, demand a further justificatory response? Nemo might say that he had no desire to make the beggar's life worse off, that doing the deed in the way he did perhaps even made life a bit easier for Jo. But this is no reply to the skeptic. It is either redundant or a reiteration of facts not questioned by the skeptic. Nemo, I think, has no further reply. In the end, the best Nemo can hope to achieve would be to make the skeptic feel somewhat ridiculous for persisting in asking his questions. Clearly, as already suggested, there are genuine grounds for disagreement over whether or not an act is kind, given the circumstances, but the point is that a genuine disagreement cannot arise over why one should try to be kind. The skeptic cannot mean by "kind" what we do if he persists in asking questions like "Why should you get rid of the beggar in as kindly a way as possible?" The fact that "kind" (the umbrella-virtue), like "murder," is a terminal concept in justificatory chains will prove significant in what follows.

We could go much further into the exploration of first-order reasons for being moral and for being kind, but that would not likely throw much more light on the present subject. Suffice it to say that first-order reasons to be MORAL exist in that doing so maintains or betters the conditions necessary for a life of worth or promotes a socially better world. The accounts so far given, however, affirmatively answer only the question, "Is there a good reason for people to be MORAL?" They provide no answer to the typically asked question, "Have *I* got a good reason to be MORAL?"

We may put that question in the form: "Have I got a good reason to do what I ought (morally) to do (or for what it would be kind for me to do)?" In another form, this is to ask "Do I automatically (*eo ipso*) *have* a good reason to do something, if it is true that *there is* a good reason for me to do it?" "I have a *reason* to do *a*" should be further distinguished from "I have a *good* reason to do *a*." A person might be quite demented but still have a reason for doing a number of odd things. I have a *good* reason for doing something if my doing it is consistent with, or furthers, what I believe to be my interests or welfare. I do not have a good reason for doing something if I have not considered or am not aware of my interests, or if I have an inadequate idea of the effect on my welfare of my doing something; I do not have a good reason regardless of whether or not there is a good reason for me to do that something to protect or enhance my interests. A statement expressing the proposition that I have good grounds for my belief that *a* is in my interests must be true for it to be true that I have a good reason to do *a*. It cannot then be true of me that I have a good reason for doing *a* solely because there is a good reason (a first-order reason) for me to do *a*. I must have good reasons for making the judgment that certain courses of action are in accord with my interests. "There is a good reason for X to do *a*" then differs from "X has a good reason to do *a*" in these respects: X must, in the latter case, actually have good reasons to believe that *a* is or will be in his interests. I take it that this, in large measure, captures the concept of economic rationality. In the former case, anyone can tell X what he ought to do just so long as either (1) they have sufficient information about the institutional circumstances of X, or (2) they are aware of the MORAL principle(s) relevant to X's situation, or (3) they have sufficient information to calculate the usefulness to X of his doing one or another of a limited number of things. The latter case also assumes, as Thomas Nagel[4] has pointed out, that X has recognized that the present, his own present, is a time among others and that the future has, in some respect, reality. "X has a good reason to do something" reports a prudential subjective decision of its subject, whereas "There is a good reason for X to do *a*" reports a more or less objective finding that may be either institutional, prudential, or MORAL.

It should be acknowledged that two rather controversial positions lie not very well disguised in the foregoing: (1) that "There is a good reason for X to do *a*" does not entail nor is entailed by "X has a good reason to do *a*" and, consequently, (2) that the supposed connection between what a person ought morally to do and what he has a good reason to do breaks down. I think that both of these positions are defensible. The latter one might be reformulated so that it does not have the apparent debilitating effect on moral behavior.

Let it be understood as: what a person ought to do may not always be consistent with what a person ought prudentially (as he understands things) to do, given the economic concept of rationality. That certainly appears unexceptionable; indeed, it is the foundation stone of many a Western moral theory.

Perhaps Kant's most important contribution to the literature of ethics is the distinction he drew between categorical and hypothetical imperatives. Kant classed as necessarily categorical all moral imperatives. "The categorical imperative would be one which presented an action as of itself objectively necessary, without regard to any other end." A hypothetical imperative "says only that the action is good to some purpose." For Kant, two basic types of hypothetical imperatives existed—those of prudence and those of "skill." Prudential hypothetical imperatives are those that instruct persons regarding their self-interests. Kant's view, of course, was that moral judgments can never be directed solely at self-interest and that hence they are not prudential. They must all be categorical. (It will be recalled that in an earlier chapter the prudential "ought" was defined in game theoretic terms, translated into best-play strategy.)

One of the virtues of Kant's position is that it provides for what he and many moral philosophers have taken to be essential in all truly moral judgments: the sense of inescapability. Categorical imperatives seemingly erase the distinction between what one has a good reason to do and that there is a good reason for one to do something, by rendering the distinction unimportant. Kant argued that categorical imperatives are true of everyone regardless of condition, state of mind, perceptions, or beliefs, and that those imperatives are in themselves the best reasons people can have for doing something. In effect, on Kant's account, categorical imperatives do more than indicate or signal that there are good reasons for people to do something, they "give reasons for acting to any man."[5]

Most people do feel bound to do what moral principles recommend, but that may only be because many people mistakenly regard moral principles (and judgments) as if they were game rules, and in regard to those specific "rules" they have developed feelings of inescapability. Mrs. Foot has convincingly shown that this sociological fact is not, however, sufficient to guarantee for moral judgments a reason-giving force.[6]

Given the distinction already drawn between "There is a good reason for X to do a" and "X has a good reason to do a," the metamoral problem is to find a bridge, if one exists, between first-order good reasons (even the best of objective good reasons) and second-order good reasons (even the best of those). The criteria for first-order good reasons are at least threefold. There are three different criteria, often generating three different recommendations: institutional rules applied to an institutional situation, MORALITY; moral principles or judgments (paradigmatically applied in conflict situations); and best-play strategy objectively determined under the assumption of safe self-interest. What criteria have we to determine that "X has a good reason to do a?" X has a good reason to do a if and only if a is, or is a significant part of, a best-play strategy (a utility maximization) for X, and X believes that it is. Furthermore, if "X has a good reason to do a" is true, then X's doing a is a reasonable (or rational) thing for X to do. The problem for moralists would be to show, so far as it is possible, that it is always reasonable for X to do the MORAL thing; that is, that whenever there is a conflict, what X has a good reason to do (better than the reasons he has to do something else) is always identical to the thing recommended by either MORAL principle or sound MORAL judgment.

My account of having a good reason to do something, it will be recognized, embodies the game theoretic or economic conception of rational behavior. Rapoport[7] provides a first approximation description of a reasonable person. An individual is acting reasonably "if he takes into account the possible consequences of each of the courses of action open to him; if he is aware of a certain preference order among the consequences and accordingly chooses the course of action which, in his estimation, is likely to lead to the most preferred consequence."[8] Usually the reasonable thing to do is the safe and prudent thing to do, given alternative courses of action.

Rescher has vehemently attacked the game theorist's account of reasonableness.[9] His argument is that the equation of rationality with self-interested prudence begs two questions: (1) whether rationality demands the prudential approach, and (2) whether rationality demands cultivation of personal advantage and not the interests of others or mutual interest. Both questions, he argues, should be answered by denying the game theorist's equation: it may be rational to take a calculated risk and it may be rational to have, as a major element in one's decision-making, a deep concern for the interest of others. Unfortunately, Rescher's attempts to defend his views are presented more as polemics than arguments ("to disregard the interests of others is not rational but inhuman"). It seems to me that all that is lost by granting the game theorist his account of individual rationality is the possibility of the appeal to Reason that characterizes Kantian and Neo-Kantian ethics, in cases where the "moral imperative" calls for some action apparently incompatible with the interests of an individual. I am not suggesting, however, that the game theorist's account of rationality is not without flaws and difficulties. Clearly in nonnegotiable, non-zero sum games its application often leads to suspect results. I am, however, in agreement with Jordan Sobel, who writes:

> Utility maximization may be inadequate as a conception of individual rationality. Perhaps there is more to individual rationality than preferences for outcomes that are representable by a utility function and actions in accordance with these preferences where actions are (as if) viewed as 'gambles' on pos-

sible outcomes. Rationality may, for example, impose addition-
al constraints on an agent's ends taken either singly or as a
system. And perhaps, moving in the other direction, utility
maximization is not even always part of practical rationality:
perhaps, for example, a rational agent would sometimes, when
possessed of only weakly based assessments of probabilities,
refuse to choose amongst his actions as if they were 'gambles'
on possible outcomes. Utility maximization may be, in any
number of ways, inadequate as a conception or total theory,
of individual rationality. I do not dispute this. *All* I claim is
that the issue, whether or not and if so how utility maximization is inadequate as a conception of individual rationality
cannot presently be settled by showing how it is inadequate
in what, on the face of it, is a quite different and possibly unrelated way, namely, as a basis for communal life.[10]

Rescher's response to the game theorist's equation of individual
rationality with utility maximization is that there is no good reason
for calling a person unreasonable if he has objectives that transcend
his interests. That seems to me absolutely correct, but in Rescher's
accounts, wrongly put. Rescher argues that by internalizing the
weal or woe of others, the "operation of vicarious affects," one can
alter the utilities maximized. Such internalizations, however, only
redefine self-interest by altering the "payoff" utiles and by so doing
sometimes change the referent of "the prudent move." For example,
if X will be made unhappier by doing *a* rather than by doing *b* because doing *a* makes the life of Y more miserable than does the
doing of *b*, then it surely is in X's interest to do *b*, even if, in the
absence of vicarious affects, *a* would have been the prudent move.
The game theoretic account of reasonableness does not preclude
such reevaluations to fit those psychological facts not purely intra-
institutional or evident to the objective observer.

For my purposes it will prove useful to restate the game theory
definitions as, X acted in a reasonable way (X had a good reason
for his actions) if and only if he was aware of possible alternative
ways of acting and the range of attendant possible consequences
(payoffs), and he chose to act in the way that he believed was most
likely to maximize his utility. No limit need be set arbitrarily on
the factors that might materially affect utility and hence alter the

matrix in any one choice situation. Of course one cannot be properly described as having acted reasonably if one did the reasonable thing accidentally. Further, that there is a reason for someone to do something, even if he is aware of it, is only relevant to whether or not he acts reasonably (whether or not he can be described as having had a good reason to do something) if its being a good reason was a contributing factor to his belief that the act would maximize his utility. Even though *there is* a good reason for X to do *a*, unless X has determined that doing *a* maximizes his utility, it is false that, even if he did *a*, he *had* a good reason for so doing. This may sound rather cold-blooded, but if the possibility of vicarious affects and other alterations of the payoff matrix are granted, I do not think it is.

On the surface it would appear that one could only be said to have a good reason for doing what MORALITY recommends when a host of other conditions (those specifically regarding the agent's utility maximization) are met. Minus such conditions the agent will not, per definition, have a good reason to perform a MORALLY endorsed act. In fact, he may well have a good reason to do something quite other than the kind thing because he may have good reasons to believe, based on some imagined matrix, that acting in some other way will best serve his interests. (One may think here of Shakespeare's Richard III or Macbeth.) The game matrix provides the data that makes true the proposition(s) that is (are) a necessary condition of there being a good prudential reason for his act. His awareness, for example, of the "saddle-point on the matrix" will serve as meeting the condition necessary for his having a good reason to believe that doing the something in question does maximize his utility (granted that the other player is rational or can be expected to play prudentially), and that is a necessary condition of his being properly described as having a good reason to do that something.

Unfortunately, further complications must be added to these matters. Undoubtedly talk of games has conjured up examples such as chess or our shepherds playing Merels, both of which are zero-sum nonnegotiable games (their conclusions always equal zero—one loser, one winner, and the play is not negotiated.) Zero-sum games do seem to fit the pattern of rationality offered above. One can either gain everything or nothing (leaving out stalemates, where one gains experience only.) Each player in such games, it may be assumed, has one basic game motive, to annihilate his opponent, to emerge the victor and take home all the marbles. If we assign arbitrary utility values to the outcomes possible in chess, we could say that +5 is victory, 0, stalemate, and −5, loss. Players will settle for 0 if +5 is out of the question. At a certain point in the game a player may be faced with a next-move decision in which choosing one course of action over one other could lead either to stalemate or his own checkmate. Any player of even modest caliber will choose to stalemate to avoid loss. Because the other player's next move at this stage in the game is in large measure determined by his opponent's move, he as well will have to settle for the stalemate. Game theorists refer to the situation in which neither player is motivated by prudence to move away from an outcome as the equilibrium point of the game. A game reaches equilibrium when neither feels he can gain more or lose less by choosing some other move. By establishing, on the game matrix, what point is equilibrium the rational solution of nonnegotiable games can be determined.

J. F. Nash[11] demonstrated that all non-zero sum games have at least one equilibrium point. When such a game has one equilibrium point, the best-play strategies for both players (assuming two-person games for the sake of simplicity) can be easily prescribed. Where there are several equilibrium points, the notion of a "prominent equilibrium" is used to provide the prescriptive solution. This method fits perfectly into the previously described model of reasonableness. The problems arise with the attempt to extend the method to certain other games, games which a number of moral philsophers have recognized as distinctly similar to classical moral conflicts.[12] The most famous of these games is that popularly referred to as "The Prisoner's Dilemma"; the other I want to consider is aptly called "Chicken." The game matrix for each game we shall stipulate as below:

X \ Y	S	C
S	5, 5	−10, 10
C	10, −10	−5, −5

"The Prisoner's Dilemma"

X \ Y	S	C
S	1, 1	−2, 2
C	2, −2	−5, −5

"Chicken"

In the tale often associated with the Prisoner's Dilemma, strategy C is to confess to the crime for which the two are held prisoner, and strategy S is to remain silent. The testimony of each is needed to convict the other, if each confesses, both divide the sentence of ten years at hard labor. If only one confesses, the ten year sentence falls on the other and vice versa. If neither confesses, they will both be released. Of first note is that for both players, strategy S is the most prudent and reasonable thing to do. But that solution assumes that the players (prisoners) can discuss their options, negotiate the conclusion to benefit each. The usual story, however, is that they cannot communicate with each other. Each must arrive at his course of action by himself. When the story is told in that way, it becomes obvious that the prudent thing to do is to confess, regardless of what the other does. To make sharper the situation let us say that they must make or carry out their "moves" simultaneously, so that neither move can be tempered by knowledge of the other move. The paradoxical conclusion seems to be that by doing the reasonable thing, the prudent thing, the prisoners will fail to realize the optimum situation that provides the most utility to both. In other words, two utility-maximizing prisoners will spend some time in jail, whereas they both could have avoided any further imprisonment if they had both chosen the non-prudent and non-safe course of action. Both must have chosen S to exact the mutually best outcome, but under conditons of uncertainty regarding the other's perceptions of the situation, including the other's assessment of whether his opponent will be prudent and safe, or risk a long imprisonment against the mutually optimal outcome, the "rational" choice must be to confess. The conditions established for the game exclude the possibility of solving the Assurance Problem, providing assurance to each that the other will not confess; and the Coordination Problem, making clear to each other which move is to be played. Hobbes, of course, introduces the sovereign to overcome both problems, thereby converting prudence to the civil good.

Even in an iterated form of the Prisoner's Dilemma the reasonable choice of courses of action is C if these problems are not solved (played one million times if you wish[13]). The outcome produced by two pursuers of reasonable personal policy, however, offends our intuitions about what results being reasonable should produce. Perhaps, one is inclined to say, in this case being reasonable is to take a nonprudential point of view, to take the point of view of the collective, ask not how my interests solely can be served, but how *our* interests can be best or mutually best served. Rapoport indeed claims that at this stage in the game theoretic analysis of the Prisoner's Dilemma we have a "genuine bifurcation of the notion of rationality into that of individual rationality and that of collective rationality, each of which prescribes a different strategy to both players."[14] In effect the equilibrium point (C,C) of the Prisoner's Dilemma holds only if the criterion of reasonableness is self-interest and neither assurance nor coordination can be attained. If the criterion of rationality is altered to one of mutual interest even in the absence of such solutions to those difficulties, the equilibrium point is (S,S). What value, however, is to be found in shifting the criterion of rationality to fit the circumstances? The *ad hoc* nature of such a proposal reduces "rationality" or "reasonableness" to a function of the kind of game. If that is the best result we can expect, then the notion of acting reasonably loses most of its usefulness. Although I see no value in using the notion of "collective reasonableness," I shall refer to the "communally optimal outcome," defined as that result in which all members (or players) realize the most possible utility consistent with the least disadvantage to any. In the Prisoner's Dilemma it is the (S,S) outcome.

In games like Prisoner's Dilemma apparently one is always better off by acting prudentially, so long as one's opponent is either not reasonable or is communally motivated, motivated to make the attempt to realize the communally optimal outcome (playing S). On the other hand, it is not reasonable, unless one has special information, to make that assumption about one's opponent. Nonetheless, even assuming, as one usually must, that one's opponent is economically rational, the prudent move (C) remains the only reasonable move. What would induce anyone to play S? A martyr or a masochist would choose that strategy, but morality cannot count on martyrs and masochists. They seem to be few and far between. It would be a sad state of affairs if the communally optimal outcome can be reached only when two such types were to be engaged in the game. Also it would be odd if the only motive that in the end provided both players with a mutually satisfactory return would involve the willingness to "give up everything." A reasonable player, however, I think need not be a martyr and yet choose to play strategy S. He might play S with the hope of a similar play from his opponent. If the game were iterated and moves were alternated and his were the initial move, he might play S to elicit cooperation from his opponent. The choice of S would then not be an act of martyrdom or masochism but one of trust. Trusting in such a way is still not consistent with prudence, however, or with being reasonable (neither assurance nor coordination secured). Can one have a good reason to play the trusting move when it is not identical to the prudential move?

The reasonable man and the trusting man are not, of course, diametrically opposite types. To be sure, the person who trusts others, without evidence of their trustworthiness or in situations clearly disadvantageous to his welfare, is a saint or a fool. "Blind trust" is anathema to prudence. There is, however, such a thing as prudential trust. The prudentially trustworthy person may be defined as the person who, according to David Gauthier,[15] accepts arguments of the form, "If it is advantageous for me to agree to do x and I do agree to do x, then I ought to do x, whether or not it proves advantageous for me to do x." Knowing, recognizing, or even having strong reasons to suspect that one's opponent is such a prudentially trustworthy man makes reasonable trusting him to play S, and hence doing so to mutual benefit. Unfortunately, however, knowing or having good reasons to believe that one's opponent is trustworthy is an excellent reason from the point of view of self-interest to capitalize by playing C. No one could say that doing so was not a reasonable thing to do.

Consider now the game of "Chicken." In many ways it seems to resemble the Prisoner's Dilemma, especially in that defection from a mutually beneficial policy seems the most likely to serve individual interests, but this time only if the other chooses the mutually beneficial course of action. If both opt for C, both suffer the worst possible outcome. The C strategy then cannot be said to dominate for either player in "Chicken." The C strategy nonetheless is the most reasonable response to the other's choice of S, and vice versa. There is then more than one equilibrium point (Cx, Sy) and (Sx, Cy).

Prudential reasoning in "Chicken" forces both players to choose S. In doing so neither can realize the highest utility possible for him in the game (2). Each must settle for 1 at best, but that for either is better than −2 which game theorists call the "security level" for this game, that is, the worst a player could do by playing the prudential strategy. Both benefit by the S,S outcome and there is, no doubt, a sense of satisfaction with that result.

We cannot easily imagine a player having good reasons in "Chicken" for not playing S and for playing C instead (remembering that moves are made simultaneously and that this is not an iterated game). Only someone behaving irrationally, that is, imprudently in "Chicken" would choose to play C. The difference between "Prisoner's Dilemma" and "Chicken" is then made clearer. In the latter game, S is the reasonable thing to do while in the former it is not the reasonable thing to do. That difference is a function of the assigned utility values of the respective games. Cooperation or noncooperation is sometimes reasonable, sometimes not. Acting toward mutual benefit is sometimes prudential, sometimes not. The variable of most importance is the assigned utility values for each participant. The only way to insure that the mutually beneficial choices are reasonable is to alter the utility values of payoffs for all participants. In large measure that is what Rescher does by "adding in" the factor of "vicarious affects." Certainly it is what Hobbes' sovereign does.

I see nothing objectionable to adjusting utility values to reflect vicarious or other affects, but I do not see how that could ultimately alter the general problem. Here and there, very sensitive people could so alter the utility values of their plays in "Prisoner's Dilemma" so as to transform the matrix and, for them, escape the dilemma. But that does not provide us with a general solution.

Where then does this leave us? We seem forced to conclude that at least in nonnegotiable noniterated games, players acting prudently do not insure mutual benefit. Mutual benefit, despite alterations in utility values to allow, for example, for vicarious affects, in the end rests on the establishment of trust. Trust, however, is not always reasonable and in many cases even trusting the person known to be trustworthy is far from the rational thing to do. Mutual benefit often, if not always, calls for someone to do something that from his self-interested point of view is disadvantageous, and it further calls for all others to do likewise. No unilateral act of self-sacrifice will insure mutual benefit. Most likely such an act will result only in someone else taking the advantage thrust on him. Perhaps even more intriguing is that choosing the mutually beneficial act (in the games considered) can never guarantee gain to a player, even if everyone else in the game chooses to play in a similar manner. He always could have chosen the prudential alternative and thus realized a greater utility. Surely if all players choose the mutually beneficial action and hence all forego the purely self-interested action, they will all fare better than if they all pursue the prudential choice of action. But, as Gauthier[16] has pointed out, that is not an adequate reason for any individual to eschew prudence, for he always does better regardless of what his fellows choose.

Where we have talked of mutual benefit above, could we have talked of MORAL acts, or at least could we say that doing the MORAL thing seems to be a subclass of the category of mutually beneficial acts? A person acting MORALLY is acting, at least in one sense, for the mutual benefit of most persons. In so acting, he may even be disadvantaging himself; there certainly is no guarantee that he will not be doing so. For example, consider the industrialist whose factory dumps untreated chemical waste into a river upstream of a town that depends on that river for its major water source. Let us stipulate that the industrialist does not live in the town, and does not get his water supply from the river. Most of us would probably make the moral judgment that he ought to end his dumping activities, since his continuing dumping deteriorates the human environment of the townspeople. The industrialist is, let us suppose, economically severely disadvantaged should he choose to act in accordance with that moral judgment. He must expend a good deal of money either to remove the dangerous chemicals from his waste or to dump the waste in some safer depository. In return, he may get some good will and publicity, but his expenditure far outweighs any possible return. He is, it would appear, virtually excluded from the class of persons directly benefitting from his act. The outcome of his acting in accord with our moral judgment then surely cannot be described, on the face of it, as mutually beneficial. The industrialist reaps little, if anything; the townspeople gain a good deal.

We seem to have no reliable way of calculating the utility to everyone of acts that preserve or tend to conserve a set of environmental conditions. Novelists and even the writers of stories for children recognizing this problem tend to bring the industrialist's interests directly into the matter.[17] Our imagined case does not. We can only say that if the industrialist gains something from his act, it is far less than the townspeople gain. One idea must be discarded—either that mutual benefit means equal benefit (that is embodied in the Prisoner's Dilemma matrix), or that behaving in the MORAL fashion is always in significant ways beneficial to all. I would like to think, with Dr. Seuss, that MORAL behavior is ultimately always significantly beneficial to all, but I do not think that is true. Sometimes being MORAL is to play S and suffer while other people receive the benefit. The notion that each of us in the end will equally benefit from the doing of MORAL deeds is a vestige of romanticism. Of course, should a moral judgment have the support of law, the utilities would be tilted, and it might then be prudential for the industrialist to expend the money necessary to alter his disposal system. Nonetheless, in the absence of legal pressure the industrialist will simply be disadvantaging himself without appreciable personal return by doing the MORAL thing. And if that is true, he cannot have a good prudential reason to do the MORAL thing that is better than the good prudential reason he has to not do the MORAL thing.

It seems to me that the identification of the moral choice with the S,S outcome of the Prisoner's Dilemma invites a serious misconception of morality's primary object, of the reason we have moral concepts at all. The S,S outcome is but the record of two individual payoffs, which happens to be the only mutually beneficial outcome for that game. If we try to extrapolate that over a population we come to expect that equal benefit, even individual benefit, is the earmark of moral action. To grasp the interests of morality, however, one must take a different perspective and to do so may often be to eschew individual interest completely. Our moral concepts are framed from the species or, at least, from the communal point of view. Morally endorsed acts tend toward the maintenance of an environment; measurable utilities do not necessarily accrue to individuals. Should the maintenance or even the betterment of the human ecosystem in certain cases advantage some and disadvantage others, that is not the prime business of morality. MORALITY, as we have conceived it, is interested more in equity than equality, in making things possible rather than certain. Quite simply, MORALITY lies outside of the standard two-person game matrix. Even if all payoffs on the matrix were negative or if all were equal negatives, MORALITY might have something to say as to the individual player's choice in the matter. Suppose a matrix to be:

	S	C
S	−10,−10	−10,−10
C	−10,−10	−10,−10

(Y across top, X down side)

Reason tells a player that his choice of move is unimportant (assuming this to be a noniterated game). Whatever he does he loses and his loss is no less or no greater whatever he does. If he must play, then he might as well do C as S and get it over with. S, however, might be endorsed by MORALITY for both players and C might not. There is nowhere on the matrix to record that fact. We could, however, imagine a matrix indicating the moral assessment of X and Y making their choices in the following fashion:

S/S	S/C	C/S	C/C
0	−5	−5	−10

Here we are assuming that if at least one of the players chooses to do S, the outcome will be better in an appreciable way from the point of view of MORALITY than if neither do. We need not, however, make that assumption and the result would be:

S/S	S/C	C/S	C/C
0	−10	−10	−10

There is a problem, however, in interpreting this matrix. To whom are these MORALITY effected payoffs to be assigned? They

might not be assignable to X and Y alone. The view of the object
of MORALITY that I have defended would imply that we should
assign them to the collective of all persons. Insofar as the collection
of all persons is an aggregate, we would need to determine utility
distributivity over the membership of the class. But that is of little
help, for we then must decide if the utilities of the whole are in the
same measure the utilities of each of its members.

If the aggregate gets −5 from S/C, does that mean −5 must be
"added" into the payoff for S/C for each member, including of
course X and Y? This would suggest that X's and Y's choices in this
matter somehow reduce the utilities of all members of the collectivity of person by −5. But from what are the 5 utiles to be sub-
tracted in the cases of those members not playing? Perhaps we
should assume that each individual has a "bank account" where all
credits and debits, regardless of who is playing what, are accounted.
But that is highly artificial. And what of X and Y? How is the "communal matrix" to be "added in" to their utile figures? Certainly we
cannot assume that if the collectivity realizes 0, −5, or −10 from
their choices it automatically means that the game matrix must be
recalculated to read

Y\X	S	C
S	−10/−10	−15/−15
C	−15/−15	−20/−20

making S the reasonable choice for both players.

Each member of the collectivity or any one of them may only be
personally disadvantaged by an infinitesimally small percentage of
the −5 utiles assigned to the aggregate; thus the matrix for X and
Y, if the collective's payoffs are distributive, may not be appreciably altered. (Actually, of course, this only demonstrates the arti-
ficiality of the notion of an aggregate's payoff in the matrix.) Although the aggregate is to benefit from people's adherence to
MORALITY, it does not seem to make sense to speak of such a
collective as "having reasons," of having a prudential stake in any-

thing; it is never a player in the marketplace in which economic rationality is rooted. The upshot of this analysis then would appear to be that, with certain exceptions, persons do not have good (prudential) reasons to be moral that are better than their good reasons to do that which accrues to their individual benefits, even when by doing so they create a situation in which none is advantaged, indeed in which all are disadvantaged (Prisoner's Dilemma).

The case for individuals being kind is no stronger; if anything it is weaker. There simply is no evidence that kindness gains advantage for its agent. It could be argued that all of us will have a better life if each is kind in his interpersonal dealings. The person being kind cannot, however, count on gaining any advantage from so tempering his behavior toward others. Often it is those very persons who can provide no utility to an individual that are the most worthy objects of kindness. Little wonder that religious systems that demand kindness have offered "eternal" rewards to those evidencing such behavior.

To summarize to this point, we should have to say that although for each of us there is a good reason to be moral and to be kind, except for persons with certain dispositions, none of us individually may have a good prudential reason in specific cases to be either moral or kind that is better than the good reasons we have to be purely self-interested. In other words, if "reasonableness" is defined in terms of utility maximization (which does not seem *prima facie* objectionable), then any individual choosing to do the moral act and/or the kind act, eschewing the prudential act, is usually doing an unreasonable thing. There are, of course, untold numbers of reasons why people hold moral beliefs and do act morally, but those reasons to act that are moral reasons are by their very nature not self-interested reasons, nor are they reducible to any other kinds of reasons to act. To act for a moral reason is to act because one believes or knows that what one is to do is right or ought to be done to maintain or better the human condition. Although one may have a self-interested reason to do what there is a moral reason to do, from the point of view of economic rationality one cannot have only a moral reason to do what there is a moral reason to do that is better (more reasonable) than the prudential reason one has to do something else in that instance. The implication seems to be that there may be nonmoral reasons to be moral in certain cases, but for the economically rational person, moral reasons cannot stand alone in the face of reasons of rational self-interest.

At least two objections appear likely to be offered. One attacks the account of reasonableness that I have accepted, Rescher's tack. The other tries to show that the definition of prudence as utility maximization is too narrow. This latter approach might stress, as previously mentioned, that being prudent or having prudential concerns essentially involves having a certain view of time, of treating the future as real as the present. By so doing, one might imagine the world of one's future made more hostile to one's attempts at maximizing utility, by the grasping play of the strategy that contains the biggest payoff in the present. After all, it is good business not to destroy the potential of a future harvest while reaping that of the present, to play the strategy that contains the biggest average payoff over time. The prudent man may play at being the moral man and/or the kind man in anticipation of either a greater future benefit to himself or a continuation of current benefits. Such a person is, however, just as vulnerable as the imprudent but trusting person to the non-other-regarding actions of the reasonable and prudent person who operates on the premise that "a bird in the hand is worth two in the bush."

The argument that prudence often dictates moral action (honesty is good business) reduces to saying that, in some cases, maximizing one's utility is not to seek the greatest utility possible for any one play as seen from the disinterested point of view, but is to average in future payoffs in a reformulation of the matrix of utilities through time, maximizing over a sequence of plays. Such a strategy, of course, assumes iterated games. If the game is noniterated, then playing the MORAL move (if it is not identical to the prudential one) is to court personal disadvantage. Being prudent does not require that I believe that the game will go on, only that I believe that I will go on to reap rewards.

II

An unbridgeable gulf seems to remain between what is reasonable (as utility maximization) for the individual to do and what MOR-

ALITY often demands. One of the major reasons for that gulf is reflected in the way we talk of reasonableness, prudence, self-interest on the one hand and morality, kindness, and goodness on the other. In regard to prudence and reasonableness, it is usually sensible to consider strategy, goals, and plans. But such notions are out of place when speaking of morality and kindness. If anything, the occasions for being moral and/or being kind arise in spite of strategy and plan. Generally speaking, persons willingly enter into institutional activities for prudential reasons, and therein find it prudential to lay and to abide by plans or strategies. The conflict situations that highlight MORALITY intrude into strategy ("the best laid plans"). Other persons must be met as fellow rational strategists, but also as fellow human beings. The recognition of the opponent as a fellow human being is sometimes sufficient to complicate the best of plans reminding each of us of our communality. The general population ignores the constraints that are our MORALITY only at the risk of destroying the climate for anyone's successful participation in any personally meaningful activity. Yet in no individual case would it seem that acting discordant with MORALITY involves risks greater than ostracism. Indeed, the greater personal risks are run in acting morally.

If the risks are so great, if prudential counsel cautions against it, why do it? We can see from the accounts given of the purpose of morality and the potential results of acting with kindness that the world of moral persons and kind persons will be (1) ultimately the only world in which the species or community can flourish and (2) the most comfortable place in which to abide as persons among other persons. Our moral and euergetical concepts are the products of the (perhaps sometimes faintly) perceived vision of not only the necessity of preserving, but the beauty of, the world realized when individuals take the risk of acting morally and kindly. The existence of our MORAL conceptual system not only attests to our primitive awareness of the importance to the community of persons of not letting that vision fade completely from our perceptions of the world and our search for personal satisfaction in it,[18] as I have earlier suggested; it also creates the very world of action that we then describe. There would be no conflict between prudence and MORALITY if we had not a MORAL conception system, because the world in which there are murders and thefts and lies would not exist. The fact that we often recognize in our own lives a tension between the demands of prudence and the urgings of MORALITY is a testament that our MORAL concepts are embedded in our descriptive apparatus for altogether different reasons than are the measurement instruments of utility maximization. It should come as no surprise that, in the absence of law and severe penalty, prudence does not always direct us to be MORAL and that MORALITY does not always direct us to be prudent.

The English poet Phineas Fletcher in 15__ wrote:

> Yet never durst his Faint and Coward heart
> (Ah foole faint heart faire Ladye ne're Could winne)
> Assaile faire Venus with his new-learn'd art
> > (*Venus and Anchises*)
> > (*Brittain's Ida*)

Frankly, MORALITY urges individuals often to act in ways that threaten personal risk, even suffering. In that sense, despite a great deal of literature on the subject, we should feel no reluctance in saying that, measured against the standards of economic rationality, moral persons and kind persons are and have been heroic. There are, of course, degrees of heroism; after a majority of people have taken the risk, doing likewise to some extent diminishes the heroism. Yet even in those cases we cannot forget that we are all at the mercy of each other, at the mercy of each other's greed.

III

A major difficulty arises in using the game theory examples as a way of characterizing MORAL predicament. The Prisoner's Dilemma, for example, leads us to always identify "the MORAL outcome" with that outcome in which both players benefit equally. The dilemma arises in the game because that outcome cannot be achieved if at least one player is purely prudent, and no solution external to the game is achieved to the Assurance and Coordination problems. But why should being MORAL be mutually beneficial to the two players of this game? The thrust of the game theory version of MORALITY is toward realized economic consequences. But only some of our MORAL concepts are directed solely at consequences, and even those are not in general aimed at the consequence of mutually cashable returns. Prisoner's Dilemma might well capture some, if not indeed the primary, puzzles that confront natural persons in a Hobbesian world. But in that state the question is not "Why be moral?" but "Why be prudent?" It is not the difference between prudence and morality that marks the change from the state of nature to the civil state but the difference between rationality-dictated selfishness and rationality-dictated long-term prudence. Hobbes argues that in the state of nature we can have no regard for the future, and that industry and other enterprises that involve anticipation of future return are not reasonable endeavors. Without the possibility of setting rather specific goals for oneself, prudence is vacuous, as Nagel has shown. In fact, the only active motives in the Hobbesian state of nature are gain, safety, and reputation and all are described as variations of selfishness. Only after the formation of the civil state, in which the third law of nature *"that men perform their covenants made"* is incorporated into civil law and enforced by the coercive power of the sovereign, is prudence a reasonable motive, only then does morality, in the form of a rudimentary theory of justice, defined as the keeping of covenants, emerge. The question, "Why be moral?" is indeed then answered in prudential terms, but prudence itself is made possible only in civil association. If justice is the keeping of covenants made, then no assumption is present in Hobbes that in all just acts mutual benefit will accrue to participants. One may well make a disadvantageous covenant. Nothing in the theory of justice so defined excludes that possibility or allows demonstration of calculation error or realization of disadvantage to void the convenant. The idea that morality always or even usually produces tabulatable mutual benefit to agents is a fiction presupposed in the game theory conception of the problem.

The main reason, however, that we are liable to be uneasy with the Prisoner's Dilemma model of a moral situation is that nothing or very little relevant to MORALITY is or can be exposed on the game matrix.

A number of conditions must be met for the question "Why should I be moral?" to be intelligible. Unless the question is made in reference to some general strategy of living, its use will be restricted to specific choice situations, that is, to situations in which an agent regards himself as at a crucial stage of act decision, and the alternatives he confronts to include one act (or course of action) that is endorsed by MORALITY and one that is not. To make the matter more dramatic, we usually assume that doing the MORAL thing may be distasteful while doing the non-MORAL thing is pleasurable to him. But that is just where the difficulties arise. For, it is only because we have a MORAL conceptual system at all that the problem arises. The decision that confronts him would not exist and the question would not be intelligible in the absence of MORAL concepts. Although Hobbes probably did not intend his position to be interpreted in the way I am, his dictum that in nature nothing is unjust can be read as a reflection on this fact. The Prisoner's Dilemma needs to be descriptively "fleshed-out" to expose whether in any particular instance the issue of choice is a moral one and what the moral choice is.

We might suppose that player X's choice is not simply to remain silent or to confess but whether to lie to Y about how he will choose (assume that X and Y are allowed to discuss their choices before they make them; this seems to me an essential presupposition of a moral predicament—civil association). In order to frame X's situation, in order to describe it, we made use of a moral concept, lie. If the question that X poses *to himself* is "Why should I be moral?" and if he understands his choice to be between lying to Y and telling Y truthfully what he will do, then his answer would seem to reside in the very description he uses to relate the question to the circumstances. To describe his situation, he uses moral concepts, and to admit that their names properly describe a contemplated act is to admit that the act is either right or wrong. If it is a lie, it is wrong. If it is a murder, it is wrong. To suggest that one ought to do what one has admitted to be wrong is to deny the appropriateness of the very conceptual apparatus that is being used to make the description of one's decision problem intelligible.

One form of decision situation in which the question "Why should I be MORAL?" typically seems to be raised is then that in which the agent is imagined to be deciding between, for example, lying and not lying, or murdering or not murdering. But, as we have seen, such a decision is only possible for him because we have the MORAL concepts of lie and murder, and he has utilized them in his way of describing his circumstances. Of course, we invented those concepts because we recognized a need to discourage such acts, to render blamable the perpetrators of such acts, in effect, to make it unnecessary for anyone to make such a decision as "To lie or not to lie?" The question "Why should *I* be MORAL?" when that means "Why should I not lie?" or "not murder?" is not intelligible. If one invokes MORAL concepts to describe one's situation, one cannot deny their validity. Kovesi writes "His problem and decision is meaningful only within our conceptual framework, which framework is not the result of his decision."[19]

If he regards the words "lie" and "murder" as being elliptical for "What people in this society call lie" and "What they call murder," he has no MORAL predicament. His raising the question "Why should I be MORAL?" is a sham, and no recitation of MORAL principles, judgments, concepts, or beliefs about the human condition can be expected to counter the prudential argument. Undoubtedly that is why the law is necessary to exact compliance by shifting the benefits. As Hobbes has written:

> There must be some coercive power, to compel men equally to the performance of their covenants, by the terror of some punishment, greater than the benefit they expect by the breach of their covenant.[20]

The law then, when it is enforced, shifts the utilities and thereby relocates the prudential "play" on the matrix. Kai Nielson[21] has seen this business in a similar way but he has not emphasized the role of law. He argues, quite straightforwardly, that it will not generally be in the interest of the nonmoral person to oppose morality, that he depends on the moral behavior of the majority to gain anything from his immoral acts, and that to succeed at all in achieving a benefit from a nonmoral act he must be moderate, not "going to the well" too often and risking alarming the general moral citizenry. Furthermore, if this type of approach is adopted by all other rational egoists the result will be a populace that generally behaves morally (with only a moderate lapse now and then).

Nielson's scenario is persuasive. Indeed it incorporates the idea of the first part of this chapter: that one might, because of circumstances, have prudential reasons to be moral. The difficulty is that Nielson and Hobbes and a number of other philosophers, in order to find good reasons for being MORAL, abandon MORALITY and the very foundations of MORAL concept formation. If we ask for the reason we have MORAL concepts, it is unlikely we will learn that we have them to insure that particular individuals will realize a gain in utiles. We would, in general, seem to have invented them to try to stem the tide of deterioration that erodes the walls of civil association.

Economic rationalists view human life in terms of the satisfaction of an individual's ends by cost accountable means. MORALITY views human life *sub specie aeternitatis*. A. Phillips Griffiths has provided a helpful statement of this Wittgensteinian idea: Griffiths writes

> My attitude is an ethical one when I look at the good life not as a possible life of this body with its history and its future and its individual wants and wishes, but as a life with no par-ticular preeminence embedded in all life.[22]

Morality is not to be conceived as a matter of somewhat isolated individuals acting in one way rather than another, accomplishing one or another aim and being rewarded or punished by the addition or the subtraction of so many utiles. The wellspring of MORALITY is an altogether different *vision*: the flourishing, not just the sur-vival, of *the species in an environment*. Our MORALITY is either adequate or not to that task.

A number of questions almost immediately are raised whenever a philosopher argues that MORAL reasons transcend individual ra-tionality in favor of the maintenance of the human environment. In particular, the standard charge is that no provision is made to pro-tect the individual from martyrdom in the cause of the species. Such a charge, of course, when further elaborated, associates an account of MORALITY such as mine with some rather strict form of utilitarianism. This is, however, a fundamental mistake. My ac-count of MORALITY is neutral with respect to the famous tradi-tional theories. I am not propounding a theory of MORALITY. As it happens, the MORAL concepts we have are not all of one cloth. Some are purely consequentialist, others deontological, others the-oretical mongrels. We discover their sources by finding out what sort of evidence is relevant to their nonapplication in a predicament. In fact, rather than with questions of the sort "To lie or not to lie?"

the situations that actually highlight moral dilemmas tend to be those in which, because of one's perception of the relevant facts, one feels he cannot adequately describe one of his alternatives by using the name of a moral concept. Some facts perceived to be pertinent to the circumstances just have not been incorporated in a MORAL mixed mode concept. The famous (or notorious) case created by Benjamin Constant (see Chapter 7, footnote 2) is such a situation, though Kant did not seem to see it as such. Because we see the myopia of Kant's perception of what is relevant, we regard his answer as rather incredible. Kant seemingly excludes from consideration what strikes most people as highly pertinent to the decision; that saying what one knows to be false in this case will save the life or limb of one's friend. The feeling of genuine predicament arises because no amount of rationalization to general consequences can wash away that fact. But that very fact is not covered by or associated in the mixed mode concept of lie, though we do recognize that its inclusion in the description of the circumstances drastically alters the applicability of the description of the case as a lie. In such a case, we are no longer certain that what is being done is lying, even though it is clearly not telling the truth. As I showed in Chapter 5, the real difficulty with euthanasia is that the descriptions of events called euthanasias are apparently incomplete unless they involve the citing of facts that we have not incorporated in the mixed mode concept of murder; as it happens, the presence of those facts in a case is sufficient to throw doubt on the using of "murder" to describe the events, even though the events are undeniably killings. These two examples, lie and murder, also show the theoretical neutrality of MORAL concept invention. In the lying case, it is motives rather than consequences that delimit the descriptive applicability of the name of the concept. In the euthanasia cases, it is also motive that is pertinent, but the way of applying the pertinent motivation information is somewhat different, because the class of murder motives is limited by the concept, whereas the class of lying motives is not. In the Benjamin Constant case, that the motive is to save the life of a friend is generally regarded as relevant in determining the rightness or wrongness of saying what one knows to be false. Surprising, perhaps, we should then say that lying must have been formed for utilitarian reasons, intention having been incompletely considered. Kant also seems to have caught this point, for he defends his position in terms of consequences.[23] Murder, however, seems to have been invented for both consequentialist and deontological reasons, as is evidenced by the rather closed class of intentions and consequences; but it might be argued that the consequences are somewhat unspecified, hence a puzzle about assassination. If that is the case, then murder has a deontological tap root.

Let us return then to the objection that martyrdom of the individual is entailed by my account of MORALITY. Of course it is true that MORALITY calls for self-sacrifice. That hardly anyone disputes. What is of concern is that the ultimate sacrifice of an individual to the human environment might also be recommended. I do not think that, as we have constructed our MORAL conceptual system, that is likely. The concept of human scapegoat was formed to discourage any such actions by a community because we do feel that the flourishing of the human environment depends on the principle that one person's well-being cannot be replaced by that of another or of a group. However, as I argued in Chapter 4, conditions can change and our MORAL concepts consequently will have to change to avoid obsolesence. People have willingly laid down their lives for much less.

If there is, however, a basic vision embedded in the MORAL conceptual scheme, it is that despite individual sacrifice and even suffering, the *raison d'être* of MORALITY, the flourishing community, is the condition of anyone's achievement of the good life. That fair lady, faint, prudential, economically rational heart never won. It is a testament to the perceptiveness of our ancestors that that fact did not escape their view.

Appendix

Appendix

SENSES OF "BLAME"

An integral element in the discussion in Chapter 1 of the requirements for entry in the moral community was an account of responsibility ascriptions. Two types of such ascriptions were distilled and it was remarked that a study of the corresponding senses of "blame" would support and illuminate the distinctions drawn. Blaming is, of course, one of the most common ways by which we indicate we are holding someone responsible for something. This appendix provides an analysis of the concept of blame by way of a study of the different senses that "blame" has in ordinary discourse.

A second reason for including this study as an appendix is that it provides a further justification for the claim made in the Preface that the imperialist view of morality is in error in interpreting its scope. Many episodes of genuine full-blooded blaming significantly are not grounded in moral judgment or based on moral principles.

I

The following sentence I take to be an ordinary, if not typical, example of the use of blaming expressions and a significant index to the concept of blame and our practices of blaming.

(S) "Charles Manson is to blame for the Tate/LaBianca murders, but he cannot be blamed, even though we do blame him."

On first reading, S is confusing. It may even sound contradictory. If he is to blame and he is blamed, then why can he not be blamed? S is, however, not only not contradictory, it is perfectly unexceptionable.

Separate the three distinct component phrases of S:

(S^1) Charles Manson is to blame for the Tate/LaBianca murders

(S^2) He cannot be blamed for the T/L murders

(S^3) Even though we do blame him for the T/L murders.

Designate the "blame" term in each phrase for reference:

(S^1) Charles Manson is to blame (B^1) for the Tate/LaBianca murders

(S^2) He cannot be blamed (B^2) for the T/L murders

(S^3) Even though we do blame (B^3) him for the T/L murders.

I propose to examine the uses of "blame," B^1, B^2, and B^3, as exemplified in S^1, S^2, and S^3. For reasons that should become clear, I shall begin with the sense of "blame" labeled B^3.

S^3 is a report that we (some of us or the communal "we") blame Charles Manson for the Tate/LaBianca murders. But what is this blaming? What have we done to Manson when we have blamed him? Has anything been done *to* Manson at all? I can blame Manson for the T/L murders although I have never met him, never talked to him. I cannot reprimand, reprove, reproach, or scold Manson if I have never met him or talked to him. My blaming Manson may have no effect on him whatever. If I (or "we" as in the example) have done nothing to Manson when I have blamed him, how is Manson involved in my act of blaming? "Blame" is a two-place predicate. We blame X for y. We "put the blame for y on S," as the old song about Mame goes. But we do not blame *to*.

"Blame" in many respects is different from "guilt." One is guilty *of*, not guilty *for*. To be guilty is to be in trespass of a specifiable code or system of rules. In some instances "X is guilty of y" entails that "X is to blame for y," and that is the intent of much of the criminal law; but that entailment does not hold in every case and is especially weak in cases where the assessment of guilt is not strictly a legal one, such as violations of codes and customs of etiquette and dress. It is of further note that only persons can be "guilty of . . .," though all sorts of things may be "to blame for. . . ." The absurdity of medieval animal trials was a product of the misconceived identification of blame with guilt that the legal model tends to foster.

Persons can "accept the blame" for something, even if they are not to blame for it, but whether or not those blamed accept blame, they are still blamed, that is to say that blaming (the speech act) can be complete without reciprocation or acknowledgement. To blame is to speak certain kinds of sentences or phrases, and to do it sincerely is to have certain beliefs and/or attitudes as well. I shall refer to the sentences and phrases we generally use to blame as "blaming animadvertives."

We have in the English language a broad class of phrases and sentences that when used in the normal way have the illocutionary force of expressing the speaker's disapprobation, disfavor, discountenance, and disapproval of, and sometimes anger, disappointment, annoyance, or irritation at/over someone or something, while also having the perlocutionary force of attempting to persuade or convince listeners to assume the same view toward the object of the utterance. I call that class of expressions "animadvertives."[1]

The word "blame" is rooted in the Greek $\beta\lambda\alpha\sigma\phi\eta\mu\sigma\varsigma$. It meant something like "evil speaking" or "speaking evil of." Most often, when not used in relation to a divine being, it should be translated "to injure the reputation." Hence "blame" has, etymologically, an animadvertive character. When we use "blame" in the standard way, however, we do more than express an adverse opinion and suggest that others view a person or thing with similar disfavor. In standard blaming utterances, coincident with the speaker's expression of disapprobation and/or disapproval of a person or thing, is his identification of a particular act(s), event(s), or occurrence(s) as untoward or substandard, and the pinning of responsibility for it (them) on that person or thing. In other words, someone sincerely using standard blaming animadvertives is performing *inter alia* at least three illocutionary acts and (generally) a perlocutionary act.

However, when "blame" B^3 is used, it is not animadvertive; it does not blame its object; its use is reportive. Sentences like S^3 are true if utterances of blaming animadversion in reference to the named person or thing have been made; otherwise they are false. There are two different ways of using blaming animadvertives, and the locution "X is to blame for y" is a standard way of expressing both. Reportive sentences containing "blame" (B^3) may be true in regard to one use of "blame" while false in regard to the other use. But, as I hope to show, it is a sufficient condition of sentences of the S^3 type being true that blaming animadvertives of one kind, those incorporating "blame" B^1, have been uttered. I further want to show that blaming animadversions of the second kind, those incorporating "blame" used in the B^2 sense, are higher-order sentences dependent on and from which blaming animadversions of the first kind can be unpacked.

II

Sentences using "blame" in sense B^1 primarily assert the proposition that X (someone or something, the object of B^1) was a cause of an event, action, or occurrence (y) and express the speaker's belief that y ought not to have happened. Anyone saying S^1 ("Charles Manson is to blame for the Tate/LaBianca murders") is, in the first instance, identifying what he believes to be one of the causes of those murders. We do not in practice, however, blame all of those events, acts, actions, things or persons that might legitimately be singled out as the causes of an untoward event, although such causes may indeed legitimately be blamed (B^1) for the event. Imagine, for example, that a waiter has mistakenly set the tables of a convention dining hall with steak knives, even though the menu called for no such cutlery. During a heated conversation at one of the tables, one conventioneer insults another. The insulted individual reaches for a utensil and grabs one of the improperly laid steak knives, which he thereupon jabs into the chest of his insulter, instantly killing him.[2] The waiter's actions might be cited as one of the causes of the insulter's death, and the waiter might be blamed. Had he not mistakenly laid out the steak knives the instrument of death would not have been present, and the insulter might still be alive. By the same token, the knife now lodged in his chest caused the death of the insulter, and there can be little doubt that the insulted conventioneer was a cause of the insulter's death. Someone might even maintain that the insulter was the cause of his own death in that he provoked it. Hence the waiter, the knife, the conventioneer and the dead insulter might all or any one be blamed for the killing.

The plausibility of blaming X is wedded to the assumption of a causal connection between X and a substandard event. A version of J. L. Mackie's analysis of statements that assert a singular causal sequence will make clearer the causal identification aspect of B^1 blaming ascriptions. Using the murder case just cited for the purpose of explanation, let A stand for the waiter's act of placing steak knives on the dinner table, B for the conventioneer's reactions to his insulter, C for the insulter's behavior toward the conventioneer, and D for the consumption of alcoholic beverage by the insulter and the conventioneer. In very rough fashion we might say that the conjunction of A, B, C, and D is a "minimal sufficient condition" of the killing. It surely is not the only conceivable "minimal sufficient condition" of the killing of the insulter by the conventioneer. E will stand for the disjunction of all of the other conceivable sets of minimal sufficient conditions of the events; then (ABCD or E) is a necessary and sufficient condition of the killing. No conjunct of ABCD and none of the conjuncts of all of the disjuncts of E is a sufficient condition, but each is, to use Mackie's term, an INUS condition of the killing.[3] If any conjunct of ABCD were also a conjunct of every set of minimal sufficient conditions (E), then that conjunct would be a necessary condition of the killing. "A is *at least* an INUS condition of the killing" means that the necessary and sufficient condition of the killing has the form of either "ABCD or E" *or* "A or E" (A itself a minimal sufficient condition) *or* "ABCD" (there being only one minimal sufficient condition) or "A" (A the only minimal sufficient condition and thereby a necessary and sufficient condition for the killing). "A was a cause of the killing" should then be understood as the conjunctive assertion that (1) A is at least an INUS condition of the killing, (2) A was present at the time of the killing, (3) the factors, if any, other than A in a set containing A that comprise a minimal sufficient condition were also present, and (4) every disjunct of E that does not have A as a conjunct was not present at the time of the killing. To generalize: if an event is believed (with justification) to be untoward or substandard, then anything that is at least an INUS condition of it, and was present on the occasion of the event, conditions (3) and (4) above having been met, is justifiably to blame (B^1) for the event.

By treating the causal assertion aspect of B^1 blaming in this fashion, the range of the class of things that are blamable is not very limited, allowing the capture of more of the ordinary use of blaming expressions than is to be found in many recent analyses of the concept. We regularly blame inanimate objects ("The battery was to blame for the car not starting"), ideas ("The idea of equality was to blame for civil unrest"), natural phenomena ("Turbulent weather was to blame for the airplane crash"), animals ("The neighbor's dog is to blame for killing my evergreen tree"), young children ("Little Johnny is to blame for breaking that priceless vase"), other adults ("You are to blame for wasting my time") and ourselves ("But I guess that I'm as much to blame as you are"). Because the notion of cause is given in terms of conditions, many of our B^1 ascriptions of blame are directed at the performance or nonperformance of certain acts or the occurrence of certain actions and not at persons: Little Johnny's racing around the room, your story telling, the waiter's placing of the steak knives. In blaming (B^1) persons, the only interesting causal questions are those related to the determination of whether an act was or was not done by that person, or whether he happened to do something, that is, matters of fact. For purposes of B^1 blaming, the distinction between actions and acts is unimportant.

Given the above account of "cause" we may also see how cases may be developed in which many different actions, acts, persons, things, etc., can be justifiably blamed (B^1) for the same untoward event by different speakers and/or by the same speaker when he takes different points of view. An example borrowed from W. I. B. Beveridge's *The Art of Scientific Investigation* (where it served a rather different purpose) may prove illustrative. An outbreak of plague may be blamed by a bacteriologist on the microbe he finds in the blood of its victims, on the microbe-carrying fleas that spread the disease by an entomologist, on rats that escaped an infested ship by an epidemiologist, and on the ship's health officer by the magistrate. Each of the above subjects of B^1 blame ascriptions is at least an INUS condition of the event (the plague) and was present in conjunction with other conjuncts of a minimal sufficient condition for the outbreak. That something is blamed by one speaker and something else by another speaker is but a matter of point of view and office. The only restriction is that it cannot be the case that the bacteriologist justifiably blames X and the entomologist justifiably blames Y and, although X and Y need not be conjuncts of the same minimal sufficient condition of the event in question, if X then not-Y (that the occurrence of X is somehow incompatiable with the occurrence of Y).

An objection might be raised in the form of a counterexample to the case of the waiter. In the example, the waiter's placement of steak knives at table was certainly at least an INUS condition of the killing and, granted that the other conditions were met, was one of the causes of the killing (though surely not a primary one) and by my account is justifiably blamed (B^1) for the killing. Now suppose, it might be suggested, that the menu had called for the setting of steak knives, the waiter acted accordingly, and the killing occurred as previously described. Would we not have to say, given my account, that the waiter's actions were to blame (B^1) for the killing even though any other waiter assigned to set that particular table would have laid those knives? The intuition that motivates this objection is that establishing a causal relationship between an action and an untoward event is somehow insufficient to justify the ascription of blame, unless something was out of the ordinary in regard to the action itself: it was a mistake, an accident, done maliciously, etc. The presence of the knives in the second case was called for by the menu. Conventionally we do not carry our exercise of blaming back to standard or given conditions. To do so would certainly weaken the practical effect of using blaming animadvertives. Nonetheless, the objection misses the major point of B^1 blaming. It is the event, the consequence of a certain set of actions or conditions that is the focus of B^1 blaming. "Blame" (B^1) is occasional. It is not directed toward issues of intention or disposition but often is correctly used even when the blamed party is not believed to be capable of helping what he does, as well as in cases when the blamed party is doing exactly what he might be expected to do. Its use simply does not involve evaluations of intelligence or states of mind. Conventional usage may, in part, be swayed by efficacy when persons are blamed, but efficacy does not govern the meaning of B^1 "blame."

The speaker of such a sentence as S^1 is invoking standards he supposes to be appropriate to the *event* that occasioned the utterance, and he is answering the question, "Who (or what) dunit?"[4] Stress on the assertion of causal responsibility in uses of B^1 "blame" should not mask the fact that the *occasions* of its use are events or occurrences the blamer believes ought not to have happened, that the blamer believes obstruct, defeat, interfere with, or in some negative way affect some human (not necessarily his own) goal, project, interest, standard, or principle.[5] As no questions of capacities, dispositions, or abilities need arise, the "ought implies can" argument does not apply to B^1 blaming.

III

When "blame" is used in the second sense (B^2), the speaker is asserting that the actions of a person (X) were one of the causes of (to B^1 blame for) an event, and that X has no acceptable excuse for his actions, that he is blameworthy; it also expresses the speaker's negative evaluation of the event and the disapprobation with which he views both the event in question and the person (X) whose actions are to blame (B^1) for it. B^2 "blame" is ascribable only to persons. It has the sense of "is to be held responsible," for which there are good lexical grounds. *The Oxford English Dictionary* lists as its fifth definition of "blame": "to lay the blame on, to fix the responsibility on, to make answerable." "To fix the responsibility upon" seems to correspond to B^1 blame, but "to make answerable" is clearly more than B^1. B^1 "blame" is, in large measure, "fixing responsibility for," while B^2 "blame," in the same measure, is "to hold responsible for" or "*make answerable* for."

The etymology of "responsibility" like that of "blame" affords an aid to the task of understanding our blaming practices. "Having a responsibility" meant something like "having a liability to answer." Of course, the home of such a use is a legal one, liability to answer a charge in a court of law or before a tribe or before a monarch. It seems as well to entail the threat of punishment in the case of failure. Ignoring the punishment aspect, and concentrating on what seem to be the important features of responsibility relationships, the following I take to be a reasonable position: (1) "X can hold Y responsible for z" entails (2) "X occupies some position of authority *vis-à-vis* Y as regards z (or $\bar{z}$)." Hence, (1) entails (3) "(X and Y are persons or collectivities and z is either an action or event)." X can hold Y responsible for z only if Y is responsible to X for z (or $\bar{z}$).[6]

"Liability to answer" or "accountability" implies, among other things, both the existence of recognized authority relationships between people and the possession of certain abilities, capacities, and even opportunities by the person deemed accountable. The accountability relationship can only hold between persons (including one type of collectivity[7]). Generally excluded are infants, mental defectives, those suffering some forms of mental illness, and so on. The argument appears to me to be intuitively plausible that for X legitimately to hold Y responsible for something, Y must be responsible to X in the case in question. Surely we would regard as infelicitous an outsider's claim that he was holding Y responsible for doing something. The problem is, of course, to determine what constitutes an outsider. What makes someone an outsider, in a responsibility relationship? We probably will all agree, however, that if X promises Y that he will take him, Y, to dinner and then fails to do so, that it would be inappropriate for a third party, Z, to enter on the scene claiming that he was holding X responsible for not taking Y to dinner. Unless he is a delegated agent of Y, it is none of his business. Similarly, if X's job in a factory is to sweep the floors and he does not do so in one room on a particular day and if Z is not his superior nor even employed at the factory nor ever has any dealings with the factory, Z has no business holding X responsible for his sloppy work. We would be quite uncertain as to how to understand any statement he might make that he was holding him responsible. It is a mark of moral responsibility issues, however, that no persons are outsiders. For that reason, we cannot construe the notion of "responsible to" in narrow terms. A person may in some instances be responsible to all of his fellow persons for doing or refraining from doing certain things. I shall proceed on the assumption that the argument is not *prima facie* defective nor counterintuitive. Its interest to the present topic is that it yields the following: Unless the speaker of a sentence using B^2 "blame" occupies a place of some authority (very broadly defined) regarding the subject of the blame predicate in the matter in question, the utterance will "misfire";[8] B^2 "blame" is appropriately ascribable only to persons not because such persons are in possession of some occult characteristic identified by "responsible" (as in "He is a responsible lad"), but because such persons can enter into and participate fully within "responsibility" relationships with each other.

The ascription of B^2 blame amounts to the assertion by a serious speaker of a conjunctive proposition about a person (or certain type of collectivity), the first element of which identifies his actions as one of the causes of an untoward event; the second asserts that he is liable to account to some extent for it, that exculpating excuses are not acceptable in his case. When, however, a person is excused, it is not so much his actions as the person himself that is the focus of concern. We may excuse the waiter (in our example), not his actions of placing the wrong knives at table and hence of supplying the instrument of death. His actions remain incorrect, but he is relieved of the liability to account. He did it by mistake or absentmindedly, perhaps having been troubled by family matters. His actions are to blame (B^1) for the presence of the weapon, but he is not to be blamed (B^2). In B^2 blaming we are to some extent, if not exclusively, concerned with, in Hume's words, "the quality of character from which the action proceeded."[9]

What one implies when he blames (B^2) a person is that at least one course of action was realistically available to the blamed person that, had he chosen it, would have altered his participation; although he still might have been at least an INUS condition of the event in question, that would not have been owing to his own decision not to take an alternative course. Excuses generally fit into one of two categories: "It was an accident, it was a mistake, it happened inadvertently, he made me do it, I was provoked," and so on, are mitigatory; while insanity, mental defectiveness, etc., are exculpatory.[10] Mitigatory excuses do not attempt to remove the subject from the class of those able to enter into responsibility relationships. They are occasional, attempting to shut the "could have" door, in that case at that time, by classifying the action in some way as unintentional. Exculpatory excuses are dispositional. They tend to slam, lock, and bolt the door in the aftermath of something having gone wrong, to lock the door on the discussion of what other courses of action the subject could have taken.

If it is said of Charles Manson that "He could have prevented the Tate/LaBianca murders," we can infer that the sincere speaker believes that Manson did not prevent the murders, that Manson possessed a certain amount of power relative to the situation, and that Manson had opportunity to alter the situation had he chosen (he was not a bystander; he was the leader of the hippie commune that perpetrated the crime). "Manson could have prevented the Tate/LaBianca murders" makes implicit reference to Manson's actual abilities, capabilities, and opportunities, and perhaps even to his state of mind. It is inappropriate to say it, unless one could specify a particular course of action that was in Manson's *province* so that had he made such a choice, the murders would not have occurred.

There is a sense of "could have" that means "there were conceivable alternative courses of action" (the logical sense), but it is unrelated to blame B^2, if only because it effectively paints the blamed person out of the picture. The "could have" implicit in B^2 ascriptions is a "factual could have" that when "fleshed in" defines what I have called the blamed person's province in the matter in question.

The differences between these senses of "could have" may be sharpened by the device of talking in terms of possible worlds. "X could have done y" might mean that in some possible world the entity rigidly designated by "X" does y. For example, imagine a possible world in which the person called "Manson" rescues Sharon Tate from an attempt by someone else to murder her. What Manson does in any possible world is limited only by logical parameters so long as the entity therein designated by "Manson" still has the "essential properties" of being Manson, for example, having been a product of the sexual union of Manson's mother and father. We are able to imagine possible worlds in which the entity designated by "Manson" does not commit petty crimes in his youth and does not spend time in prison and never meets Susan Adkins, and so on. It is in the actual world that Manson commits his crimes. What Manson can do in that world, however, is limited by more than logical parameters. Factual parameters by and large determine his province in the actual world, for example, that he has certain abilities, capacities, and background. What Manson could have done in the actual world cannot be freely stipulated. Of course Kripke does not allow free stipulation across possible worlds either. A thing cannot do something in a possible world if it would have to have properties to do it that it is not possible for it to have and still retain its essential identifying properties.

The transworld sense of "could have" suggests a rather important related point about transworld identity. It might seem that the entity designated by "Manson" in the possible world in which "Manson saved Sharon Tate from an attempt by someone else to murder her" can only be identical to the entity designated by "Manson" in the actual world under conditions of factual stipulation limitation. Insofar as no spatial/temporal continuity could, by definition, ever be established between "actual Manson" (AM) and "possible Manson" (PM), it would seem that, to show that AM = PM, it must be shown that AM's abilities and capacities are such that saving Sharon Tate from an attempt by someone else to murder her is something he actually could do. If PM must have had certain kinds of training, a certain sort of upbringing, must not have cultivated certain values, and so on, and those things are all incompatible on factual grounds with being AM, then it would seem to follow that AM cannot be identical to PM. Putting the argument a bit differently: AM = PM if and only if AM could become PM, given AM's abilities, capacities, etc. AM can only do that if doing what PM does is factually possible for AM in the actual world (excluding the possibility of a miracle brain exchange or memory exchange). Logical parameters on "could have," it would then be argued, are irrelevant to the identity issue. Failing to have a bodily continuity identification of AM with PM, stipulation of acts of PM that are counterfactual to AM's acts takes us nowhere toward understanding what AM could have done in any relevant sense. PM does everything we stipulate PM does because PM≠AM.

It is one thing to ponder what AM would have been like, the argument may continue, if he had had a different upbringing, developed a different character, and learned other skills in the actual world; it is another to say that he could have done the sort of things that only those with certain capacities and abilities do. Suppose that AM (that is in the actual world) were to suddenly undergo a change of such a magnitude that everything stipulated of PM is now true of AM, and nothing that is now actually true of AM remains so, except that he has the same body. We would be startled, to say the least, but continuous bodily continuity would seemingly provide a sufficient ground to judge that $AM = AM^1$ (AM^1 being the actual Manson as changed). Such a criterion, however, would seem to be absent in transworld identification, so the identity of AM and PM seems to be lost, and hence what it is possible to say about PM is irrelevant if we are concerned with AM's province.

This argument does not say that we cannot usefully stipulate a possible world in which Manson does not engineer the killings of Sharon Tate and the others. He might very well have killed Raquel Welch, or Richard Nixon or no one. What it says is that if we intend to stipulate a possible world in which it is Manson who does something, then we must have grounds for saying that the Manson who is in that world is Manson. There being no way of doing so by use of bodily continuity criteria (after all, as Kripke frequently reminds us, a possible world has no geographic location), we seem to have to fall back on capacity and capability criteria; there logical parameters must give way to factual ones, rendering the possible world's analysis of "could have" useless. But this is not really so. Kripke[11] maintains that the essence of a human being is his zygote. Hence AM can be PM if AM's zygote could have existed in the possible world of PM or, better still, $AM = PM$ only if the possible world that contains PM contains AM's zygote. The existence of that particular zygote is, of course, dependent on the sexual union of a particular set of parents who have, geneticists tell us, a particular set of natural abilities, a number of which are genetically transmitted to their offspring and hence are in some sense present in the zygote. The particular set of natural abilities of any human being that develops from the zygote's genetic structure contributes, in no small way, to the creation of the boundaries of the "factual could haves" of that human being in the actual world. By genetic engineering, however, actual natural traits and capacities, apparently even including sex, can be altered after fertilization. Hence, it makes sense to say that in some possible world the zygote could have become a human being so different from what it actually became that it is a female not a male, with blue eyes not green, five feet tall not six, a genius not a blithering idiot though it is still transworld identical to the human being in the actual world who is a green-eyed, six-foot tall, male blithering idiot. Transworld identity then provides no answer to the important questions for the justification of B^2 blame; whether a person could have done something other than he did. In getting the kind of answer we need, we must amass actual world (factual) data about that person's province. We can only do that if we can determine the factual parameters on his behavior and to do that we need, in part, a criterion of actual world reidentification. By my account such a criterion primarily must be bodily continuity. Should that fail, we can only fall back on a capacities and capabilities criterion. Furthermore, "He could have done . . ." will be true only if a number of conditions regarding his rather peculiar actual capacities, opportunities, and capabilities are satisfied and not true if conditions favorable to his doing it would have been a matter of chance or luck.

As B^2 "blame" is directed at the agent and not the acts of the person, no reevaluation of his acts or their consequences is involved in determining whether B^2 blame is justified, whether he should be held responsible or accountable for the event of which he was a cause.

IV

This analysis of the senses of "blame" has made no reference to peculiarly MORAL concerns. No attempt has been made to distinguish moral from nonMORAL blame. Many philosophers have identified "MORAL blame" with what I have called the second sense of "blame," and some, such as G. P. Henderson[12], argue that the only important use of blame in the case of persons is a MORAL one. Henderson writes: "If we 'blame' John Fowler at all, it appears, we do so in a full-blooded moral way. . . . the notion of non-moral blame ascribed to persons remains, it would seem, suspect. . . . As directed to persons, then, moral blame alone comes naturally. . . ."[13] Henderson's view, however, is wrongheaded, a symptom of "moral imperialism" that blurs an important distinction that may be drawn along lines similar to those Aristotle uses to distinguish between intellectual and moral virtue.[14] Human beings, Aristotle pointed out, may fail in the intellectual arena as well as the moral one, and may be blameworthy for such failures. Put simply, not every failure for which a human being may be held responsible or to B^2 blame is a MORAL failure; some are failures of office and understanding; some are failures in practical reasoning. Consider, for example, the following tale.

On a remote island lives a tribe of cannibals, possibly Melville's vicious Typees. Head chefs, junior chefs, and apprentices are selected with great care and are highly regarded by the tribe. The Supreme Chef had gained that lofty position by introducing to the menu an entree in which the whole tribe delighted: white Anglican missionary. The proper selection, preparation, and cooking of such missionaries had become the mark of a head chef.

On one occasion the tribe welcomed a group of white missionaries to their shores. After ceremonial greetings the chief of the tribe abruptly ordered the startled missionaries bound and imprisoned. Shortly thereafter a head chef arrived to select the main course for the evening meal. Each missonary was stripped to his crucifix and thoroughly inspected by the head chef. After a long period of apparent deliberation, the head chef pointed to one of the missionaries. . . .

Almost on first bite it was widely remarked at table that the meat was stringy and tough. The tribal chief even suffered a bit of a dyspeptic stomach. The head chef was confronted: "You're to blame for this, you should have known better. You could have been more discerning in making your choice. Have you not been instructed in the finer points of selection? He tasted more like a Lutheran than an Anglican." The head chef was thereupon himself bound and imprisoned with the others, who, as he discovered, were members of an ecumenical expedition. By the time night darkened the prison hut he had struck up a friendship with all of the missionaries save one. He simply could not bring himself to so much as nod at the Anglican in the group.

There seem to me to be no reasons whatever for denying that the head chef is justifiably to blame (B^2) for his failure in office, although there seems not to be a morsel of MORAL issue about it. It is a culinary matter.[15] The facts are that the chef had the training and the competence to make a proper selection; after all, he was a head chef. Furthermore, an Anglican was available for the choosing. Whatever excuse the head chef might have offered would, given the circumstances, be unsupportable. Had he, for example, pleaded mistake, that given his office would not have been accepted.

What then is MORAL sense of "blame?" There simply is no special MORAL *sense* of "blame," though "blame" B^1 and B^2 is often put to a MORAL use when, in the case of persons, the act or event that is the occasion for blaming someone is identified as or is believed to be incompatible with (in the sense of having a strong potential deteriorative effect on) the human environment believed to be necessary for members of the community to live worthwhile lives.

In summary, I have attempted to show that at least three distinct senses of the word "blame" exist, as revealed in common usage and distinguishable also in terms of the grounds for ascription of each to persons. I have tried to show why there is nothing necessarily contradictory in saying of a person that he is both to blame for y and not to be blamed for y and that he is blameworthy for y. Ascriptions of B^3 blameworthiness are parasitic on ascriptions of B^1 "blame," while saying of a person that he is (or was) blamed for y is not to ascribe blame at all.

We may conclude that we cannot learn much about MORALITY from a study that focuses primarily on our blaming practices and the senses of the word "blame," if that study is carried on in isolation from an attempt to understand the distinguishing marks of moral judgments and principles. We characteristically blame people for a variety of non-MORAL reasons, based on a number of practical non-MORAL judgments, and we do so in a "full-blooded" way—even though in most of those cases we do not pass MORAL judgment. It is simply not true, as some philosophers would have us believe, that all judgments of blameworthiness are if not evident then disguised MORAL judgments. We often fail and are blamed for our failures at tasks we set ourselves to perform, and MORALITY often remains mute in the face of those failures.

Notes

Notes

Preface

1. Arthur Schopenhauer, *On the Basis of Morality*, trans. by E. F. J. Payne (Indianapolis: Bobbs-Merrill Co. Inc., 1965), p. 39.

2. *Ibid.*, "Judicium," p. 216.

3. For an excellent collection that includes seminal works by Richard Price, Frances Hutcheson, and John Balguy, see D. D. Raphael, *British Moralists 1650–1800*, Volumes I and II (Oxford: Clarendon Press, 1969).

4. Schopenhauer, p. 121.

5. See for examples, Richard Taylor, *Good and Evil* (London: Collier Macmillan Publishers, 1970); and J.L. Mackie, *Ethics: Inventing Right and Wrong* (Harmondsworth, Middlesex, England: Penguin Books, 1977).

6. Mackie, p. 18.

7. Baron de Montesquieu, *The Spirit of the Laws*, trans. by T. Nugent (New York: Hafner Press, 1949), p. 293.

8. *Ibid.*, p. 115.

9. Robert Baum and James Randell, *Ethical Arguments for Analysis* (New York: Holt, Rinehart and Winston, Inc., 1973).

10. R. M. Hare, "Nothing Matters" in *Applications of Moral Philosophy* (London: The Macmillan Press, 1972), pp. 32–47.

11. William H. Prescott, *History of the Conquest of Peru* (London: Dent & Sons, Ltd., 1847).

12. *Ibid.*, p. 103.

13. See Bertrand Russell's Chapter III "Incomplete Symbols" in A. N. Whitehead and Bertrand Russell, *Principia Mathematica* (Cambridge: Cambridge University Press, 1910); also for a good account of scope problems, see Arthur F. Smullyan, "Modality and Description," *The Journal of Symbolic Logic* 1948, pp. 31–37.

14. W. V. Quine, *Methods of Logic* (New York: Holt, Rinehart and Winston, Third edition 1972), p. 166.

15. W. V. Quine, "Logic as a Source of Syntactical Insights," *The Ways of Paradox* (Cambridge: Harvard University Press, 1966, 1976), pp. 44-49.

16. See *Ibid.* for a good account of this. Also see W. V. Quine, *Word and Object* (Cambridge: MIT Press, 1960), p. 138 ff.

17. *Ibid.*

18. R. M. Hare, *Freedom and Reason* (Oxford: Oxford University Press, 1963), p. 119.

19. Richard Robinson, "Ought and Ought Not," *Philosophy*, July 1971, pp. 193-202.

20. *Ibid.*, p. 201.

21. See Hector-Neri Castañeda, *The Structure of Morality* (Springfield: Thomas, 1974), especially Chapter 7.

22. H. A. Prichard, "Moral Obligation" in *Moral Obligation and Duty & Interest* (Oxford: Oxford University Press, 1968), pp. 89-95.

23. R. M. Hare, *The Language of Morals* (Oxford: Oxford University Press, 1952).

24. Mackie, p. 106.

Chapter 1

1. John Locke, *An Essay Concerning Human Understanding* (1690), Book II, Chapter XXVII.

2. See Peter A. French, "The Corporation as a Moral Person," *American Philosophical Quarterly*, Volume 16, Number 3, July 1979, pp. 207-215.

3. See John Rawls, *A Theory of Justice* (Cambridge: Harvard University Press, 1971).

4. J. L. Austin, "Three Ways of Spilling Ink," in *Philosophical Papers* (Oxford: Oxford University Press 1970 ed.), p. 273.

5. Donald Davidson, "Agency," in *Agent, Action, and Reason*, ed. by Binkley, Bronaugh, Marras (Toronto: University of Toronto Press, 1971), p. 4.

6. Alan White, *The Philosophy of Action* (Oxford: Oxford University Press, 1968), p. 2.

7. See Nicholas Rescher, "On the Characterization of Actions" in *The Nature of Human Action*, ed. Myles Brand (Glenview, IL: Scott, Foresman and Company, 1970), pp. 247-254.

8. See W. J. Sinclair, *Semmelweis: His Life and His Doctrine* (Manchester: Manchester University Press, 1909). The example was used with great success by Carl Hempel in *Philosophy of Natural Science* (Englewood Cliffs, NJ: Prentice Hall, 1966), Chapter 2.

9. Locke, Book II, Chapter XXI, #72.

10. Davidson, p. 7.

11. See James Cornman, "Comments on Davidson's 'Agency,' " in *Agent, Action, and Reason*, ed. by Binkley, Bronaugh, Marras (Toronto: Toronto University Press, 1971), pp. 26-37.

12. The example is used by Davidson.

13. A number of confusions have crept into current theories on "seeing" that lead to the incorrect view that seeing is an act, or the equally incorrect view that a sentence of the form "X saw Y" records an achievement of the subject. In the justifiably popular works of Hanson, that view is expressed as a "Seeing an object x is to see that it may behave in the ways we believe xs do behave. In effect, this view equates "seeing" with "seeing that," and it further seems to take "seeing that" as equivalent to "observe." A corollary of Hanson's view is that "seeing is . . . an amalgam of . . . pictures and language." [N. R. Hanson, *Patterns of Discovery* (Cambridge: Cambridge University Press, 1958), p. 22] Surely this is an attractive theory in that it seems to alleviate many of the problems of talking about scientific knowledge as arising from sensation, memory, association,

interpretation, and comparison. Unfortunately, Hanson's theory also blurs important distinctions between the terms "seeing," "seeing that," "observing," and "observing that." When one is reminded of those distinctions, it becomes obvious that Hanson's theory is false.

Consider the following example, which is similar to many of Hanson's examples: A child and an astronomer alternately look through a telescope that the astronomer has pointed in a particular direction. The child reports seeing only a white blotch in a black background. The astronomer tells the child, "That is a nebula." The child had known nothing previously of nebulae. Given Hanson's theory, it would seem that the child cannot be said to have seen a nebula; the astronomer and the child must have seen different things when they looked through the telescope at the heavens. If the child were to report to his mother, "I saw a nebula today," he would be lying. But that view offends our sensibilities. I am inclined to say that the child *did* see a nebula, even if he did not see that it was a gaseous mass, etc.

"Seeing that" usually indicates "seeing," though not always, but in "seeing" there is not a "seeing that" to be unpacked. It is true that the child cannot see that the blotch of white is a nebula; he would have to know about nebulae. Yet the child certainly can see the nebula. "Seeing" is not, contrary to Hanson's view, theory-laden.

What can we say of "seeing"? In the first place, "seeing" seems closer to "laying eyes on" than to "knowing that," or "noticing." "I saw the nebula" does not entail that at the time I saw it I was able to describe it correctly, or that I can describe it now. Suppose I were to say that I saw Laurence Olivier in a play last week. Although I might be able to describe correctly what Olivier looked like costumed and made up for the part, I cannot describe accurately what Olivier looks like. I might not, as a matter of fact, be able to describe correctly his appearance in the play. It might have happened that someone told me after the play that I had just seen one of the world's greatest actors, but that he had played a minor role. Try as I might, I cannot recall what he looked like. Yet I would not be lying were I to tell my grandchildren that on one occasion I saw the great Laurence Olivier in a play. Here another aspect of "seeing" is revealed. I need not be able to identify correctly what I see. Suppose that I were to say that I saw Olivier play the part of the bishop. My learned friend, however, tells me I could not have seen that. What I saw was Olivier playing the king.

I saw Laurence Olivier, even though Laurence Olivier did not appear to me to be Laurence Olivier, nor did he appear as Laurence Olivier normally does (what Laurence Olivier looks like minus make-up is a mystery to me). Yet it cannot be said that I did not see Olivier. I could not have watched the play and failed to see him. What cannot be said, of course, is that I saw Laurence Olivier play the king.

I may *see* someone kidnap a child without *seeing that* he is kidnapping a child. Someone might say of me, "He saw the kidnapping take place," but surely that does not entail that I knew a kidnapping was taking place. I might, however, be an excellent witness for the state when the kidnapper is apprehended. I might on examination admit that I saw a man usher a child into an automobile. I might truthfully say that I saw the child struggle with the man. Of course, if I never were to find out about the kidnapping, someone else could say, but I never would say, that I had seen the kidnapping. At the risk of overburdening this example, it is worth mentioning that the kidnapper might have seen me and that he could truthfully say, "He saw the kidnapping," even though I would not say I saw it. A common plot in television and movie scripts has the criminal attempting to eliminate a witness who does not even know he is a witness nor of what he is a witness. The criminal's concern is well-grounded, because one can see something even though he does not see that it is what it is. Similarly, though I saw a white ball that looked red, I would have to say "I see a red ball," unless I had the requisite knowledge to see that the ball is really white. Only then could I say "I see a white ball that looks red."

Ryle and Rescher claim that a statement such as "I see the nebula" records a success, that the verb "to see" is an achievement word in a group including also "to hear," "to taste," "to smell." But what is the achievement in seeing? When the child sees the nebula, what has he achieved? Ryle suggests that the achievement in seeing is noticing. But that cannot be the case.

Suppose that I have accidentally dropped a straight pin. I know that it must be on the rug by my chair somewhere, but I have looked and looked for it. I must find it or one of my children will surely find it in his foot. You glance over my shoulder, bend down, pick it up, and hand it to me. I never saw it there. "Saw" in this context does seem to mean "noticed." But I also saw the rug while I was looking for the pin, though I could not be said to have noticed the rug. Of course, if the rug had suddenly risen, as Aladdin's rugs did, I surely would have noticed it. To notice anything is to be disposed to say, "I see it," though one can see it without noticing it. Had the rug been painted with some magic invisibilizing paint or had I been blindfolded before entering the room it could be said that I did not see the rug, but only in such drastic circumstances would one be able to say that. As it happens, most of the things we see are not worth noticing. In short, "to see" is not an achievement in the sense that "to notice" is. Failure to see the straight pin is just not seeing it. If the child fails to see the nebula he is not necessarily failing to notice it. Instead he is just not seeing it.

Now suppose that the child is led to the telescope and asked, "What do you see?" He reports that he sees flickering lights or white dots or masses of light. In effect, he starts to notice. Often the order, "Tell me what you see," starts one noticing, but it does not start one seeing. One cannot be taught to see, nor does one learn to see. One sees or one does not see. A child may be outfitted with new glasses to improve his seeing, but he cannot learn seeing as he can walking, writing, or subtraction.

"Seeing that," however, does seem to be to some extent, as Hanson would have it, theory-laden. The child cannot see that this patch of white is a nebula unless he possesses a good deal of knowledge about astronomy. I cannot see that the theatrical king is Laurence Olivier unless I know what Sir Laurence looks like or, failing that, unless I have some knowledge of Olivier's acting techniques, the special marks he brings to his performance. Unless I had such knowledge or had read his name on the program, it would be wrong of me to say, "I see that the king is Laurence Olivier."

One usage of "I see that" does not seem on first examination to be knowledge-dependent. Suppose that after glancing at the program of the play I announce, "I see that Laurence Olivier is to play the king," and showing my abysmal lack of knowledge regarding the theatre, I add, "Who is he? I do hope that he can carry off the part." Of course I must know a number of things even to see that Olivier is playing the king. One might see Olivier playing the king without knowing that Olivier is an actor, or that he is watching a play, or that actors only assume roles on the stage, or that the program announces the cast and their roles. But one must know all of those things to see that Olivier is to be the king.

Further, many uses of "seeing that" do not involve seeing at all. I might at the dinner table, for example, notice that the salad has a strong taste of vinegar. Since I know from past experience that Jones always puts too much vinegar in the salad dressing, I might remark, "I see that Jones is cooking tonight."

"See that" and its cognates as well as "observe that" and its cognates do function very much like "know that." They are epistemic notions. It would be absurd to append the expression "but I might be wrong" to such expressions. We would not know how to take someone's statement, "I see that the glass will break when I hit it with a hammer, but I might be wrong." The reason for this is that in every "I see that . . ." an "I know that" is to be unpacked. Hanson argues that to "see that" one must know something. I want to argue that when saying that one "sees that x" one is also claiming to "know that x." This is especially clear in the past tense usage. When I say "I saw that x is y," I am both giving others my authority for saying that x is y and reporting on the way I came to know it. Consequently others hearing my utterance of "I saw that x is y" are entitled to say that they saw that x was y, though they might say that because of my utterance, they had come to see that x is y for themselves. "I saw that x is y" and "I see that x is y" offer the speaker's guarantee (his transmissible authority) as well as his support for his guarantee that x is y.

When the child looks through the telescope he sees the nebula, but he does not know anything of what he sees. Suppose then that he asks the astronomer what he (the astronomer) saw when he looked through the telescope and the astronomer answers, "I saw a nebula." The child asks, "How do you know that it is a nebula?" The astonomer, realizing that the child has not the training to understand a technical explanation of the subtle signs of a nebula, responds that he saw that the white blotch at which he was looking was a nebula. If asked, "How do you know that?" the child may cite the astronomer's words: "The great astronomer saw that it was nebula." Of course the astronomer might have been wrong. He may not even be a very good astronomer. But all that it would show if he were wrong is that he should not have uttered the sentence prefixed by "I see that. . . ." It would have been better for him to have said something like "I think I see" or "It might be," or "That could be," or "I believe we are looking at," or "It is my opinion that it is," or "It looks like," etc.

I argued earlier that seeing is not learned. "Seeing that" is, as Hanson rightly points out, intimately related to language use and theory. I offer no major objections to the view that learning a language is learning to see that this is happening, did happen, or will happen. It should be pointed out, however, that one is not trained to "see that," although one is trained "to observe." We learn to "see that" without being taught to "see that"— which is not to say that we are self taught. We can, in one sense, be taught to "see that" in that we can be taught a more sophisticated dialect of our native language. Astronomy students are taught that certain objects are nebulae. But we are not taught either all that we "see that" or the way (whatever that might be) or the rules (whatever they are) of "seeing that."

14. Joel Feinberg, *Doing and Deserving* (Princeton: Princeton University Press, 1970), p. 134.

15. Davidson, p. 17.

16. For example, Jaegwon Kim and Alvin Goldman.

17. Hector-Neri Castañeda, *Thinking and Doing* (Dordrecht, The Netherlands: Reidel Publishing Co., 1975), Chapter 12.

18. *Ibid.*

19. *Ibid.*

20. J. L. Austin, "Three Ways of Spilling Ink," in *Philosophical Papers* (Oxford: Oxford University Press, 1961), p. 275.

21. I have in mind those philosophers who defend a theory of agent causality. See for example Alvin Goldman, *A Theory of Human Action* (Princeton: Princeton University Press, 1970), especially pp. 80–85.

22. Davidson, p. 15.

23. Frederick I. Dretske, "Referring to Events," *Midwest Studies in Philosophy*, Volume II, 1977.

24. Donald Davidson, "Actions, Reasons, and Causes," *The Journal of Philosophy* 60, No. 23 (November 7, 1963), pp. 685-700. Reprinted in Brand, op. cit., pp. 67-79 (references will be made to the Brand book), pp. 74-75.

25. A similar argument is used for different purposes by Stuart Hampshire in *Freedom of Mind and Other Essays* (Oxford: Oxford University Press, 1972).

26. Davidson, "Actions, Reasons, and Causes," p. 79.

27. F. H. Bradley, *Ethical Studies* (Oxford: Clarendon Press, 1876), Essay I.

28. Locke, Book II, Chapter XXVII, #26.

29. J. L. Mackie, *Problems from Locke* (Oxford: Oxford University Press, 1976), p. 177.

30. Locke, Book II, Chapter XXVII, #26.

31. Bradley, Essay I, p. 5.

32. Aristotle, *Nichomachean Ethics*, trans. by M. Ostwald (Indianapolis: Bobbs-Merrill, 1962), p. 55.

33. *Ibid.*

34. J. L. Mackie, *Ethics: Inventing Right and Wrong* (Harmondsworth, Middlesex, England: Penguin Books, 1977), p. 204.

35. Mackie defends a similar principle which he calls the "straight rule of responsibility." *Ibid.*, pp. 208-215.

36. *Ibid.*

37. Bradley, Essay I.

38. *Ibid.*

39. "Types of Collectivities and Blame," *The Personalist*, Spring 1975.

40. Leonard and Goodman, "The Calculus of Individuals and Its Uses," *The Journal of Symbolic Logic*, Volume 5, Number 2, June 1940, pp. 45-55.

41. "The Corporate Moral Agency," in Bowie and Beauchamp (eds.) *Ethical Theory and Business* (Englewood Cliffs, NJ: Prentice Hall, 1978). Also see P. A. French "The Corporation as a Moral Agent," *American Philosophical Quarterly*.

42. Rawls, p. 146.

43. John Rawls, "Justice as Reciprocity" in John Stuart Mill, *Utilitarianism*, ed. by Samuel Gorovitz (Indianapolis, 1971), pp. 244-45.

44. See R. S. Downie and E. Telfer, *Respect For Persons* (New York: Schocken Books, 1970); S. I. Benn, "Privacy, Freedom and Respect for Persons," *Nomos*, XIII; David Gauthier, *Practical Reasoning* (Oxford: Oxford University Press, 1963), pp. 119-120; B. A. O. Williams, "The Idea of Equality," in *Moral Concepts*, ed. by Joel Feinberg (Oxford: Oxford University Press, 1970); Carl Cranor, "Toward a Theory of Respect for Persons," *American Philosophical Quarterly*, Volume 12, Number 4, October 1975, pp. 309-319.

45. Immanuel Kant, *The Doctrine of Virtue*, trans. by Mary J. Gregor (Philadelphia: University of Pennsylvania Press, 1964), p. 99.

46. Pepita Haezrahi, "The Concept of Man as End-in-Himself," *Kant-Studien*, Band 53, 1962.

47. Cranor, p. 309.

48. Kant, *The Doctrine of Virtue*, p. 117.

Chapter 2

1. Seán O'Faoláin, *Finest Stories* (New York: Bantam Books, 1959), p. 181.

2. Julius Kovesi, "Against the Ritual of 'Is' and 'Ought'," *Midwest Studies in Philosophy*, Volume III (1978), p. 14.

3. John Locke, *An Essay Concerning Human Understanding*, (1690) Book II, Chapter XXII, #2.

4. *Ibid.*

5. *Ibid.*, #2.

6. *Ibid.*, #9.

7. Julius Kovesi, *Moral Notions* (London: Routledge & Kegan Paul, 1967), Chapter 1.

8. Locke, *Essay*, #4.

9. *Ibid.*, #9.

10. R. M. Hare, *The Language of Morals* (Oxford: Oxford University Press, 1952), p. 80 f.

11. Jaegwon Kim, "Supervenience and Nomological Incommensurables," *American Philosophical Quarterly* Volume 15, Number 2, April 1978, p. 149-156.

12. *Ibid.*, p. 150.

13. Actually in the world of perception we don't even find this—but that complication need not concern us here.

14. J. L. Mackie, *Problems from Locke* (Oxford: Oxford University Press, 1976), p. 91.

15. Saul Kripke, "Identity and Necessity" in *Identity and Individuation*, ed. Milton Munitz (New York: New York University Press, 1971), p. 160 ff.

16. *Ibid.*; and "Naming and Necessity" in *Semantics of Natural Language*, ed. by D. Davidson and G. Harman (Dortrecht, The Netherlands: Reidel, 1972), pp. 253-355, p. 319 f.

17. Locke, *Essay* III, Chapter VI, pp. 44-51.

18. *Ibid.*

19. Mackie, *Problems from Locke*, p. 93.

20. See Kovesi, *Moral Notions*, Chapter I.

21. J. L. Mackie, *Ethics: Inventing Right and Wrong* (Harmondsworth, Middlesex, England: Penguin Books, 1977), Chapter 1, esp. pp. 48-49.

22. Locke, *Essay* I, Chapter III, #10.

23. *Ibid.*, Book IV, Chapter IV, #6.

24. *Ibid.*, #8.

25. Kovesi, *Moral Notions*, pp. 26-27, 103, 109, 124.

26. Locke, *Essay*, Book IV, Chapter IV, #9.

27. Gilbert Harman, *The Nature of Morality* (Oxford: Oxford University Press, 1977), p. 106.

28. Hector-Neri Castañeda, *The Structure of Morality* (Springfield: Thomas, 1974), p. 13. Castañeda includes more in the euergetical dimension than I do. I would, for example, not include, "Do not kill a man except in self-defense" as an euergetical requirement, but as a moral one (see p. 215 of *The Structure of Morality*). I would, however, include Casteñeda's Eu. 2-Eu. 8 injunctions in euergetics (Castañeda p. 216); see chapter VII.

29. *Ibid.*, p. 214.

30. *Ibid.*, p. 217.

31. As for example W. D. Ross does in *The Right and the Good* (Oxford: Clarendon Press, Oxford University Press, 1930).

32. See for a similar view: Kovesi, *Moral Notions*.

33. Mackie, *Ethics*, p. 106.

34. G. J. Warnock, *The Object of Morality* (London: Metheun & Co. Ltd., 1971), p. 26.

35. Plato, *Protagoras*, especially the "Great Speech" of Protagoras.
36. Hobbes, *Leviathan* (1651).
37. *Ibid.*
38. Montesquieu, *The Spirit of the Laws*, trans. by Thomas Nugent (New York: Hafner Publishing Co., 1949), Book I, p. 2.
39. *Ibid., Book* I, 2., p. 4.
40. See for example George Edgin Pugh, *The Biological Origin of Human Values* (New York: Basic Books, 1977), Chapter 11.
41. Montesquieu, *Book* I, 3., p. 5.
42. *Ibid., Book* I, 3., p. 6.
43. Warnock, p. 17.

Chapter 3

1. J. L. Mackie, *Ethics: Inventing Right and Wrong* (Harmondsworth, Middlesex, England: Penguin Books, 1977), p. 234.
2. Thomas Hobbes, *Leviathan* (1651), Part II, Chapter 21.
3. See Kurt Baier, "Moral Reasons," *Midwest Studies in Philosophy*, Volume III, 1978, p. 70.

Chapter 4

1. See Norman Bowie and Robert Simon, *The Individual and the Social Order* (Englewood Cliffs, NJ: Prentice Hall, 1977), Chapter 7.
2. See Bertram Gross, ed., *Social Intelligence for America's Future* (Boston: Allyn & Bacon, 1969).
3. Alan Donagan, *The Theory of Morality* (Chicago: University of Chicago Press, 1977).
4. Julius Kovesi, "Against the Ritual of 'Is' and 'Ought,'" *Midwest Studies in Philosophy*, Volume III, 1978, p. 15.
5. Garrett Hardin, "Living on a Lifeboat," *BioScience*, October 1974.
6. Richard A. Watson, "Reason and Morality in a World of Limited Food," in *World Hunger and Moral Obligation*, ed. by Aiken and LaFollette (Englewood Cliffs, NJ: Prentice Hall, 1977), p. 123.
7. Immanuel Kant, *Foundations of the Metaphysics of Morals* (Lewis White Beck translation) (Indianapolis: Bobbs-Merrill, 1969), p. 45.
8. See Onora O'Neill, "Lifeboat Earth," *Philosophy and Public Affairs*, Volume IV no. 3 (1975), pp. 73–92.
9. See Kenneth Boulding, "The Economics of the Coming of Spaceship Earth," in *Environmental Quality in a Growing Economy*, ed. by Henry Jarrett (Baltimore: Johns Hopkins Press, 1966).
10. For further elaboration on these equations and the economics of the spaceship see William Ramsay and Claude Anderson, *Managing the Environment* (New York: Basic Books, 1972), pp. 277–278.
11. O'Neill, "Lifeboat Earth."
12. Thomas Hobbes, *Leviathan* (1651), Chapter 14.
13. See Garrett Hardin, "The Tragedy of the Commons," *Science*, Volume 162, December 13, 1968, pp. 1243-1248.
14. Carolyn Morillo, "Doing, Refraining, and the Strenuousness of Morality," *American Philosophical Quarterly*, Volume 14, Number 1, January 1977, pp. 29-41.

15. See Robert Nozick, *Anarchy, State and Utopia* (New York: Basic Books, 1974), pp. 178-182.

16. Peter A. French, "The Corporation as a Moral Person," *American Philosophical Quarterly*, Volume 16, Number 3, July 1979, pp. 207-215.

17. O'Neill, "Lifeboat Earth."

18. Rom Harré, *An Introduction to the Logic of the Sciences* (London: Macmillan and Co. Ltd. 1960), p. 87 ff.

19. This I take to be a version of N. R. Hanson's account of retroductive inference. See his "Retroductive Inference," in B. Baumrin, ed., *The Philosophy of Science, Delaware Seminar* (New York: John Wiley and Sons, 1962); his *Patterns of Discovery* (Cambridge: Cambridge University Press, 1958); and his *Observation and Explanation* (New York: Harper and Row, 1971).

20. Gen. 1:28.

21. For example see Joshua Lederberg, "Experimental Genetics and Human Evolution," *The American Naturalist*, Volume 100 (September-October, 1966), pp. 519-531.

22. Joseph Fletcher, *The Ethics of Genetic Control* (Garden City: Doubleday, 1974), pp. 118-119.

23. G. J. Warnock, *The Object of Morality* (London: Methuen & Co. Ltd., 1971), p. 26.

Chapter 5

1. These examples are all derived from Agatha Christie's *Murder is Easy* (London, 1945). It is interesting to note that the publishers chose for the American title of the novel *Easy to Kill*.

2. R. M. Hare, *The Language of Morals* (Oxford: Oxford University Press, 1952).

3. *Ibid.* and also R. M. Hare, *Freedom and Reason* (Oxford: Oxford University Press, 1963).

4. Hare, *Freedom and Reason*, p. 26.

5. *Ibid.*, pp. 75-76.

6. Hector-Neri Castañeda, *The Structure of Morality* (Springfield: Thomas, 1974), p. 153.

7. Paul Grice. "Causal Theory of Perception," *Proceedings of the Aristotelian Society*, Suppl. Vol. 35, 1961, p. 121 ff.

8. Julius Kovesi, "Against the Ritual of 'Is' and 'Ought,'" *Midwest Studies in Philosophy*, Volume III, (1978); also see Julius Kovesi, *Moral Notions* (London: Routledge & Kegan Paul, 1967).

9. See Ludwig Wittgenstein, *Philosophical Investigations* (Oxford: Blackwell, 1953).

10. See F. Waismann, "Verifiability," *Proceedings of the Aristotelian Society*, Suppl. Vol. (1945).

11. Kovesi, *Moral Notions*, p. 14.

12. Stuart Hampshire, "J. L. Austin 1911-1960," in *Symposium on J. L. Austin*, ed. by K. T. Fann (London: Routledge & Kegan Paul, 1969), p. 35.

13. A similar account of the ideas associated in the concept of murder is suggested by Kovesi.

14. J. L. Austin, "Three Ways of Spilling Ink," in *Philosophical Papers*, 2nd Ediition (Oxford: Oxford University Press, 1970), p. 273.

15. This is a central point in a number of recent articles in moral philosophy. See for example: Philippa Foot, "Abortion and the Doctrine of Double Effect," *Oxford Review*,

5 (1967); Gilbert Harman, "Moral Relativism Defended," *The Philosophical Review*, January, 1975, pp. 3–22, and "Relativistic Ethics: Morality as Politics," *Midwest Studies in Philosophy*, Volume III, 1978; Richard Trammel, "Saving Life and Taking Life," *The Journal of Philosophy* 72, 1975, pp. 131–137.

Chapter 6

1. John Rawls, *A Theory of Justice* (Cambridge: Harvard University Press, 1971), p. 55.
2. See for example: William Alston, "Linguistic Acts," *American Philosophical Quarterly*, Volume 1, Number 2, April 1964, pp. 138–46; John Searle, "How to Derive 'Ought' from 'Is,'" *The Philosophical Review*, Volume 73, 1964, pp. 43–58; John Rawls, "Two Concepts of Rules," *The Philosophical Review*, Volume 64, 1955, pp. 3–32.
3. Searle, "How to Derive 'Ought' from 'Is'"; *Speech Acts* (Cambridge: Cambridge University Press, 1969).
4. I am indebted to my colleague, Professor Howard Wettstein, for this most useful definition of a constitutive rule.
5. Searle, *Speech Acts*.
6. This form is based on a discussion with Haskell Fain. He is not responsible for my employment of it in the manner herein.
7. M. G. Singer has maintained that there are three different kinds of rights: action rights (rights to act in certain ways); receivatory rights (rights to receive certain things or be treated in certain ways); and property rights (rights in or to something). See *Generalisation in Ethics* (London: Eyre Spottiswoode, 1961), p. 312. Because I am not concerned with right-granting rules, I shall not comment on Singer's types of rights.
8. It is of passing note that "merel" was often corruptly used for both "moral" and "miracle."
9. Shakespeare in *A Midsummer Night's Dream* (Act II, sc. 1, lines 96–98) refers to the game:

> The fold stands empty in the drowned field,
> And crows are fatted with the murrion flock.
> The nine men's morris is filled up with mud

10. Research by a number of my students has shown that the game is such that two knowledgeable and careful players who do not commit major blunders will always stalemate. One must lose the game; it cannot be won. Morals indeed!
11. For example, the fact that I have the right to sell my house does not entail that I have an obligation to do so.
12. From the rules of Merels, obligations of two sorts can arise for players. From (a), the statement, "Players have an obligation to play alternately" can be derived; and from the factual report that X has completed his play and the game is not ended, it follows that Y has an obligation to make his play. From (b) or (c) conjoined with the factual report that X has formed a new line of three men and has exercised his right, it follows that Y has an obligation not to reenter his removed man into the game; similarly from (b) in conjunction with the factual report that X has formed a new line of three, that Y has a line of three and at least one other man, it follows that X has an obligation not to remove one of the men making up Y's line of three. The steps needed to show that these derivations hold are straightforward and unexceptional. The force of the first type of obligation is requisitive, while that of the second is prohibitive.

An obligation is requisitive if it obliges one to do something and not specifically to refrain from or avoid doing something. Suppose that Bill is a lifeguard at the beach. On accepting that position, he assumes obligations, among which are included (1) being on guard during specific hours of each day and (2) trying to rescue distressed swimmers. Requisitive obligations of type (1) are met only when that which is to be done is actually accomplished. If he fails to be on guard during his assigned hours, he will be fired. Often the requisite obligations within an institution are in a class with (2). Bill's obligation is not to save lives, it is to try to do so when a swimmer is drowning. To meet that obligation he *must* endeavor, seriously strive, but he need not succeed. There is a temptation to read all requisite obligations as obligations only to endeavor to do something, which gains support, no doubt, from the frequency of use and general acceptance of the supposedly justificatory, "I tried."

Many requisitive obligations within institutions, however, are not met just by trying, even by trying hard. In some institutional situations, "I tried" is utterly senseless. Imagine in the Merels game that Shepherd X completes his play and the game is not ended. Spaces are available to which Y may move his men. The rule of alternate play requires Y to make his move. Y raises his hand over one of his men, then moves his hand to another, shakes his head, mutters to himself, then proclaims with finality, "I tried." Have all of Y's men become inexplicably attached to the layout? Struggle as he might, he cannot budge them! X leans across the layout with a sneer: "Are you going to play, or do you concede?"

An obligation is prohibitive if meeting it specifically involves abstaining, avoiding, refraining, in short *not* doing something. Hence the Merels rule that includes the clause "he (the player who has formed a line of three) cannot take one (of his adversary's men) from a line of three unless there are no others remaining on the layout," conjoined with the true statements that X has formed a new line of three and Y has a line of three plus other men on the layout, yields the obligation on X not to remove any of the three men from Y's line. There appears to be but one type of prohibitive obligation. We do not have institutional obligations to try not to do something. We do have institutional obligations not to do that something (although trying not to in some institutions is often mitigatory when a penalty is involved).

13. Anatol Rapoport, *Two Persons Game Theory* (Ann Arbor: University of Michigan Press, 1966), p. 135.

14. And it can alternatively be stated as "_____ is obliged to XXX."

15. Richard Brandt, "The Concepts of Obligation and Duty," *Mind*, Vol. 73, No. 291 (1964), p. 378.

16. Ludwig Wittgenstein, *On Certainty*, trans. by C. Paul and G. E. M. Anscombe (Oxford: Basil Blackwell, 1969).

17. See Alan White, *Modal Thinking* (Ithaca: Cornell University Press, 1975), Chapter 10 for a good discussion of this aspect of "ought."

18. A. C. Ewing, *The Definition of Good* (London, 1947); and *Ethics*, (New York: The Free Press, 1953).

19. Alan Gewirth, "The Golden Rule Rationalized," *Midwest Studies in Philosophy*, Volume III, 1978.

20. *Ibid.*

21. *Ibid.*

22. Wittgenstein, *On Certainty*, #95-98.

Chapter 7

1. For quite a different view see many of the papers of William Frankena.

2. Although morality does not provide goals for living, some people apparently do try

to make "being moral" their primary goal, and some philosophers may be read as encouraging just that. Both Aristotle and Kant can be read, albeit, I think, cursorily as sharing a certain outlook on what we might call the "ultra-moral person." In Aristotle's case, charity would seem to demand that we regard his "great-souled" man, in the words of D. J. O'Connor, as "a ponderous joke." ("Aristotle," in D. J. O'Connor, *A Critical History of Western Philosophy*, New York, 1964, p. 55.)

Aristotle describes his "great-souled" or "high-minded" (*Megalopsychia*) person as follows:

> A man is regarded as high-minded when he thinks he deserves great things and actually deserves them . . . high-mindedness implies greatness . . . the high-minded are concerned with honor. For they regard themselves as worthy of honor above all else, but of an honor that they deserve. . . . he will utterly despise honors conferred by ordinary people and on trivial grounds, for that is not what he deserves. . . . A high-minded person is justified in looking down upon others for he has the right opinion of them, but the common run of people do so without rhyme or reason. . . . He will not go in for pursuits that the common people value, not for those in which the first place belongs to others. He is slow to act and procrastinates, except when some great honor or achievement is at stake. . . . He speaks and acts openly; since he looks down upon others his speech is free and truthful, except when he deliberately depreciates himself in addressing the common run of people.
>
> (*Nicomachean Ethics* 1123b–1125a 35)

Little wonder most philosophers reading these sections of the *Nicomachean Ethics*, wanting to be as generous as possible with their author, pass them off as aberrative. What is described is not the sort of person one would recommend or aspire to be. Instead it is an excellent account of a proud, conceited, condescending snob. Enshrining such a person as the model of goodness and virtue tends to offend our intuitions about praiseworthy character. It is not important to provide an account of the course of Aristotle's reasoning that culminates in this description of the "great-souled" person. I want to use it only to suggest that pursuit of the moral life as an end in itself might result in a character not unlike that described by Aristotle.

From quite another philosophical point of view, Immanuel Kant draws a portrait of a comparable character. Kant quotes Benjamin Constant as having criticized his (Kant's) view that it is always one's moral duty to tell the truth, even if the lie one might have told would have saved a friend from a murderer bent on killing him. Kant writes:

> Truth in utterances that cannot be avoided is the formal duty of a man to everyone, however great the disadvantage that may arise from it to him or any other, and although by making a false statement I do no wrong to him who unjustly compels me to speak, yet I do wrong to men in general in the most essential point of duty, so that it may be called a lie (though not in the jurist's sense) that is, so far as in me lies I cause that declarations in general find no credit, and hence that all rights founded on contract should lose their force; and this is a wrong which is done to mankind. (Immanuel Kant, "On the Supposed Right to Tell Lies from Benovolent Motives," from *Kant's Critique of Practical Reason and Other Works on the Theory of Ethics*, translated by T. K. Abbott, London, 1873.)

Kant draws a distinction between actions done to harm or wrong someone and actions that do harm accidentally. Telling the truth in the case where one must answer something does harm, given the situation sketched by Constant, but the intent is not to do wrong.

In fact the intent is to do right, to act according to duty, according to the dictates of the categorical imperative, the argument that lying in any circumstance destroys the credibility of all contracts. Kant tells us, "It is merely an accident (*casus*) that the truth of the statement did harm. . . . Every man has not only a right, but the strictest duty to truthfulness in statements which he cannot avoid, whether they do harm to himself or others. . . . Veracity is an unconditioned duty."

Kant seems to identify the person who is moral with the person who is good. It follows, of course that if doing *a* is right then anyone doing *a* is right then anyone doing *a* cannot be doing wrong by doing *a*. What does not follow is that anyone doing *a*, even if he does if "from duty," is necessarily doing good by doing *a* in the way that he does *a*. Constant's example provides an adequate case to test intuitions. Sanctioning a lie certainly weakens the foundation upon which all promising and thereby all contractual arrangements are built. But it cannot be that I am doing good by revealing the whereabouts of my friend to his would-be murderer. I am doing something that seems to be rather bad and I am surely not doing it accidently, inadvertantly, unintentionally, etc. That act seems to be "right but bad." The officious moral snob, we might say, piously does the moral thing despite doing something most of us would recognize as bad or, better, he does it in a way we would recognize as a bad way to do it.

3. In *The Southern Journal of Philosophy*, summer 1971, pp. 113–118, reprinted in Peter A. French, *Philosophical Explorations* (Morristown, 1975), pp. 96–104.

4. *Ibid.*

5. *Ibid.*

6. Jo's remark, quoted from *Bleak House*, is made about a law-writer known by the name of "Nemo" who has been found dead of an overdose of opium in squalid lodgings. No one at the coroner's inquest can give much in the way of useful evidence as to Nemo's lifestyle or provide reasons why he would have killed himself in such a manner. Jo is not permitted to give testimony because he is incapable of providing what the court deems to be proper answers to its preliminary queries. After the court has adjourned, Jo tells the coroner and solicitor, Mr. Tulkinghorn, of his acquaintance with the deceased. He says that Nemo has showed him various kindnesses, providing Jo with money for food and lodging and, when he could not give money, had spoken comfortingly with the boy. Jo knew nothing more of the law-writer's life and deeds and certainly could not say why "Nemo" had committed suicide. To Jo, Nemo was a good man. At the end of his own short life, Jo's last request is to be buried in the same "berryin' ground" alongside the body of Nemo.

7. See Chapter 6.

8. Hector-Neri Castañeda, *The Structure of Morality* (Springfield, 1974), p. 217.

9. W. D. Ross, *Foundations of Ethics* (Oxford: Oxford University Press, 1939), p. 309.

10. George Nakhnikian, "Love in Human Reason," *Midwest Studies in Philosophy*, Volume III, 1978.

11. *N.E.*, 1103a 15-20.

12. See W. D. Ross, *The Right and The Good* (Oxford, 1930); and Ross, *Foundations of Ethics*, Chapter XII.

13. See Chapter 5.

14. See for example George Edgin Pugh, *The Biological Origin of Human Values* (New York, 1977), especially Part III.

15. I hold what I take to be an Austinian view that every distinction of word usuage in common speech is in the language for good and sufficient reason. See Stuart Hampshire,

194 / Notes

"J. L. Austin, 1911–1960," in *Symposium on J. L. Austin*, ed. by K. T. Fann (London, 1969), for an exposition of this view.

16. *The Philosophy of The Active and Moral Powers of Man* (Edinburgh, 1828); see especially Book First.

17. *Ibid.*, Chapter Second.

18. *Ibid.*

19. See for examples: Pugh, *The Biological Origin of Human Values*; Edward O. Wilson, *Sociobiology* (Cambridge, 1975); Desmond Morris, *The Naked Ape* (London, 1967); Konrad Lorenz, *On Aggression* (New York, 1966).

20. For a counter-thesis in sociobiology see Richard Dawkins, *The Selfish Gene* (Oxford, 1976).

21. See Pugh, Part III, Chapter 14. See also Ralph W. Burhoe, "The Source of Civilization in the Natural Selection of Coadapted Information in Genes and Culture," *Zygon* Volume 11, No. 3, September 1976.

22. For a sociobiological definition of "value" see Pugh, Part One, Chapter 1.

23. Ross, *Foundations of Ethics*, p. 309.

24. *Ibid.*

25. Colin Turnbull, *The Mountain People* (New York: 1972).

The Ik are a small tribe of formally nomadic hunters who live in the mountains of northern Uganda. Their current plight is the result of many factors, not the least of which is African nationalism. As nomadic hunters the Ik had recognized no national boundaries and wandered over a territory that extended into parts of the Sudan, Uganda, and Kenya, but their prize hunting ground was the Kidepo Valley of Uganda. In recent years those African states restricted the Ik's hunting territory and Uganda declared the Kidepo Valley a National Park, outlawing all hunting there. The tribe was confined to the mountainous area between the Kenya-Uganda escarpment and Mount Morungole in Northern Uganda. Their villages, ironically, overlook the forbidden hunting grounds of Kidepo. These events forced the Ik to adopt a new style of life, to become farmers. Then the great drought came to Central Africa and the Iks began to starve to death.

Before being confined to the mountain area, the Ik society, Turnbull tells us, was basically family oriented, though the concept of family was not understood as restricted to biological kinship and was instead defined in terms of prime social unit, the nomadic hunters of a camp. All adults living in the camp were treated as parents by camp children and all people of like age treated each other and were reciprocally treated as siblings. The "virtues" of kindness, generosity, charity, honesty, hospitality, etc., were normally manifested in the behavior of the hunters, toward all members of the tribe.

The territorial restriction placed on the Iks by the Uganda government and the abrupt change in the weather produced one pervasive, inescapable fact of life for every Ik: starvation. With starvation came the inevitable reduction in numbers so that within a few years only a thousand or so Ik remain. The established social structure of the tribe collapsed and was replaced by a life-style of survivalist individualism reminicient of Hobbes' man in nature, or the droogs of Anthony Burgess' *Clockwork Orange*. Iks now "live" or barely so and then only for a short life-span, at the very edge of survival. They think nothing of stealing food from the mouths of children and the aged and they entertain themselves by watching each other injure themselves and/or die. Their children are put out of their homes and allowed to die if they can find no sustenance for themselves. The elderly, anyone over 25, have little or no energy to perform daily tasks, and sit absentmindedly gazing out across the forbidden Kidepo Valley awaiting death or the slight diversion of someone else's death. There is no passion, no remorse, no joy—just, and barely,

Notes / 195

survival and ever-present starvation. The Iks did have a chance at a salvation of a sort. The rains did come and the crops flourished yet, as Turnbull reports, the potential harvest was left to rot in the fields. Any Ik that had the strength filled only his own stomach and made no effort to lay in stores for the future or to feed those of his tribe dying at the threshold of his hut.

The Ik do not allow nourishment or medicine to be squandered on the dead, defined by the Ik to those nearly dead. For example, Turnbull reports discovering a dying Ik (one who had befriended him when he had arrived in the village) on his doorstep and gave him a cup of tea. The cup was promptly stolen from the dying man's grasp by his biological sister, who drank as she ran, laughing and delighted with herself! There was no censure of such behavior by the tribe; it was in fact encouraged and often repeated. Turnbull, not the sister, was reproached. Ik entertainment amounts to watching the agony of each other and, when possible, increasing the woeful plight of a tribal member in order to heighten the entertainment value. Suffering members apparently recognize a kind of duty to the other Iks to fulfill their roles without complaint, "Old people had joined in the merriment when they had been teased, knocked over or had a precious morsel of food taken from their mouths. They know that it was silly of them to expect to go on living, and, having watched others, they knew that the spectacle really was quite funny. . . . (they) would die laughing, happy that (they) were at least providing (their) children with amusement."

26. John Rawls, *A Theory of Justice* (Cambridge, 1971) p. 190.
27. Plato, *The Republic* I, 335.

Chapter 8

1. See Bernard Gert, *The Moral Rules* (New York: Harper & Row, 1966), Chapter 10.
2. Karl Menninger, *The Crime of Punishment* (New York: Viking Press, 1968).
3. Russell Grice, *The Grounds of Moral Judgement* (Cambridge: Cambridge University Press, 1967), p. 137.
4. Thomas Nagel, *The Possibility of Altruism* (Oxford: Oxford University Press, 1970), especially Part Two.
5. For an account of Kant's position on these matters see Philippa Foot, "Morality as a System of Hypothetical Imperatives," *The Philosophical Review*, July 1972, pp. 305-316.
6. *Ibid.*
7. Anatol Rapoport, *Two-Person Game Theory* (Ann Arbor: University of Michigan Press, 1966).
8. *Ibid.*, pp. 17-18.
9. Nicholas Rescher, *Unselfishness* (Pittsburgh: University of Pittsburgh Press, 1975).
10. Jordan H. Sobel, "Utility Maximizers in Iterated Prisoners' Dilemmas," *Dialogue* March 1976, pp. 38-53.
11. J. F. Nash, "Non-cooperative Games," *Annals of Mathematics* 54, 1951, pp. 286-295.
12. See in particular David Gauthier, "Morality and Advantage," *The Philosophical Review*, LXXVI, No. 4, October 1967, pp. 460-475; Gauthier, "Rational Cooperation," *Nous* 8, 1974, pp. 53-65; R. B. Braithwaite, *Theory of Games as a Tool for the Moral Philosopher* (Cambridge: Cambridge University Press, 1955); and Rescher.
13. See Rapoport, *op. cit.*, pp. 131-137.
14. *Ibid.*, pp. 130-131.

196 / Notes

15. Gauthier, "Morality and Advantage."
16. *Ibid.*
17. One is reminded of Dr. Seuss' *The Lorax.*
18. The notion of conscience is but another aspect of that perception. Consciences are nurtured as depositories of that shared vision. To obey one's conscience is not to act in order to maximize some "hidden utility"; it is to appease the sensation that one has contemplated or acted harmfully (not necessarily to oneself).
19. Julius Kovesi, *Moral Notions* (London: Routledge & Kegan Paul, 1967), p. 113.
20. Thomas Hobbes, *Leviathan* (1651) Part 1, Chapter 15.
21. Kai Nielson, "Why Should I Be Moral?" *Methodos* XV, No. 59–60 (1963), pp. 275–306.
22. A. Phillips Griffiths, "Wittgenstein, Schopenhauer, and Ethics" in *Understanding Wittgenstein* (London: Macmillan, 1974), p. 97.
23. Immanuel Kant, "On the Supposed Right to Tell Lies from Benevolent Motives"; see Chapter 7, Footnote 2.

Appendix

1. According to the *Oxford English Dictionary*, the word "animadvert" is derived from the two Latin words for "mind" and "to turn to." Hence "to turn the mind to." The fourth definition cited is: "to comment critically (on), to utter criticism (usually of an adverse kind), to express censure or blame." Note examples: "I see no reason why her modesty should be so severely animadverted on." "To animadvert on this modest and courteous picture belongs not to the present subject," and "The academics began to animadvert on defects beyond the province of grammar." A list of words one would usually find in animadvertive utterances would include:

delinquent, vile, offensive, criminal, despicable, reprehensible, devilish, naughty, contemptible, satanic, wicked, barbaric, diabolical, insufferable, irresponsible, evil, malicious, murderous

and a host of phrases which are animadvertive in some circumstances, if not in every case.
2. This story was suggested to me by Sidney Morganbesser.
3. J. L. Mackie, "Causes and Conditions," *American Philosophical Quarterly*, Volume 2, Number 4, October 1965, pp. 245 ff. The term INUS is derived from the initial letters of the words italicized in the definition, "an *insufficient* but *necessary* part of a condition which is itself *unnecessary* but *sufficient* for the result."
4. Elizabeth Beardsley, "A Plea for Deserts," *American Philosophical Quarterly*, Volume 6, Number 1, January 1969, pp. 33–42, correctly identifies this sense of "blame" as the "whodunit" or "whatdunit" sense, but she then laments that this sense of "blame" is confusing and regrettable because it merely singles out culprits. Here she is incorrect, if what I have argued is consistent with our practices, for not only is this use of blame animadvertive; it is, as I hope to show, the basis for the ascription of the other sense of B^2 blame, which Professor Beardsley has also wrongly wedded to moral notions and judgments.
5. "The great glacier is to blame for creating thousands of lakes" is a clear misuse of the word "blame." I find it impossible to imagine anyone who could seriously utter such a statement, for in saying it one would be identifying the great glacier as the cause of the formation of thousands of lakes that he believes obstruct some human goal.
6. G. E. M. Anscombe has maintained that most of our moral notions are derived from a law conception of ethics that was founded in Christianity and which necessitated a "re-

sponsibility to" relationship to God as a law-giver. ("Modern Moral Philosophy," *Philosophy*, 33, 1958, pp. 1-19.) I see no reason, however, to abandon the notion or the insight if we abandon the divine law-giver conception.

7. See my "Types of Collectivities and Blame," *The Personalist*, Spring, 1975; also Chapter 2 of this book.

8. The term is borrowed from J. L. Austin.

9. *A Treatise of Human Nature* (Oxford: Clarendon Press, 1888), p. 575.

10. For a fuller catalogue of excuses, see Jonathan Glover, *Responsibility* (London: Routledge & Kegan Paul, 1970), Chapter 3; and H. L. A. Hart, "The Ascription of Responsibility and Rights," *Proceedings of the Aristotelian Society*, 1948-49.

11. See Saul Kripke, "Naming and Necessity," in *Semantics of Natural Language*, ed. by G. Harman and D. Davidson (Dordrecht, The Netherlands: Reidel Publishing Company, 1972).

12. "Censure Under Control," *Ratio*, 15, June 1973, pp. 44-56.

13. *Ibid.*, p. 46.

14. Aristotle wrote: "We call some virtues 'intellectual' and others 'moral': theoretical wisdom, understanding, and practical wisdom are intellectual virtues. In speaking of a man's character, we do not describe him as wise or understanding, but as gentle or self-controlled; but we praise the wise man, too, for his characteristic, and praiseworthy characteristics are what we call virtues." *Nicomachean Ethics*, Book I (1103a).

15. Which is not to say that cannibalism should not raise genuine moral concerns, even for a cannibal, just that it does not do so here.

Selected Bibliography

Selected Bibliography

I. Classical Works

Aristotle. *Nichomachean Ethics*, trans. by M. Ostwald (Indianapolis, 1962). An analysis of the way by which persons may achieve the good life towards which their actions aim. Includes analyses of many important moral and political concepts. One of the great works in the Western moral tradition.

Bradley, F. H. *Ethical Studies* (Oxford, 1876). Idealist view that self-realization is the goal of ethical behavior and that self-realization, in part, involves identification of one's station in the social structure and performance of its related duties. Also provides an account of "the vulgar notion of responsibility" that is compared with Locke's views in Chapter 1 of this book.

Hobbes, Thomas. *Leviathan* (1651). Account of civil association that provides an argument that positive law is based on natural law. Hobbes' account of the state of nature is contrasted with that of Montesquieu in Chapter 2 of this book. Also in Hobbes' account, rational self-interest dictates the decision to form a civil state, an act of mutual benefit. Contrast this to the account given in Chapter 8.

Kant, Immanuel. *The Doctrine of Virtue* (or *Part II* of *The Metaphysics of Morals*) trans. by M. Gregor (Philadelphia, 1964). Provides the argument that from the universalization principle formulation of the categorical imperative can be derived the special duty of all rational animals to act only according to a maxim of ends that one could will everyone to have.

Kant, Immanuel. *Foundations of the Metaphysics of Morals*, trans. by L. W. Beck (Indianapolis, 1959). Famous deontological analysis of morality. Defends the position that being moral involves conscious choice of the morally correct action for its own sake and that the grounds of morality lie in reason rather than in the anticipation of consequences of actions. Analyzes moral duty in terms of universalization, respect for the intrinsic worth of persons, and the preservation of the autonomy of moral agents.

Locke, John. *An Essay Concerning Human Understanding* (1690). Fountainhead of British Empiricism. Contains mixed-mode account of moral concepts that is defended in this book. Of particular interest are Books III and IV of the *Essay*.

Montesquieu, Baron de. *The Spirit of the Laws*, trans. by T. Nugent (New York, 1949). Somewhat eclectic account, often from an historical perspective, of various solutions to the problem of reconciling right and coercion in civil associations. Anti-Hobbesian approach to the state of nature found in Montesquieu is reflected in Chapters 2 and 3 of this book.

Schopenhauer, Arthur. *On the Basis of Morality*, trans. by E. F. J. Payne (Indianapolis, 1965). Anti-objectivist theory of the foundations of moral concepts and moral judgments; includes a very strong attack on Kantianism.

Stewart, Dugald. *The Philosophy of the Active and Moral Powers of Man* (Edinburgh, 1828). Defends the position that moral values can be ascribed to the operations of a moral sense in persons, but expands that idea by trying to show that innate human proclivities to social association and concern for the welfare of others underlie our convictions about proper conduct. Stewart's views are discussed in the context of recent sociobiological theories in Chapter 7 of this book.

II. Contemporary Works

Austin, J. L. *Philosophical Papers* (Oxford, 1968). Collection of Austin's papers. Includes "Three Ways of Spilling Ink," an analysis of act-modifiers such as "deliberately," "on purpose," and "intentionally." Contains a number of clever examples, some of which are utilized in Chapter 1 of this book. Also many of the papers by Austin evidence the "Principle of Sufficient Linguistic Reason" mentioned in Chapter V.

Castañeda, Hector-Neri. *The Structure of Morality* (Springfield, 1974). Presents a three-dimensional structural account of the "institution of morality." Includes an examination of the basic assumptions about human behavior that underlie the structure. The division of MORALITY into morals and euergetics is found in Castañeda's account, but he includes a third aspect of MORALITY, a "metathetical dimension," from which issues the moral duty to act so as to bring about revision of the moral code to correct errors, omissions, etc. This aspect of MORALITY is not distilled out in my account, but is subsumed within the discussion in Chapter 4. Castañeda's book also contains an excellent account of the logic of imperatives.

Castañeda, Hector-Neri. *Thinking and Doing* (Dordrecht, The Netherlands, 1975). Further development of the logic of imperatives and deontic judgments. Also includes a discussion of agency compatible with that presented in Chapter 1 of this book.

Donagan, Alan. *The Theory of Morality* (Chicago, 1977). Defense of the traditional Hebrew-Christian morality as the only moral system binding on rational persons. Argues that the tenets of that system can be derived from the basic principle that all rational creatures must be treated with respect.

Feinberg, Joel. *Doing and Deserving* (Princeton, 1970). Collection of essays on various topics in moral and legal philosophy and the theory of action. Of special interest is "Action and Responsibility," which includes a discussion of the "accordion effect."

Grice, G. R. *The Grounds of Moral Judgement* (Cambridge, 1967). Utilizes the social contract theory to establish the grounds of moral obligation. Of particular interest is Grice's account of motivation, which has much in common with the distinction drawn in Chapter 8 of this book between the meaning of "There is a good reason for someone to do something" and that of "Someone has a good reason to do something."

Hare, R. M. *Freedom and Reason* (Oxford, 1963). Further development and modification of the prescriptivist theory of *The Language of Morals*.

Hare, R. M. *The Language of Morals* (Oxford, 1952). *Locus classicus* of the prescriptivist account of moral judgments. Discussed in detail and contrasted with my account in Chapter 5.

Kovesi, Julius. *Moral Notions* (London, 1967). Analysis of the logic and use of moral concepts. Treats moral concepts as inventions used to encourage and discourage types of behavior that create the world they describe. Of particular interest is Chapter 4 on moral judgments and principles, which has much in common with my account. Also, although he does not identify his view with Locke's in *Moral Notions*, he acknowledges similarities to the mixed-mode account in a recent article, "Against the Ritual of 'Is' and 'Ought,'" *Midwest Studies in Philosophy*, Volume III, February 1978, pp. 5–16.

Mackie, J. L. *Ethics: Inventing Right and Wrong* (Harmondsworth, Middlesex, England, 1977). Defends a subjectivist theory of ethics and applies it to practical problems. His views are, in large measure, compatible with the approach I take in this book. His claim that morality is an all-inclusive theory of conduct, however, contrasts with the more limited view of the scope of morality that I have defended.

Mackie, J. L. *Problems from Locke* (Oxford, 1976). Critical analysis of certain key topics in Locke's *Essay Concerning Human Understanding*. See Chapter 3 for a clear analysis of Locke's account of mixed-mode concepts that complements Chapter 2 of this book.

Nagel, Thomas. *The Possibility of Altruism* (Oxford, 1970). Defends the thesis that being altruistic is a basic requirement of rationality on action. Contrasts with Chapter 8 of this book.

Nozick, Robert. *Anarchy, State and Utopia* (New York, 1974). Maintains that the minimal state is the only morally justifiable state. Develops and defends an entitlement theory of distributive justice.

Pugh, George Edgin. *The Biological Origin of Human Values* (New York, 1977). Attempts to locate moral values in biological structure, and hence as products of genetics and evolution. Compare to the account of the foundation of euergetical concepts given in Chapter 7 of this book.

Rawls, John. *A Theory of Justice* (Cambridge, 1971). Major work in moral and political theory that derives and defends nonutilitarian principles of justice that Rawls believes would be agreed to by free and rational persons under conditions of equality, describes the social system that would appear to satisfy those principles, and then associates his theory to a concept of the good. Rawls' description of persons in the "original position" is used in the discussion of moral personhood in Chapter 1 of this book.

Rescher, Nicholas. *Unselfishness* (Pittsburgh, 1975). Attack on the game theorists' account of rationality conjoined with an attempt to defend the importance of vicarious affects in human action. Contrasts with the argument of Chapter 8 of this book.

Ross, W. D. *Foundations of Ethics* (Oxford, 1939). Further analysis of the theory set forth in *The Right and The Good*. Of particular interest is that the complete divorce of rightness from goodness in the earlier work is modified in the final chapter of *Foundations of Ethics*.

Ross, W. D. *The Right and The Good* (Oxford, 1930). Analysis of the concepts of right, good, and morally good. Argues that rightness and goodness are unanalyzable properties. Contrast Ross' position with that discussed in Chapter 7 of this book.

Searle, John. *Speech Acts* (Cambridge, 1969). Development of the speech act theory of language use based on assumptions of J. L. Austin's views on language; includes an elaboration on the derivation of "ought"-statements from "is"-statements using institutional rules. Searle's analysis is attacked in Chapter 6 of this book.

Taylor, Richard. *Good and Evil* (New York, 1970). Nonobjectivist, voluntaristic theory of good. Compare with Chapter 7 of this book. Also contrast Taylor's account of the function of principles with that presented in Chapter 6.

Warnock, G. J. *The Object of Morality* (London, 1971). Analysis of the subject matter of morality based on the view that a morality is an instrument created to better or preserve the human predicament against the tendency in society of things to go badly. That tendency arises primarily because of our limited sympathies for each other in the face of limited resources. Warnock's account of the object of morality is similar to that maintained throughout this book.

III. Articles

Alston, William. "Linguistic Acts," *American Philosophical Quarterly*, Vol. 1, No. 2 (April 1964).

Anscombe, G. E. M. "Modern Moral Philosophy," *Philosophy*, Vol. 33 (1958).

Austin, J. L. "Three Ways of Spilling Ink," *Philosophy Papers* (Oxford: Oxford University Press, 1970).

Beardsley, Elizabeth. "A Plea for Deserts," *American Philosophical Quarterly*, Vol. 6, No. 1 (January 1969).

Benn, S. I. "Privacy, Freedom, and Respect for Persons," *Nomos*, Vol. XIII.

Brandt, Richard. "The Concepts of Obligation and Duty," *Mind*, Vol. 73, No. 291 (1964).

Burhoe, Ralph W. "The Source of Civilization in the Natural Selection of Coadapted Information in Genes and Culture," *Zygon*, Vol. II, No. 3 (September 1976).

Cornman, James. "Comments on Davidson's 'Agency,'" *Agent, Action, and Reason*, ed. by Binkley, Bronaugh, Marras (Toronto, 1971).

Cranor, Carl. "Toward a Theory of Respect for Persons," *American Philosophical Quarterly*, Vol. 12, No. 4 (October 1975).

Davidson, Donald. "Actions, Reasons, and Causes," *The Journal of Philosophy*, Vol. 60, No. 23 (November 7, 1963).

Davidson, Donald. "Agency," *Agent, Action, and Reason*, ed. by Binkley, Bronaugh, Marras (Toronto, 1971).

Dretske, Frederick I. "Referring to Events," *Midwest Studies in Philosophy*, Vol. II (1977).

Foot, Philippa. "Abortion and the Doctrine of Double Effect," *Oxford Review*, Vol. 5 (1967).

Foot, Philippa. "Morality as a System of Hypothetical Imperatives," *The Philosophical Review*, Vol. LXXXI, No. 3 (July 1972).

French, Peter A. "Corporate Moral Agency," *Ethical Theory and Business*, ed. by Bowie and Beauchamp (Englewood Cliffs, 1979).

French, Peter A. "Types of Collectivities and Blame," *The Personalist* (Spring, 1975).

Gauthier, David. "Morality and Advantage," *The Philosophical Review*, Vol. LXXVI, No. 4 (October 1967); and "Rational Cooperation," *Nous*, Vol. 8 (1974).

Gewirth, Alan. "The Golden Rule Rationalized," *Midwest Studies in Philosophy*, Vol. III (1978).

Grice, Paul. "Causal Theory of Perception," *Proceedings of the Aristotelian Society*, Suppl. Vol. 35 (1961).

Haezrahi, Pepita. "The Concept of Man as End-in-Himself," *Kant-Studien*, Band 53 (1962).

Hampshire, Stuart. "J. L. Austin 1911-1960," *Symposium on J. L. Austin*, ed. by K. T. Fann (London, 1969).

Hanson, N. R. "Retroductive Inference," *The Philosophy of Science, Delaware Seminar,* ed. by B. Baumrin (New York, 1962).

Hardin, Garrett. "Living on a Lifeboat," *BioScience* (October 1974).

Hardin, Garrett. "The Tragedy of the Commons," *Science,* Vol. 162 (December 13, 1968).

Hare, R. M. "Nothing Matters," in *Applications of Moral Philosophy* (London, 1972).

Harman, Gilbert. "Moral Relativism Defended," *The Philosophical Review,* Vol. LXXXIV, No. 1 (January 1975).

Harman, Gilbert. "Relativistic Ethics: Morality as Politics," *Midwest Studies in Philosophy,* Vol. III (1978).

Kim, Jaegwon. "Supervenience and Nomological Incommensurables," *American Philosophical Quarterly,* Vol. 15, No. 2 (April 1978).

Kovesi, Julius. "Against the Ritual of 'Is' and 'Ought,'" *Midwest Studies in Philosophy,* Vol. III (1978).

Kripke, Saul. "Identity and Necessity," *Identity and Individuation,* ed. by Milton Numitz (New York, 1971).

Kripke, Saul. "Naming and Necessity," *Semantics of Natural Language,* ed. by Davidson and Harman (Dordrecht, The Netherlands, 1972).

Lederberg, Joshua. "Experimental Genetics and Human Evolution." *The American Naturalist,* Vol. 100 (Sept.-Oct. 1966).

Leonard and Goodman. "The Calculus of Individuals and Its Uses," *The Journal of Symbolic Logic,* Vol. 5, No. 2 (June 1940).

Mackie, J. L. "Causes and Conditions," *American Philosophical Quarterly,* Vol. 2, No. 4 (October 1965).

Morillo, Carolyn. "Doing, Refraining and the Strenuousness of Morality," *American Philosophical Quarterly,* Vol. 14, No. 1 (January 1977).

Nakhnikian, George. "Love in Human Reason," *Midwest Studies in Philosophy,* Vol. III (1978).

Nash, J. F. "Non-cooperative Games," *Annals of Mathematics,* Vol. 54 (1951).

Nielson, Kai. "Why Should I be Moral?" *Methodos,* Vol. XV, No. 59-60 (1963).

O'Neill, Onora. "Lifeboat Earth," *Philosophy and Public Affairs,* Vol. IV, No. 3 (1975).

Prichard, H. A. "Moral Obligation," *Moral Obligation and Duty & Interest,* (Oxford, 1968).

Quine, W. V. "Logic as a Source of Syntactical Insights," *The Ways of Paradox* (Cambridge, 1966, 1976).

Rawls, John. "Justice as Reciprocity," in John Stuart Mill, *Utilitarianism,* ed. by Samuel Goroqitz (Indianapolis, 1971).

Rawls, John. "Two Concepts of Rules," *The Philosophical Review,* Vol. 64 (1955).

Rescher, Nicholas. "On the Characterization of Actions," *The Nature of Human Action,* ed. by Myles Brand (Glenview, 1970).

Robinson, Richard. "Ought and Ought Not," *Philosophy,* Vol. 46 (July 1971).

Searle, John. "How to Derive 'Ought' from 'Is,'" *The Philosophical Review,* Vol. 73 (1964).

Smullyan, Arthur F. "Modality and Description," *The Journal of Symbolic Logic* (1948).

Sobel, Jordan H. "Utility Maximizers in Iterated Prisoners' Dilemmas," *Dialogue* (March 1976).

Trammel, Richard. "Saving Life and Taking Life," *The Journal of Philosophy,* Vol. 72, No. 5 (March 13, 1975).

Waismann, F. "Verifiability," *Proceedings of the Aristotelian Society,* Suppl. Vol. (1945).

Watson, Richard. "Reason and Morality in a World of Limited Food," *World Hunger and Moral Obligation,* ed. by Aiken and La Follette (Englewood Cliffs, 1977).

Williams, B. A. O. "The Idea of Equality," *Moral Concepts,* ed. by Joel Feinberg (Oxford, 1970).

Index

Index